THE NEW AMERICAN CINEMA

At the movies

Elliott Moss Landy

THE NEW AMERICAN CINEMA

A CRITICAL ANTHOLOGY

Edited by

GREGORY BATTCOCK

A Dutton  *Paperback*

New York
E. P. DUTTON & CO., INC.

LEWIS & CLARK LIBRARY SYSTEM

P. O. BOX 368

EDWARDSVILLE, ILL. 62025

PERMISSIONS

Grateful acknowledgment is made to the following for permission to quote
from copyright material:

JONAS MEKAS: "Where Are We—the Underground?" Reprinted by per-
mission of the author and the Philadelphia College of Art.
KEN KELMAN: "Anticipations of the Light." Reprinted from *The Nation*,
May 11, 1964, by permission of the author.
DAVID EHRENSTEIN: "No Story To Tell." Printed by permission of the
author.
FRED WELLINGTON: "Liberalism, Subversion, and Evangelism: Toward
the Definition of a Problem." Printed by permission of the author.
TAYLOR MEAD: "The Movies Are a Revolution." Reprinted from *Film
Culture*, No. 29, Summer, 1963, by permission of the author and editor.
ANDREW SARRIS: "The Independent Cinema." Reprinted from *Motive*,
November, 1966, by permission of the author and editor.
RUDOLF ARNHEIM: "Art Today and the Film." Reprinted from the *Art
Journal*, Vol. XXV, No. 3, by permission of the author and editor.
PARKER TYLER: "Is Film Criticism Only Propaganda?" Printed by per-
mission of the author.
HENRY GELDZAHLER: "Happenings: Theater by Painters." Reprinted
from *The Hudson Review*, Vol. XVIII, No. 4, Winter 1965-66, by per-
mission of the author and editor. Copyright © 1966 by The Hudson
Review, Inc.
ANNETTE MICHELSON: "Film and the Radical Aspiration." Printed by
permission of the author.
KEN KELMAN: "The Reality of New Cinema." Printed by permission of
the author.
CHARLES BOULTENHOUSE: "The Camera as a God." Reprinted from
Film Culture, No. 29, Summer, 1963, by permission of the author and
editor.
RONALD TAVEL: "Shortcomings of the Sexual Metaphor in New York's
Independent Films." Printed by permission of the author.
KENNETH KING: "23Toward Re:Programming *Nature* with Mirrors: Films,
Theater &." Printed by permission of the author.

116462

For her assistance in the preparation of this anthology I wish to thank Jill Siraisi. Gratitude is also due Ken Kelman and P. Adams Sitney for their suggestions and advice. I thank Jonas Mekas, Editor and Publisher of Film Culture, *for allowing me to reprint so much material that he published first.*

Most of the films mentioned in this book can be rented for showings. Those interested should write for a catalogue of films to:

Film-Makers' Cooperative
175 Lexington Avenue
New York, N.Y. 10016

Gregory Battcock, painter, holds degrees in art history from Michigan State University, Hunter College, and the Accademia Di Belle Arti in Rome. He is lecturer in art history and criticism at Hunter and Queens colleges and Assistant Professor of Art at Fairleigh Dickinson University. Mr. Battcock is editor of *The New Art: A Critical Anthology* (1966) and has written criticism for several journals, including *Art and Literature, College Art Journal, Film Culture, 57th Street Review,* and is New York correspondent for *Arts Magazine.*

peace, Jonas

"Film critics are writers, and they are hostile and uneasy in the presence of a visual phenomenon."—Jack Smith

CONTENTS

ILLUSTRATIONS

INTRODUCTION

The New American Cinema is a term sufficiently elastic to embrace an extraordinary variety of artistically and sometimes technically amateurish ambitious productions that have recently attracted critical attention in New York City and elsewhere. In New York, indeed, what are sometimes referred to as "underground" movies have almost achieved the status of cult objects among the art public. All this in a country where the Old American Cinema—Hollywood—has long since achieved the highest pitch of technical excellence, and where the showing of films from almost every moviemaking country under the sun serves to supply some of the imagination and spontaneity that Hollywood notoriously lacks. The lack is felt even in its best efforts, which, like Sara Lee cakes, are delicious and stuffed with good ingredients but always automated beyond the expectation of variation.

The films of the New American Cinema are by contrast intensely personal and idiosyncratic statements even when the personality of the filmmaker is deliberately hidden within his work. Each film is the creation of a single artist, usually working on a budget so limited as to preclude any display of smooth proficiency in camera work, editing, directing, and the like. The actors are nearly always drawn from the artist's circle of friends and are neither professional nor paid. The entire, and only, purpose of every production is to express the artistic intention of its maker.

There are several reasons why the New York movement has sprung into prominence at the present time. Of course, it goes without saying that the New American Cinema is very far from being the first attempt to transform the movies into an art medium. Nor are all of the leading artists in the movement new to the field—several of them have been working in film for a decade or more. In historical and personal terms, much can be attributed to the influence of Jonas Mekas, publisher and editor of *Film Culture* and film critic for *The Village Voice*, who has tirelessly publicized the work of these artists and by so doing has perhaps helped to weld

12

them into a more or less cohesive group. More importantly, at the aesthetic level, cinema is a peculiarly appropriate medium for further exploration of today's chief artistic concerns. Not only is it free of many of the traditional restrictions and preconceptions that surround painting and sculpture, but, above all, its physical and technical properties are ideally suited to the necessary forms of experimentation.

The impact of twentieth-century technology upon the arts and upon our response to them has necessarily been enormous. The spread of automation, the extremely rapid and widespread diffusion of superficial information through the mass media, and the increasingly consumption-oriented nature of our society cannot fail to affect both artist and observer, although in very different ways. It is the artist's reactions that are of prime importance, for ultimately they will mold not only the pattern of response to the information conveyed by the media, but the very framework of society itself.

In coming to terms with contemporary conditions, many artists have developed apparently depersonalized styles from which the human element seems to be more or less completely removed. The artist's own role can no longer be considered as that of a craftsman whose unique and individual skill stamps everything he makes. Whether painter, sculptor, inventor of Happenings, or filmmaker, he now stresses his position as an originator; he functions primarily as the creator of new ideas which, being much more rapidly diffused, at least in general terms, than was ever possible before, may well prove to be social catalysts. Thus we have a situation in which we are confronted by a rapid succession of art statements that apparently have in common only a scorn for traditional techniques, but that in reality all reflect the current interest in exploring how far an artist can withdraw from the art object before it ceases to be art. Certain discoveries of the Abstract Expressionists produced the liberating concept that the object need no longer be, in the traditional sense, entirely the artist's own creation. But if his control is now no longer total, to what extent should it be exerted? How can the artist best fulfill his fundamental role as an innovator who redefines the nature of art itself? What is the role of the accidental? What is the place of craftsmanship or indeed artistic expression on the part of the artist's employees and assistants? And, ultimately, need the artist have any direct contact with the art object at all in order to call it his? All these are queries that contemporary filmmakers have tried to answer in their work.

In evaluating the work of the filmmakers of the New American Cinema, we should remember that it is not only the artist who is called upon to struggle with the continuing redefinition of art; the same responsibility also falls upon the critic. Art and criticism interact, as Lionello Venturi once remarked, and, ideally, the role of the critic should expand and change with that of the artist. We have to be prepared to face the necessity of developing new standards of judgment and perhaps, ultimately, a new aesthetic.

The contents of this anthology have been collected from a variety of sources and include both criticism and statements by film artists. It should be stressed that no attempt has been made to cover all aspects of contemporary independent filmmaking or the work of every filmmaker in the field. The most glaring omission, of course, concerns the technical inventiveness of the new cinema artist, which none of the articles printed in this book purports to consider in any depth. The omission is, alas, essential. There is simply too much material that may be included under this loosely defined subject, and, quite naturally, most people just aren't interested in reading it all. In a letter to Gregory Markopoulos, Stan Brakhage wrote: " . . . exchange of technical information . . . might prove dull reading . . . it oughtn't: for I have discovered it impossible to communicate certain aesthetic information to technically ignorant audiences, have found it like trying to explain a pun to a child who doesn't even know the same sound can have several meanings. . . ." [1] It is enough to say, however, that while the new filmmakers are very much aware of their position as aesthetic revolutionaries, they are at the same time exploring a wide variety of new technical and technological possibilities.

The present book aspires to be no more than a general introduction to today's independent cinema, but it is hoped that it will convey something of the vitality and dedication of the many artists who are contributing fresh insights to the value and meaning of film as an art form today.

GREGORY BATTCOCK

[1] *Film Culture,* Winter 1964–65, No. 35, p. 52.

PART I

SURVEY

WHERE ARE WE—
THE UNDERGROUND?

By Jonas Mekas

In 1965 Jonas Mekas wrote in The Village Voice: *"For a number of years now, the avant-garde artist (in cinema, and in other arts) felt, and publicly insisted, that he is creating something so different from the traditional art that his work, he felt, could be defined as anti-art. And he was right." Mekas also sees film art as both new and timeless: " . . . we are the true cineasts, each of us, crossing space and time and memory—this is the ultimate cinema of the people, as it has been for thousands and thousands of years."*

Mekas is founder and publisher of Film Culture, *as well as founder of the Film-Makers' Cooperative (Film Distribution Center) and the Film-Makers' Cinematheque in New York City. He is critic of experimental cinema for* The Village Voice. *His most famous film,* The Brig, *is an outstanding record of the Beck-Malina production at the old Living Theater. The film, an anti-military, anti-authoritarian statement that is shocking in its immediacy, won the Grand Prix de St. Mark at Venice.*

The following remarks were made by Mr. Mekas at the June, 1966, commencement exercises of the Philadelphia College of Art.

When I was asked to accept the highest award of the Philadelphia College of Art, I hesitated for a moment. I said to myself: Who am I? Really, I haven't done much in my life. Everything I want to do, all my dreams, are still in the future. Then I thought again. What the College is really doing by awarding this honor to me, is directing people's attention to the avant-garde arts. This award doesn't, really, go to me; it goes to the new cinema—to all those avant-garde artists who are trying to bring some beauty into a world full of sadness and horror.

17

What are we really doing? Where are we—the Underground? What's the meaning of it all? I will try to answer, or to indicate, some of the meanings connected with our work—meanings that are closely connected with all of us.

There was a time, when I was sixteen or seventeen, when I was idealistic and believed that the world would change in my own lifetime. I read about all the suffering of man, wars, and misery that took place in the past centuries. And I somehow believed that in my own lifetime all this would change. I had faith in the progress of man, in the goodness of man. And then came the war, and I went through horrors more unbelievable than anything I had read in the books, and it all happened right before my eyes—before my eyes the heads of children were smashed with bayonets. And this was done by my generation. And it's still being done today, in Vietnam, by my generation. It's done all over the world, by my generation. Everything that I believed in shook to the foundations—all my idealism, and my faith in the goodness of man and progress of man; all was shattered. Somehow, I managed to keep myself together. But, really, I wasn't one piece any longer; I was one thousand painful pieces.

It's really from this, and because of this, that I did what I did. I felt I had to start from the very beginning. I had no faith, no hope left. I had to collect myself again, bit by bit. And I wasn't surprised when, upon my arrival in New York, I found others who felt as I felt. There were poets, and filmmakers, and painters—people who were also walking like one thousand painful pieces. And we felt that there was nothing to lose any more. There was almost nothing worth keeping from our civilized inheritance. Let's clean ourselves out, we felt. Let's clean out everything that is dragging us down—the whole bag of horrors and lies and egos. The Beat Generation was the outgrowth, the result of this desperation; the mystical researches came out of this desperation. No price was too high, we felt, to pay for this cleaning job, no embarrassment too big to take. Let them laugh at us and our shabby appearances; let them spit into our beards. Even if we had nothing—some of us still have nothing to put in the cleared place—we couldn't remain as we were. We had to clean out not only the present but, through the drug ex-

perience or through meditation, to go back by several generations, to eliminate our egos, our bad faith, our mistrust, our
sense of competition, of personal profit—so that if there was
anything beautiful and pure, it would find a clear place and
would settle in us and would begin to grow. It was a painful
search, and it still is. We are still in the beginning of this
search and growth, and many minds get broken to pieces.
We are going through a dramatic end of the Christian Era
and the birth of what we begin to call the Aquarian Age,
and there are violent happenings taking place in man's
spirit and they aren't always in our control. But it's a little
bit easier because there are today many of us in various
places of the country, of the world; we keep meeting each
other, and we recognize each other; we know we are the
traveling pioneers of the new age. We are the transitional
generations. My generation, your generation, we have been
marked by the sign of travel. We kept going and searching
(we still do) in constant movement, from one side of the
continent to another, between San Francisco and New York,
between India and Mexico, and through all the inner
journeys of the psychedelics and yoga systems, and macro-
biotics. No generation since Columbus has traveled more
than the current two generations of America. Yes, other
generations have also traveled, but they always traveled as
conquerors, to conquer the others, to teach them their own
way of life. Our parents are still traveling through Vietnam
as conquerors; they travel, yes—but how useless and unreal
all their journeys and their conquerings seem to us today!
For we are traveling, collecting the broken bits and pieces
of knowledge, of love, of hope, of old ages; not the wisdom
of our parents, nor our mothers' wisdom, but that wisdom
which is as old as the earth, as the planets, as man himself—
the mystical, the eternal—collecting, gathering ourselves bit by
bit, having nothing to offer to others but taking gladly whatever is invested with love and warmth and wisdom, no matter
how little that may be.

In cinema, this search is manifested through abandoning
of all the existing professional, commercial values, rules,
subjects, techniques, pretensions. We said: We don't know
what man is; we don't know what cinema is. Let us, therefore, be completely open. Let us go in any direction. Let us

be completely open and listening, ready to move to any direction upon the slightest call, almost like one who is too tired and too weary, whose senses are like a musical string, almost with no power of their own, blown and played by the mystical winds of the incoming Age, waiting for a slightest motion or call or sign—let's go in any direction to break out of the net that is dragging us down. Our mothers' wisdom! Don't get tied down to any of the establishments; they will go down and they will drag us down. The sun, that is our direction. The beauty, that is our direction—not money, not success, not comfort, not security, not even our own happiness, but the happiness of all of us together.

We used to march with posters protesting this and protesting that. Today, we realize that to improve the world, the others, first we have to improve ourselves; that only through the beauty of our own selves can we beautify the others. Our work, therefore, our most important work at this stage is ourselves. Our protest and our critique of the existing order of life can be only through the expansion of our own being. We are the measure of all things. And the beauty of our creation, of our art, is proportional to the beauty of ourselves, of our souls.

You may be wondering, sometimes, why we keep making little movies, underground movies, why we are talking about Home Movies, and you hope, sometimes, that all this will change soon. Wait, you say, until they begin making big movies. But we say, No, there is a misunderstanding here. We *are* making real movies. What we are doing comes from the deeper needs of man's soul. Man has wasted himself outside himself; man has disappeared in his projections. We want to bring him down, into his small room, to bring him home. We want to remind him that there is such a thing as home, where he can be, once in a while, alone and with himself and with a few that he loves close to him, and be with himself and his soul—that's the meaning of the home movie, the private visions of our movies. We want to surround this earth with our home movies. Our movies come from our hearts—our little movies, not the Hollywood movies. Our movies are like extensions of our own pulse, of our heartbeat, of our eyes, our fingertips; they are so personal, so unambitious in their movement, in their use of light, their imagery. We want to surround this earth with our film frames and warm it up—until it begins to move. We could continue expressing our own surroundings, being mirrors of the dirty cities, the black dailiness. But we have done that job already. There is pain in the arts of the last few decades. The whole period of so-called modern art is nothing but the pain of our ending civilization, the last decades of the Christian Era. Now we are looking, we are being pulled by a desire for something joyful deep within us, deep in the stars, and we want to bring it down to earth so that it will change our cities, our faces, our movements, our voices, our souls—we want an art of light. You'll see more and more of luminous colors and heavenly sounds coming through our art. The brush strokes will be charged with a different energy, not to express our egos, not to promote ourselves "as artists" (that is gone, all that is gone and gone), but to bring down the whispers of heaven to serve as strings, as instruments of ethereal winds, with our own personalities almost disappearing. I see it all over the country, and humble, unknown artists keep coming from various and distant countries, passing the town like monks stopping on their way somewhere, showing glimpses brought down from heaven. There is a renaissance, a spiritual renaissance coming upon us, and it's through artists that this new age is bringing to us its first voices and visions; it's through their intuition that the eternity communicates with us, bringing a new knowledge, new feelings. Let us then be very open to our art, to this new art, and to our work as artists. This isn't time for lowering ourselves, but for being ready to sing the most beautiful note.

I was talking in the beginning about my own disillusionment after the war. Today, for the first time in a long time, I suddenly again begin to see the broken pieces of myself coming together. I am listening, very openly, with all my senses, with my eyes and ears open, and I begin to hear and see a new man emerging. After fifteen years of disillusionment, slowly, during the last few months, I have gained again the belief and trust in man, and the knowledge that this is the generation that is building the bridge from horror to light. You, me—we are the one thousand painful pieces that are beginning to come together in one beautiful note. As if a completely new race of man were emerging on earth. Do you know what the rock 'n' roll group called *The Byrds* do with their money? They are making huge signs and putting them all along the roadsides of California, and the signs say one word: Love. But our parents would say: This is crazy, you should put your money into the bank. That's the difference. That's what I mean. That's where we stand in 1966 and mid-summer.

ANTICIPATIONS OF THE LIGHT *
by Ken Kelman

Ken Kelman writes about himself: "I was born, and grew up in New York City. I am first of all a playwright no theater can afford to recognize (major and most recent unknown work: Mortality, *or* The Passion Play of the Fall of the Austro-Hungarian Empire) *and secondly a semi-retired film critic (*Film Culture, Filmwise, Clyde, The Nation, Moviegoer). *My most accurate biography, written by three crippled angels, is preserved in a cave, latitude 121°, longitude 73°."*

"Anticipations of the Light" appeared in The Nation *in 1964. In it, Kelman surveys the various filmmakers and their most significant works up to that date. The second section, "Further Developments," reviews the independent filmmaking scene since then.*

If movements are thought of as schools and neat categories, I would rather just speak of movies. If movements mean processes, then I will speak of that movement which has been called New American Cinema. But it can no more be defined than any other form of life; it can be autopsied only when dead. No vivisection.

What it is, is Brakhage and *Dog Star Man*, Smith and *Flaming Creatures* (see *The Nation*, April 6), Markopoulos and *Twice a Man* and others, all alive. We like to petrify such life for our schizoid and rationalistic nonpurposes. Our current reduction of the totality of things is precisely what New American Cinema goes against, and I would give co-

* Reprinted from *The Nation*, May 11, 1964.

hesion to this Cinema first in terms of its response to the
prevalent modern superstitions. Again, I would not call it a
movement so much as a release of energies, whose various
aspects are related not so much by common purpose as by
common necessity.

Two necessities underlie New American Cinema. One is an
aesthetic need, born of the exhaustion of film form by mid-
century. A pertinent analogy here is that of music at the turn-
of-the-century, when composers like Schönberg and Stravinsky began to react in major ways against an art which had
overevolved. The type of diatonicism which reached a sort
of perfection with Mozart had become, with Mahler and
Strauss, a growingly, groaningly, unwieldy idiom. Its sheer
material opulence was easy to swallow but hard to digest;
compositions gave more and more predominance to expressive
detail over organic vitality. The only way to develop such a
form was to enlarge it still further; and further growth would
only choke on itself. A radical reversal was needed.

Like that music, contemporary movies have gone as far
as they can. As the standard half-hour symphony of Mozart
ended up in the hour-and-a-half Mahler opus, the old ninety-
minute film becomes three, four hours long. As instruments
were added, melodies endlessly elaborated, and harmonies
more and more richly thickened, the motion picture acquired sound, color, 3-D, wide-screen, smells, electrical shocks,
and developed multi-plotted, multi-directed, star-clustered
and omnibus films. Unfortunately, nothing as gorgeous or
powerful as the music of Strauss or Mahler has come out of
the overripe movie period. It is especially too bad because the
end is as surely at hand here and now as it was in Vienna fifty
years ago, though we lack a "Resurrection Symphony" to im-
mortalize our own dead art. No knight of the past has transfigured that art, and now it is just too late.

In old Europe, itself, a reaction is evident, which both the
Continentals and many of us tend to take seriously as the
new cinema. This centers around Resnais, Antonioni and
Godard (surely not Bergman or Fellini). But two aspects of
their work mitigate against any real evolutionary or revelatory
significance. First, they are merely manipulating the old
dramatic narrative to obviate the formal excesses into which
it has (necessarily) fallen. If Schönberg had gone to a spare
sonata form in 1910, that would have been the musical

equivalent of such procedure; of Antonioni's dilution of Godard's ellipsis of plot, anyhow. Resnais's reaction has been more that of late Mahler or very early Schönberg—to stretch the traditional form as far as it will go, to cast the old plot-film in as dense and complicated a guise as possible. Another element in the work of these three which seems to me reactionary in a bad sense is, as Jonas Mekas has remarked, a tired determinism, a rationality that is restrictive on more levels than just the formal.

Which leads to the second necessity, the second pressure for coherence in the New American Cinema. This can be most simply stated as the need for freedom in an increasingly restrictive world. It is, as they say, not within the scope of this essay to analyze social infirmity. But surely we know at the very least that man is more and more estranged from nature, from his fellow man, and from himself. Through our powers of reason we have isolated certain truths and principles out of whole nature, rejecting the nature of ourselves, separating body and spirit, and enthroning one consciousness as the most efficient means of ordering the material external world. New American Cinema is a release of different forms of consciousness, as well as a reaction on several levels against the repressive pressures of our culture.

Old American Cinema is not only glutted and cluttered with expensive sets, actors, and union members, with all the respect for material power that characterizes our culture today. The Old is also completely calculated, with believable characters, developed and motivated actions, clockwork time, everything to confirm our belief—or hope?—that the universe is a causal, rational place. Our films have become a function not of energy, interest and rhythm—not of the human spirit— but of economic greed and compulsive hypertrophy.

The New American Cinema is a spiritual medium; *and* more physical than Hollywood ever dreamed. In it the conscious and the deep images are reunited, man himself is reunited, with passion and no apologies. It seeks to project genuine experience and direct vision. Its primary drive is to replenish the human spirit which has been eroded as much as our earth has been by "progress." The new cinema attempts to restore subjectivity to its proper realm, and urges the balance of human nature.

The Old is sluggish, its reflexes are gone. It *removes* experience, making us see things along with (or through) a protagonist with whom we identify, and a plot in which we are caught. Such an approach tends toward not only a lack of viewpoint, of definition of *whose* experience it is, but also filters the power of sight into mere habit, and dissolves insight into a mere vicariousness. The spectator is reduced to a voyeur—which is, increasingly, the individual's role in our society at large. Old American Cinema is doped, hooked, and preconditioned by all the oughts and noughts of our society. It is a docile pet which apes the way things are not; it is the tame creature of an invalid culture.

At present, the filmmakers who are trying to refresh us may be divided into three major groups, according to their central reactions to our culture, although there is a great deal of overlapping and individuality which it would take too long to discuss here.

The first is that of outright social criticism and protest: those whose films indict the repressive and unnatural aspects of our world. Here I would include Dan Drasin (*Sunday*); Jonas Mekas (*Guns of the Trees*); Bruce Conner (*A Movie: Cosmic Ray*); Richard Preston (*Black and White Burlesque, Nightscapes*); and Stan VanDerBeek (*Science Friction, Skulduggery*). Drasin is most straightforward as propagandist, with his documentary on authoritarianism (police coercion) which is photographed with great spontaneity and feeling of presence. Mekas makes a good try at expressing the defeats and triumphs of the human spirit in a dehumanized society, through episodes connected by meaning rather than dramatic causality. The intensity of vision which might fuse and sustain a full-length film of this type is not achieved, but Mekas remains the guiding spirit of the New American Cinema as a result of his recognition some four years ago of two crucial early works, *Shadows* and *Pull My Daisy*; his magazine *Film Culture;* and his championing of other new filmmakers, which includes the creation of a cooperative to distribute their work.

Conner, VanDerBeek, and Preston operate by various collage techniques, Conner assembling film itself, re-editing stock movie footage to transform its values, and Preston and VanDerBeek animating magazine illustrations, ads, photos, etc. A common fault here is the overworking or repetition of material for formal purposes at the expense of the expression itself. Their approach is abundant in visual pun, and largely satiric, except for the agonized *Nightscapes*. But all three go beyond mere parody in their strong affinities with the next group.

And this consists of the films of liberation, films which suggest, mainly through anarchic fantasy, the possibilities of the human spirit in its socially uncorrupted state. The central works here are those of Vernon Zimmerman (*Lemon Hearts, To L. A. with Lust*); Ron Rice (*The Flower Thief, The Queen of Sheba Meets the Atom Man, Chumlum*); Ken Jacobs (*Little Stabs at Happiness, Blonde Cobra*—in association with Jack Smith and Bob Fleishner, *Star Spangled to Death*); Jack Smith (*Flaming Creatures, Normal Love*); and George and Mike Kuchar (*Tootsies in Autumn, Pussy on a Hot Tin Roof*). They all allow the utmost freedom to actors and actions, and catch on film the deepest urges, the most delightful and often "obscene" whimsies of their characters, with only the loosest sort of prearrangement. Zimmerman perhaps tends most closely to observe a format, and is least spontaneous in camera work. Rice and Jacobs rely more than the others upon editing for the final structure of material, Rice being the superior editor and the more inventive director of incident while Jacobs, the foremost new cinema singer of common experience, expresses humble human values with less brilliance. Smith is the supreme photographer of the group, both in black and white and previously unimaginable color, as well as the most poetic inspirer of actors and the greatest creator of soundtrack (that of *Flaming Creatures* is unequaled in all cinema). The Kuchar brothers may be considered the primitives or Pop artists of this category. They absolutely avoid continuity of action, logic of motivation, consistency of character or economy through edition, which makes for a lack of shape and looseness of effect; largely compensated by excellent color and composition, and gorgeously libidulgent overacting. The Kuchars typify the flaws of their group as a whole, whose strength is surely not the technical smoothness or structural precision we are used to.

The third major group is the mythically oriented. While the first expresses, out of a need for protest, a generally negative reaction; and the second presents, out of a need for freedom, an antithesis or antidote to merely conventional values and emotions; the third creates, out of a need to fill our rationalistic void, those actual inner worlds which fall within the realm of myth. Primary here are the works of Gregory Markopoulos (*Twice a Man, Serenity*); Charles Boultenhouse (*Handwritten, Dionysius*); Kenneth Anger (*Scorpio Rising*); and Stan Brakhage (*Anticipation of the Night, Window Water Baby Moving, The Dead, Blue Moses, Dog Star Man*).

Twice a Man and *Dionysius* utilize Greek myth, the former a modern setting of the Hippolytus theme and the latter an explicit ritual. Markopoulos is the most important experimenter with nondramatic narrative form, particularly noteworthy for his use of nonchronological, subjective time; he is also one of the three or four supreme colorists in film history. On the basis of marvelous rushes of *Dionysius* (the finished version of which I have not seen) Boultenhouse appears to have attained a measured sureness and pictorial simplicity which should add a significant element of classicism to New American Cinema. Anger, after ten years' lapse and many broken projects, again blazons out his demonic mythology.

Brakhage's myth is less specific than any of the others, indeed less derivative; for which reason P. Adams Sitney, editor of *Filmwise*, has referred to *Dog Star Man* as the cinematic instance of mythopoeia—the making of new myth. However, this process can be found in *Anticipation of the Night* and *The Dead* and even in earlier works, though not with the definition achieved in *Dog Star Man*. In all ways a master of technique, Brakhage gives filmic substance to the spirit of matter and to the flesh of spirit, to the life which our culture denies. What a pity Jung could not see these movies. (To those who complain of headaches from certain Brakhage films, I can only suggest that their eyes have been too long focused on the wrong things; it is not easy to pour new visions into old eyes.)

To the above three categories I would add a less pivotal one, which is concerned with fresh perception of the physical world around us. The two filmmakers who thus try to wash our eyes clear of grime, smoke, and other pollution are Marie Menken (*Bagatelle for Willard Maas, Notebooks, Go! Go! Go!*); and Joseph Cornell (*Nymphlight, A Fable for Fountains*). Menken is the surer technician and stylist as she reveals natural beauties which still survive among us; while Cornell's glimpses of the ordinary seem ready

to break with holding some inner mystery. Finally, there
are Robert Breer (*Blazes, Horse over Teakettle*); Carmen
D'Avino (*The Room, A Trip*); and Ed Emshwiller (*Life-
lines, Thanatopsis*), who make decorative films, "plastic
enterprises," in which we can enjoy form and color at play,
alive, and not just animated.

The New American Cinema has arisen at this time precisely
because of the great possibilities of film which the Old
smothers, possibilities of cultural counteraction. Film still
offers the formal freedom of a relatively new and unexplored
medium, unshaped by the centuries. More pointedly, there
is the potential spontaneity of cinema, especially in the recording of the moment, with later reshaping of the vital
matter. This freedom, which has chance as well as anarchic
implications, according to who uses it, has of course dis-
pleased those who prefer the old tidiness to the new life.
And then there is the immediacy of the moving image, its
impact and "realism." Film, in relation to other arts, can be
comparatively nonsymbolic; a power useful to counteract an
environment ever more alien and abstract, as Siegfried
Kracauer has pointed out in his *Theory of Film*. (This power
can either reproduce the material qualities of the physical
world with the conviction which the machine's accuracy
engenders; or can take on the aspect of dream, fantasy, the
unconscious, through its unrivaled achievement of a stream
of direct images.) The great example of such immediacy
does not seem to me to lie in the realism advocated by
Kracauer and fulfilled par excellence by Rossellini, and
Neorealism in general; nor in Buñuelian surrealism; nor even
in the improvisatory cutting loose of Rice's people or the
unleashing of Smith's and his actor's fantasies. Rather it is
in Brakhage's use of basic experience as material, unmediated
by acting or action, where the power of cinematic immediacy
is manifested most definitively.

Further Developments

The preceding article was published in May, 1964. This
extension is concerned with the major events since then. To
begin with, there are two filmmakers whose work deserved
mention above, which omission I remedy here. One is Harry

Smith, whose work was unknown at the time, to me as well as to the world at large. He has since emerged as one of cinema's consummate artists. His *Heaven and Earth Magic Feature* (dating from the late 1950's or early 1960's) is an exceptionally fine cartoon; a very deliberate play of images of people, creatures, and objects constantly metamorphosing, in a hallucinogenic or ritual trance structure; an ironic and incredibly precise articulation of the illusory sense of life, in its infinite variety. Over the period 1939–1950, Smith made numerous excellent abstractions, which employ in a more formally complex manner the changing (indeed the permutation) of shapes. The other filmmaker missing from my earlier piece was George Landow, whose major work is *Fleming Faloon* (1963), a quite nonliterary and uninterpretable work questioning all of the viewer's cinematic experience and expectations. Since then Landow's most distinguished achievement has been an untitled loop (1965) showing a girl blinking over and over again for eleven minutes, plus everything else (like numbers and frame divisions) that occurs on the filmstrip; a cogent exploration of the nature of film itself.

Many of the artists mentioned in the earlier article have done some of their most important work since it was written. Stan Brakhage has made twenty-two *Songs* (1964–66), a landmark in directness of seeing, where the unedited spontaneity of home movies manifests as never before its own special and undeniable *form*. Brakhage also made *Pasht* (1965), a treatment and transfiguration of the death of his cat in terms of the ebb and flow of light upon its fur and flesh. In 1966, Kenneth Anger re-created his masterpiece *Inauguration of the Pleasure Dome* (originally made in 1953), stressing and elaborating the psychedelic elements in this ritual, magical exaltation of the power of man's imagination. From Bruce Conner in 1965 there was *Report*, a meditation—using a few basic images repeated and varied, and a lot of flickering whiteness—on the assassination of Kennedy; and *Vivian*, an appropriately capricious treatment of a glamorous personality. The Kuchar brothers have gone their separate ways, Mike making the imaginative science fiction *Sins of the Fleshapoids* (1965); and George his first truly economical film, *Hold Me While I'm Naked* (1966), a perfect fusion of mock-Hollywood and mock-avant-garde styles

to very funny and very sad effect. Ed Emshwiller also
created his best work so far in 1966, the feature-length
Relativity, an exploration of the forms and textures of nature, and the place of man among them. As this suggested
the influence of Brakhage's *Dog Star Man*, so Gregory Markopoulos's *Galaxie* (1966), a series of vignettes of friends and
acquaintances, seemed inspired by the portrait section of
Songs. Markopoulos has also completed two as yet unshown
works, *Himself as Herself*,* and a major project, *The Illiac
Passion*.

   The most important new filmmakers to have emerged in
the last two years are Andy Warhol, Bruce Baillie, and Carl
Linder. Warhol has been the most prolific filmmaker, or
more properly, producer, of this decade. Using ideas of his
own, scripts by others, and various cameramen, he has
turned out an enormous number of works. This speed of
production has been facilitated by Warhol's method of presenting his material "straight" or "raw"—i.e., leaving it
unedited. Whatever the merits of his individual films may
be—and some are among the purest and most uncompro-
mising of all documentaries—it is in the totality of Warhol's
work that his achievement is most truly seen; for each film
takes its place as one band in a vast spectrum, one slice of
life in a peculiar and perhaps sick, but utterly credible and
living world. I would here single out the the silent *Sleep*
(1963) and *Eat* (1964); and the soundtracked *Vinyl* (1965),
Screen Test (1965), *Space* with Edie Sedgwick (1966), and
The Chelsea Girls (1966). After Warhol and Brakhage,
Bruce Baillie has been the most productive in terms of
quantity in recent years. His best long works, *Mass* (1964)
and *Quixote* (1965), have taken the form of journeys incor-
porating images of city and country, man and nature, the
personal and the documentary, in such a way that the viewer
"goes through" their experience as an odyssey of contemporary America. More recently Baillie made the short lyric
Tung (1966), his most fully realized work; again in the form
of a journey, but through the realm of reverie rather than
the physical world. Carl Linder's reputation rests on little
more than a half-hour of film, *The Devil Is Dead* and *Skin*
(both 1964); but that reputation is secure, and indeed, vir-

---

   * This film received its first showing in New York in May, 1967.
—Ed.

tually unchallenged. Linder is now the foremost creator of surrealistic movies, assuming the grand old mantle that has been worn by, among others, Luis Buñuel and Sidney Peterson. Two new Linder works, *Detonation* and *Overflow*, are nearing completion as this article is written.

Three individual films of special significance were made in the period under consideration. The most sensational and unusual was *The Flicker* (1966) by Tony Conrad, an avant-garde musician. This was a pioneer attempt (along with the Austrian Kubelka's *Arnulf Rainer*, made in 1960) to create a film of absolute light, using pure imageless blacks and whites. *The Flicker* built from relatively simple slow alternations of dark and light, to an overpowering effect where waves radiated over the audience as if some cold sun had risen in the theater. An even more explicitly psychedelic movie was John Cavanaugh's fragmentary *Acid Man* (1966), which included a passage I consider the most successful orchestration of pure colors anywhere in cinema. Also in *Acid Man* was a series of superimpositions of a man making faces, over his serene face, a powerfully direct vision of the varieties of human "role-playing," of the many manifestations assumed by the spirit in this world. The third film is Stanton Kaye's *Georg* (1964), remarkable for its innovation in narrative technique, including the first true use of the subjective camera-eye throughout an entire film. Moreover, in its play with the style of *cinéma vérité*, shifting from nuance of "reality," *Georg* is the most brilliantly Pirandellian movie I know.

Other films I would at least mention are Nathaniel Dorsky's *Summerwind* (1965), a beautiful evocation of his home town; Peter Goldman's *Echoes of Silence* (1965), an indictment of the corrupting spirit of New York City; Robert Nelson's *Plastic Haircut* (1963) and *Oh Dem Watermelons* (1965), two elaborate and bizarre jokes; and Storm De Hirsch's *Divinations* (1964) and *Peyote Queen* (1965), delicately wrought fantasies combining photographed and brilliantly hand-painted objects and abstractions.

To sum up briefly, the two tendencies that have most clearly emerged since 1964 are (1) the psychedelic (as prefigured in the work of Harry Smith), in Anger, Conrad, and Cavanaugh; and (2) the documentary, pure and direct as never before, as realized supremely on the one hand in

Peter Emanuel Goldman: From *Echoes of Silence*, 1965

Warhol's great "inhuman comedy," the panorama of contemporary decadence, and on the other in Brakhage's *Songs*,
the refreshing images of life in its essential simplicity.

NO STORY TO TELL
by David Ehrenstein

Born in New York in 1947, David Ehrenstein writes for
Film Culture *and is majoring in English at Pace College.
He defines the film critic as "10 percent writer, 20 percent
soapbox orator, 5 percent sociologist, 15 percent inside in-
formant, and 50 percent frustrated film director." This frustration he hopes to remedy in the near future. His favorite
actors are Anna Karina and Dirk Bogarde, and his favorite
directors are Max Ophuls and Carl Dreyer.*

A raised platform, with actors and sets and bound sheets
of paper on which letters have been imprinted, obviously
has little in common with moving strips of celluloid through
which light is projected. Yet the general critical insistence
that film follow a theatro-literary tradition is perhaps the
major factor in keeping film criticism (especially in this
country) in such a backward state.

Pauline Kael's plea for the good old-fashioned plot seems
somewhat archaic in the light of developments in the last
few years. Mass audiences have long since abandoned it,
and the seemingly endless parade of spy spoofs and so on
that they consume in such large quantities contains not a
vestige of the tightly woven narrative that characterized
what used to be known as the "well-made film." In more
creative commercial work, the recent films of Bergman
(*The Silence*), Losey (*Modesty Blaise*), Antonioni (*Red
Desert*), etc., show a marked leaning away from tradition,
and toward a more visual orientation. In Godard's *Pierrot
le Fou* the characters and the elements that surround them
appear in a manner not related to plot in the usual sense,
but rather to the moments "in between." On a more complex

level, Dreyer in *Gertrud* does not avoid the film's dramatic and literary origins, but rather transforms them as an ever-so-gently floating camera tracks around couches that serve (in Dreyer's eyes) as sacrificial altars on which the great issues of life are placed and summarily dealt with. The resulting effect is not possible to duplicate in any other medium.

Films, of course, are and will remain a mixed form. But the prevailing dogma of the critical hierarchy is of little use in creating an understanding of film in general, and is of no use whatsoever in relation to the films of the "New American Cinema" in particular. For it is here that all previous notions must be laid to rest in order for eye and mind to widen. This is not to say that American experimental cinema killed cock robin, but simply that the strides that it has made in the last five years have little or no relation to the cinema of the past and what was thought of it.

A glance at the beginnings of the experimental American cinema would not lead one to anticipate this development. Maya Deren's call for a new cinema of poetry had its roots in the more literary avant-garde tradition of Duchamp, Ray, and Richter, and some of the works of those who responded to that call (Brakhage in *The Way to Shadow Garden*, Anger in *Fireworks*, Markopoulos in *Swain*) show a continuation of this style. But with the radical change of approach in Brakhage (*Anticipation of the Night*), the growth and development of Markopoulos and Anger (*Twice a Man* and *Inauguration of the Pleasure Dome* respectively) and the discovery of Andy Warhol (*Sleep*) and Harry Smith (*Heaven and Earth Magic Feature*) the focus began to shift.

In *Scorpio Rising*, Kenneth Anger examines the phenomenon of the motorcycle cult in America, tracing it, as he says, "from toy to terror." The cyclists are observed at work and play, and relationships are drawn between them and the myth-symbols (Brando, Dean, Hitler, Christ) with which they identify. But the portrayal of a dramatic incident is deliberately avoided. For example, the death of a cyclist at the end of the film could have served as a dramatic climax. Instead it is offhand, casual, and disturbing in a way that the other approach could not have been. The witty use of rock and roll on the soundtrack sets up an audio-visual friction. What is heard does not "explain" what is seen as the usual soundtrack does. All the parallels made (audio-visual, myth-symbol and cyclist, etc.) are drawn casually and never forced, free for the viewer to correlate—not imposed within a literary context.

Gregory Markopoulos's film *Galaxie* consists of 30 portraits of sundry friends and acquaintances. One roll of film (100 feet or 3 minutes) was used for each subject. All editing and superimposition were done in the camera, so that the film in its final form consists of these rolls spliced end to end. The images presented consist of the face of the subject (one or two poses) together with background materials from his or her work or environment or suggestive of his or her personality (thus, Shirley Clarke is juxtaposed with a sta-tuette of Felix the Cat and a skull, Susan Sontag with photos of Garbo and Dietrich). The images flicker on and off (the screen is often black for several seconds), intercut, and superimpose. Hence relationships between figure and object can be drawn in a far more subtle way than if a particular action were dramatized. Not one, but many meanings are suggested. The imagination of the spectator is completely liberated.

In Stan Brakhage's *Dog Star Man*, a man accompanied by his dog climbs a mountain to cut down a tree. On the way up the man is assailed by visions of his past. Certainly a dramatic incident, one thinks, but no. The figure, actions, and thoughts of the man are presented in an entirely visual manner. The man is not a character in the usual sense and one is not made to "identify" with him in order to under-stand his situation. There is no sense of objectivity as there is in a movie by Hitchcock, where one may observe the character while sharing his experience. In Brakhage, both character and experience are applied directly and simulta-neously. The "memory" of the man is a totally visual phenom-enon revolving around a set of basic elements: birth, mother, tree, sun, sky, mountain, dog, etc., and cannot be inter-preted or discussed in any other manner. Even the tree chop-ping does not come across as drama. Having reached the point of action Brakhage has each chop of the tree shown as a chop of an image. The images throughout the film are gathered, interrelated, set aside, then reinstated. If an analogy

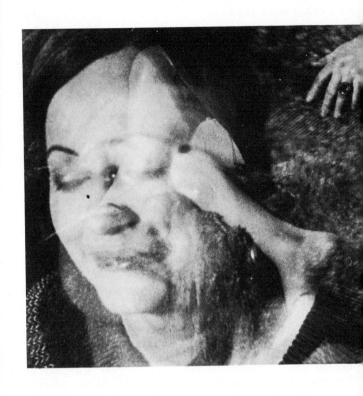

Gregory Markopoulos: From *Galaxie*, 1966

must be drawn, only a musical one would be appropriate.*

In the films of Harry Smith, one sees that former cinematic hybrid the animated film finally come into its own. For a period of over thirty years Smith worked on short abstract films, and his *Heaven and Earth Magic Feature* (as well as a live action superimposition film), showing results only to close friends. In 1965, he released his work at last and reduced such "serious" animators as Lenica and Borowczyk to the Walt Disney level. It is not humor, but horror that he seeks to induce. In his feature film, Mickey Mouse has been supplanted by the god Siva in an endless dance of death of turn-of-the-century postcard cut-outs. The symbols speak directly through their presence alone, as well as through Smith's clever juxtaposition, without benefit of dramatic structure.

For those who feel that the artistic technique of all the works described so far constitutes dehumanization for the sake of the image, one need only turn to the recent work of Andy Warhol, *The Chelsea Girls*—one of the most human pieces of cinema ever created. Here people, not characters, are displayed and at length. No excuses are made, no incidents avoided. Warhol knows that every cut would be a lie. The moments of boredom that come enhance, not detract, from the high spots, and often transform themselves into a new point of interest not originally considered by the spectator. The camera remains stationary, but by using the zoom lens in rhythmic counterpoint to the actions and reactions of the subjects, the filmmaker is able to follow, emphasize, and visually organize whatever is at hand. The people are all that is necessary; what drama need be created?

But decline of one tradition need not result in the establishment of another. Artists whose importance is just beginning to emerge include George Landow, who is at the moment completely involved with the filmstrip itself; Jack Smith, who is presently taking the surrealist tradition into new unchartered regions; and the recently discovered Viennese independent filmmaker Peter Kubelka, who is working with some original and complex audio-visual notions in his film *Unsere Afrikareise (Our Trip to Africa)*. The new film artist

* The best analysis of Brakhage extant is Dan Clark's book *Brakhage* (Film-Makers' Cinematheque Monograph series #2), in which he takes the films apart, image by image.

has responded to the challenges of the medium, and it remains only for the audience to respond to the challenge of the artist.

LIBERALISM, SUBVERSION, AND EVANGELISM: TOWARD THE DEFINITION OF A PROBLEM

by Fred Wellington

Fred Wellington emphasizes in this article the essentially subversive nature of all avant-garde art, whatever its apparent subject. In his view, the selection or avoidance of films for presentation at the New York Film Festival provides an illustration of this.

The author is a graduate of Berkeley, now resident in New York. His articles have appeared in several film journals. A veteran, he recently completed a film for the 1967 project, "The Angry Arts Against the War in Vietnam."

Again and again intelligent people question the validity of New York's Film Festival. This questioning is directed not only at specific programming but at the very idea of a film festival.

"Why does New York need a Festival?" they say. "The Festival only serves as a market place for films that will be seen anyway, films that already have distribution." "The Festival is too expensive. The people who should come, 'the people,' can't afford it." "The Festival is 'Establishment.' It is fundamentally indifferent to the real cinema, the Independent American Film." "It is a special thing—too much for the film buffs." "Everything worth seeing comes to New York City sooner or later."

Le Petit Soldat, Gertrud, Balthazar, Gare du Nord, in short the best of current European commercial cinema were first screened in America at the New York Film Festival. These films, with the exception of *Gertrud,* have not been released in America. *Gertrud* has had only cursory release.

Most of the charges show a willful misunderstanding of the problems involved. Of course the Film Festival is Establishment. It is held in a center of Establishment Art, a grotesque clump of buildings known as Lincoln Center specifically erected to house those forms academically recognized as the performing arts. The Film Festival is supported by power and money—Establishment power and Establishment money.

Mr. Bosley Crowther may not feel that the Festival represents cinema or the Establishment because Hollywood cannot control the programming: " . . . there are several American films of an artful and popular nature that commend them highly for showing here. But one can understand why their distributors did not wish to put them cheek by jowl with an old Bernardo Bertolucci picture or Cecil B. DeMille's 1915 film 'The Cheat.' " [1] Mr. Crowther is Establishment, *New York Times* Establishment—a very powerful man.

I am sure Amos Vogel would be delighted to lower his admission charge. But the Film Festival still runs at a deficit, it still has to fight for funds to cover this deficit, and it seems to have little access to the accumulation of wealth that is wasted yearly by the people of power and wealth of this city of New York on that archaic, circulating sideshow known as the Opera Hilton. According to *The New York Times* " . . . this year's expenses will reach $17 million." [2]

I would be curious to know just how many of "the people" attend the Metropolitan. " . . . The top price for a seat at the Metropolitan, now at $13 the most expensive theatre seat in the city, will be increased to $15.50. The prices for other seats will be increased by roughly 20 percent. . . . " [3]

Of course I am mistaken in this complaint—a philistine—because, as I am constantly reminded, the Met is CULTURE. But then again I remember my reading of Curzio Malaparte's *Kaputt* and that particular section on the occupation of Warsaw, *Cricket in Poland,* the casual shooting of Jews and Poles, the anal rape of a city amid the constant talk of KULTUR by the officers, ladies, and guests of Governor General Frank's

[1] *The New York Times,* September 25, 1966.
[2] November 12, 1966.
[3] *The New York Times,* November 12, 1966.

command; and my own enthusiasm for words like CULTURE
wanes .

For four years the New York Film Festival has been fundamentally concerned with the commercial "art house" film:
films designed for the mass audience, designed to make
money, but made with integrity and felt to have an appeal
limited to the better educated or the more curious. It is the
type of film with which most festivals are concerned. It is a
type of film for which there are recognized production and distribution patterns—inadequate and unsound as these patterns
may be. When these films come from foreign countries they are
less objectionable to the American Establishments than the
equivalent American phenomenon, The Independent Cinema.
This is because—irrespective of their commitments—they are
exotic foreign art.

Independent art, in this age of organization, is considered
subversive. It threatens the myths upon which the organiza-
tions and the society are based. Annette Michelson told us, in
a provocative and intelligent talk given at the 1966 New York
Film Festival, that there is a spirit of subversion connected
with the New American Cinema. The implication of her development is that the recent European Cinema has escaped
being considered subversive by assimilating a narrative convention developed by Hollywood and so successfully has
threaded the tricky path between entertainment, esoterica,
and offensiveness. "It is the acceptance of these limits and
conventions and their ultimate conversion into aesthetic principles which characterizes recent advanced film making in
France and largely elsewhere in Europe." [4]

This is a succinct and accurate summing up of what has
come to be known as the *Cahiers du Cinéma* position. It is,
however, an oversimplification of what has not been a successful conversion. The limits and conventions were never
wholly accepted. Georges de Beauregard and Jean-Luc
Godard's *Le Petit Soldat* was banned in France. In essence it
was considered politically subversive. Georges de Beauregard
and Jacques Rivette's *La Religieuse*, although shown at
Cannes in 1966 through the intercession of André Malraux,
the Minister of Culture, has also been banned. The Catholic
Church in that very Catholic country, France, considers the
film subversive. Mai Zetterling could not get her film *Night*

[4] Annette Michelson, lecture, New York Film Festival, 1966.

Games shown in open screenings at one of the world's major film festivals, the annual event in Venice. The portrayal of sex was considered subversive by the Italians. *The War Game* was made by Peter Watkins for the BBC. It is not just a good film, it is a shattering film. And it was banned by the BBC because it did so shatteringly attack the myths of civilian defense. It was considered subversive. A document of its tribulations appears in the Fall, 1965, issue of *Film Comment*.

The French of the *Nouvelle Vague* performed a remarkable feat in understanding and synthesizing a crass, commercial cinema form for their own purpose; however, when they have tried to go beyond that original purpose or when they have stood still they have found themselves in trouble. Jean-Luc Godard has gone ahead. *Les Carabiniers*, which is adventurous both in style and story, was rejected. It failed in France and has not been released in the States. It is a film of exceptional merit. François Truffaut seemed to go backward with *La Peau Douce*. The picture was not particularly interesting. *Fahrenheit 451* is a banal regression. Resnais went forward with *Muriel*. Audiences found the form and the implications of the picture difficult to accept. *La Guerre Est Finie* is, for Resnais, a regression.

An artist must go where his perception takes him. The important cinema in Europe will either decline artistically or be considered increasingly "subversive." It is doubtful if a "subversive" film, under the present combination of distributional, governmental, and critical systems can do more than just exist. According to *Variety*: "French Studios Put Hex on Sex —with TV one of the growing outlets for French films in the U.S., it is generally felt that this consideration may be causing a sort of softpedaling of daring sex scenes and nudity. Some Yank buyers have reported that French filmmakers have sometimes submitted scripts or discussed scenes with them which were felt too risqué or an impediment for TV usage. As a result, suggestions would lead to some changes in local pix slanted for video, or some touchy scenes being made in two ways. . . . Some U.S. buyers note that they sometimes think twice about buying controversial pix which, although they have potent theatrical qualities, are impossible for later TV use. . . ." [5]

There is a difference between subversion, as an act, and

[5] *Variety*, November 2, 1966.

what is considered subversive. "Subversion as an act" is an insidious attempt to destroy and has strong negative elements. "What is considered subversive" is often no more than wholesome synthesis, analysis, or criticism. These two categories are usually confused, sometimes willfully, by an Establishment. This article will concern itself with the latter category.

An interesting question might be: How many "subversive" American films can an Establishment Festival be expected to show without commiting suicide? Godard—and he is an exotic Frenchman—receives the full hostility of the two most powerful art-film critics in the United States, Bosley Crowther and Judith Crist. It would be nice to believe that Mr. Crowther and Miss Crist represent isolated mentalities. They don't. The reaction of many people of power in New York City to Godard is incendiary. It is not enough that the Festival showings of *Masculine Feminine* and *Pierrot Le Fou* sold out almost immediately; it is not enough that 22 percent of the 1966 Festival sellouts were Godard pictures; that, in short, Godard is one of the Festival's monetary backstops. None of this is enough. What is enough is to please the people in power.

"Subversion," especially mass media "subversion," is rarely defined by the one term that can provide *carte-blanche* accolades. No one in the Establishment is going to question the fundamental validity of CULTURE. CULTURE is a sacred pig. The Met and Leonard Bernstein are CULTURE. To a certain extent avant-garde painting and sculpture are CULTURE. But the mass-media avant-garde, especially when it concerns itself with the issues of the day, is generally considered an uncomfortable if not unpleasant phenomenon—for no power structure likes to be publicly challenged. By internal necessity, it will consider the implications of the modern artist's work subversive.

But power structures love CULTURE. CULTURE does not analyze. CULTURE does not challenge. CULTURE is always in good taste. Good taste is the sophistic gloss used to mask the real world and lull us into deceiving ourselves as to what we perceive. Art is seldom in good taste. Depending on the obliqueness and subtlety of the artist, art may appear to be in good taste. But its implications never are. They can't be. It would be a contradiction in terms.

The New American Cinema is curious and diverse, but there are three generalizations one can make about it. First, it is almost never in good taste. This is a sign of its great strength. Secondly, it has no financial justification. This is also a sign of its great strength. Dropouts abound. Those who remain form a resolute, tough, and desperate cadre. The term "underground" has specific point, for many of the independent filmmakers are indeed partisans at war. There is no valid financial structure that supports the independent cinema in any but the most cursory way. There is virtually no monetary reason for making an independent short, just a little more for making an independent feature. This knowledge paralyzes the diffident or those who, after many years in the world of film, find themselves suffering battle fatigue. Few people have the money or the craft to make the extended-form film (feature) without having first tried shorts. If a feature is made and does show independent spirit—in short, is "subversive"—its opportunities for distribution will be inversely proportionate to its independence. For example, the films of Stan Brakhage, Andy Warhol, and Gregory Markopoulos are shown only in a few museums and the theatres and student film societies closely aligned with the Film-Makers' Cooperative. This ostracism has little to do with artistic value. It may have more to do with esoterica (esoterica is a function of audience sophistication). The ostracism has a great deal to do, however, with "subversion," which is the third characteristic of the New American Cinema.

In 1966, for the first time, the New American Cinema was recognized by the New York Film Festival as a distinct phenomenon. The recognition took place, not in Philharmonic Hall, but in the small, two-hundred-seat library auditorium—a fitting place for Subversia. None of the 9:30 PM evening programs in Philharmonic Hall, the place and time reserved for what seems to be a combination of popularity and artistic importance, varied from the conventional art-house programming. Yet three evenings were devoted to films whose merits, in either category, are doubtful. A shrewd combination of popularity and artistic success should be the only qualification that would justify a 9:30 PM screening in Philharmonic Hall. Interesting, unreleased failures should, by all means, be seen; but they should be screened in the smaller library auditorium while those films, to quote Annette Michelson quoting André Breton, " . . . aquiver with a sense of the future," [6] such as

[6] Lecture, New York Film Festival, 1966.

Tony Conrad's *The Flicker,* Peter Emanuel Goldman's *Echoes of Silence,* and Ed Emshwiller's *Relativity,* deserve only one treatment. They should be projected in the big Philharmonic Hall before the big Festival audience for all to see.

Amos Vogel, in a short article entitled "What Is and What Will Be" published in the Festival program, wrote, "The most modern Xenon-type 16mm projectors have been installed in Philharmonic Hall. 16mm, because of low cost and easy accessibility, has traditionally been the gauge of creative experimentation and young filmmakers in this country."

Peter Emmanuel Goldman and Tony Conrad are, by any definition, young filmmakers.

The problem is not one of technique. Nor is the problem one of artistic level or even popularity. (The latter word is a euphemism for audience sophistication.) When *Pierrot Le Fou, Masculine Feminine, The War Game, Wholly Communion,* and *La Guerre Est Finie* (shown the last day of the Festival) all sell out the first few days of the 1966 Festival one does not worry about audience sophistication.

Amos Vogel, who is noted for his taciturnity, told me, "*Flicker* is a great film." [7] If the director of the New York Film Festival says a film is "great," and that film is not shown in Philharmonic Hall, then the reason for its exclusion must be found in concerns other than aesthetic.[8]

The problem is one of "subversion," American "subversion." *The Flicker, Echoes of Silence,* and *Relativity* are considered too "subversive." Andrew Sarris, one of the four members of the Festival Programming Committee said, "A lot of the people disagree with the particular attitude these films express [Mr. Sarris was not specifying the three films in question.] . . . When you get some of these films that deal quite frankly with things like homosexuality I think the majority of the people are very violently opposed, the majority of the critics are very

[7] Interview, October 1966.

[8] It may be argued that *Troublemakers* was shown in the big hall and that *Troublemakers,* by my definition, is indeed "subversive." This is true. *Troublemakers* has had great difficulty achieving distribution, which for a film of this quality certainly supports the thesis. But the basic iconoclasm of *The Flicker, Echoes of Silence,* and *Relativity* far surpasses the literary "subversion" of *Troublemakers,* which is weakened by its dependence on the compulsive, limited, mannered aesthetic of "Direct Cinema."

violently [opposed], and I think this is one of the issues that keeps coming up all the time, of subject matter. . . ." [9]

The Festival Programming Committee was diffident about showing a mass audience these works. This is a deplorable example of paternalistic thinking. The avant-garde film should not be relegated to the castrating safety of the small room, the art gallery, the museum, or the private collection. Film is designed to be shown in big rooms and on television night after night before large, diverse audiences. According to *Variety,* "Nielsen's demographic data, according to the research boys, gave 'Kwai' a viewer count of some 71,000,000 while an ARB audience comp awarded the Oscar shindig some 62,000,000." [10]

Of course we are expected to be grateful that the New American Cinema has been recognized by the Establishment. And, in truth, we are. But not that grateful. Someone else should be grateful that it exists to recognize. To quote Amos Vogel, "The onus, as always, is not on the artist; he is merely man's most nakedly sensitive radar instrument toward an understanding of this world. It is we who must learn to read him." [11]

In America, which is a provincial, pseudo-democratic plutocracy, the Establishments are many but their thinking is uniformly tribal in its conservatism. The sophisticated artist in such a society, especially the mass-media artist working in an expensive medium, is placed in an untenable position.

Parker Tyler, in a 1966 Festival lecture entitled "Is Film Criticism Only Propaganda?" [12] attacked much of what has appeared in *Film Culture.* Although he did not specify, Mr. Tyler seemed to have Jonas Mekas in mind. Mr. Tyler misses the point. Mr. Mekas is not a critic. He is an evangelist concerned with "The Word," and writing is only an adjunct component of other equally important redemptive activities. "Propaganda" is the wrong term in this context and only

---

[9] Lecture, New York Film Festival, 1966. Three months after this statement was made Andy Warhol's *The Chelsea Girls* opened for what turned into an extended and profitable run in midtown Manhattan.

[10] *Variety,* November 2, 1966.

[11] Program, New York Film Festival, 1966.

[12] Published in *Film Culture,* Fall 1966.

implies that Mr. Tyler simply does not comprehend what is happening in the reckless, autonomous world of independent cinema. Rudolf Arnheim wrote in *Film as Art*, "It is the business of the theorist to inspect the tools and to ask that they be cleaner. At the same time he is darkly aware of what the reckless practice of the arts has done to his standards in the past and will do to them in the future. Having delivered his admonition, he secretly puts some trust in the messy shrewd-ness that for so long has been the hope of the human con-dition." Adrienne Mancia of the Museum of Modern Art told me, "I think that a group that's really done a tremendous job— in any event I feel like saying it because I think it's so true— with all the polemics, with all the sensationalism is Jonas, single-handedly, and the whole group he's spokesman for. It is something we are beginning to accept as standard today but when he began there was no place for filmmakers to show their films, there was no group that would distribute their films. No one talked about their films. If nothing else, it en-couraged young people to go ahead and make them—to say, 'if nothing else I can show them at the Cinematheque, if noth-ing else I can give it to the Cooperative.' On their own the Cooperative sends films traveling overseas. This is something the Museum hasn't even been able to do yet, although this is a goal we eventually hope to achieve." [13]

If Mr. Tyler had chosen to criticize the point of redemptive activity, had chosen to explore the very probable relation-ship between the evangelist, the romantic, and the revolu-tionary, his shafts might have had point. To quote a very favorable review of Jack Smith's *Flaming Creatures* written by Susan Sontag: "Nowhere in the world has the old cliché of European romanticism—the assassin mind versus the spon-taneous heart—had such a long career as in America. Here, more than anywhere else, the belief lives on that neatness and carefulness of technique interfere with spontaneity, with truth, with immediacy." [14]

A provincial, compulsive, plutocratic industrial society at-tempts and largely succeeds in relegating the mass-media

[13] Interview, October 1966. Since this the Museum of Modern Art has sent a twenty-year retrospective of independent personal films to Japan.

[14] *Against Interpretation*, p. 228. New York: Farrar, Straus & Giroux, 1966.

artist to a subservient position. The consequent trauma experienced by those relegated provides the foundation for the
violent polarity, the underlying bitterness, the deep resent-
ment, and the polemic extremism that is so much a part of
avant-garde films, so much a part of the writing that concerns
itself with the avant-garde film. The filmmakers believe they
are at war, and indeed they are. There is no other choice.

THE MOVIES ARE A REVOLUTION *

by Taylor Mead

*Taylor Mead is a poet. He has acted in numerous films pro-
duced by the new filmmakers, including Ron Rice's* The Flower
Thief *and Gregory Markopoulos's* The Illiac Passion. *He has
been a spokesman for the New American Cinema in both
America and abroad.*

The movies are this exciting thing, you see. The movies are a
revolution. That which the public desires that excitement
inherent in a star or director or script or all three (though in
America which needs a revolution they have been able to sup-
press everything but the star—only Ronnie Rice and I are
correcting that though we are a little bit suppressed and
money does not exactly flow for us but what do we care much
—we are a revolution and will be seen.

Listen to our mad crazy audiences which are you—babies
—you beautiful ones—even our haters—all of you have got to
dig—we are the bank robbers, rapists, sodomists, all the yearn-
ing mad desires of the populace which the government has
to let be seen or else wow an explosion—what if Truman
arrested James Dean? WOW! and James Dean—the epitome
of every house breaker, mad fiend, lost asylum resident—a
typical star like Bette Davis or Marlon or Magnani all a
desperate gang—either they speak on street corners and toss
aside you lousy government(s) or you let them breed with
vast audiences the secret thoughts hopes and frustrations that

* Reprinted from *Film Culture*, No. 29, Summer, 1963.

gestate new personalities new ways of looking at and understanding and undermining and building new countries worlds
people—oh most insidious triumphant ponderous art oh big bad
beautiful sick chromium plated phony real lost Hollywood. If
you don't give the people good pictures this year Ron Rice and
Taylor Mead will storm the palace with howling hungry public
one way or another—you are dangerously boring the public this
year you phony stuffed tight dungarees and padded bra no
nakedness land— The people may be laughing at Jerry Lewis
and crying with Ava but that is because they haven't anything
better to laugh and cry with and when the empty hungry feeling persists watch out!

I myself am getting tired of making movies for forty people
to see and may retire—and last best bet I saw to replace James
Dean was arrested as a housebreaker according to this week's
March 26 *Look*—what a beauty—when your movie stars have
to break and enter the people will be right behind them.

The world weariness of Antonioni is strictly European and
however interesting and beautiful can not satisfy America. Besides, it's not beat. It's not mongrel, wild, uncouth, naive,
heartless, heartful, pornographic, licentious, insane, bold, bald,
fat, monstrous, square enough for America—strong enough to
release the monolithic freeze which periodically grips this
land and is settling in again this year along with the weather.

America's great movements are too little—we *must* have the
screen. The enormous 12,800 mile SCREEN! He says, falling
all 500 stories to the *cement*.

America, loosen up, or strangle.

PART II

THEORY
AND
CRITICISM

THE INDEPENDENT CINEMA *

by Andrew Sarris

In this article, Andrew Sarris lists several unusual arguments for the support of experimental and independent films and cites reasons why the existence of such films contributes toward the improvement of all film production. Mr. Sarris is film critic for The Village Voice *and New York editor of* Cahiers du Cinéma.

The Independent Cinema is in many respects a fiction of the journalist's imagination. What makes a film independent? And independent of what? Hollywood? Commercialism? Plot? Production values? Entertainment? In short, how much independence can we bear? At what point does liberty degenerate into license?

Patrons of Lincoln Center's Fourth New York Film Festival were initiated recently into the rites and revels of the "underground" with a Special Events series entitled "The Independent Cinema" described as "a program of 27 events covering various aspects of independent filmmaking in the United States today." The events included lectures by and discussions with filmmakers, screenings of new works and works-in-progress, and open interviews with visiting directors from abroad. As it turned out, most of the programs were well attended, but the series as a whole failed to generate much excitement. It was no one's fault, particularly, but the fact remains that the Special Events Program became a subdued sideshow to the Festival proper. Festival Director Amos Vogel and Festival Coordinator John Brockman did their best to bring the underground to the surface. The advance publicity was astoundingly impressive. Tactful overtures were made to all the warring factions in the Independent Cinema, and Andy Warhol was pointedly excluded from the proceedings so as not to offend the regular reviewers. Brockman was

* Reprinted from *Motive*, November, 1966.

particularly anxious to avoid the stigma of neo-Dadaism by focusing attention on optically oriented spectacles that fall into the category of "intermedia" or "mixed media" or even "McLuhanist happenings." Marshall McLuhan's "the medium is the message" has replaced Sergei Eisenstein's montage-collision credos of an earlier era.

At any rate, by opening night some of the independent film-makers, unrepresented either in the Festival proper or the Special Events, began picketing the proceedings. A black mass was threatened around the Revlon fountain in Lincoln Center's piazza, but the alleged protest eventually degenerated into personal publicity. Jonas Mekas, the official spokesman of the New American Cinema, criticized Vogel and Brockman in *The Village Voice,* but, far from boycotting the proceedings, Mekas actually participated in some of the Special Events panels.

What galled Mekas and his followers most was the im-plication that Independent Films were not yet ready to charge admission at Philharmonic Hall, but had to be shown free in Lincoln Center's Library Auditorium. Was it money or pres-tige at stake? Stan Brakhage flatly refused to allow his film to be shown for free. After all, Lincoln Center was loaded and he was living from hand to mouth, and why not give him a $75 rental fee? What Mekas and Brakhage failed to realize was that Lincoln Center itself was not all that generous to the Film Festival, and that if a precedent of paying rentals to Festival films were established, it would be difficult to get anything for free. Anyway money is always a more crucial issue with artists than with promoters, and one can recall the telegrams exchanged between Bernard Shaw and Sam Goldwyn in which the producer wired that he was more interested in art than in money, and the playwright wired back that he was more interested in money than in art. Although Brakhage announced his conditions in advance, Tony Conrad and Victor Grauer screened two flashing light films (*The Flicker* and *Archangel* respectively) at a special event, and then, when the house lights went on, proceeded to attack the Festival for not paying rentals for their films. As for these new-styled LSD-licensed flickers themselves, all I can say is that they represent an extreme form of passive experience. If you stare long enough, you begin to see colors merging on the flickering screen, but you can get the same effect by staring at a blinking neon light. It is like the girl who wants to be seduced without having a meaningful relationship. The creator is replaced by the stimulator, and we find ourselves back in a can of Andy Warhol's Campbell Tomato Soup—at least as far as aesthetic distinctions are involved.

Aesthetic distinctions! That is usually what is most lacking in inquiries about the Independent Film. New, different, way-out: these are the adjectives of fashionable journalism. Good—bad: these are the relics of academe. What counts here is not what the scene is, but who is making it. That is why all the mumbo jumbo of Happenings fits so well into the promotion of resorts and night clubs. What is a night club, after all, but a Happening with dim lights, loud music, perfumed odors, gleaming flesh, swirling incense, and liquid LSD? This swing to the religious, the rapturous, the irrational, the oblivious, the orgasmic is not without social implications. One might say (though I do not) that this flight from coherence involves a complete rejection of conscious existence and the monstrous movement of history. There is possibly also a reaction against the systematic social consciousness of the "independent filmmakers" of the thirties and forties. Acceptance of one's environment, the corollary of Pop and Camp, would seem to be the most reactionary response possible to the ancient schools of documentary seeking to make films more "honest" than Hollywood's hallucinations, to borrow a phrase from Parker Tyler, one of the more skeptical lecturers at the Independent Film Series. In fact, a recent series of Independent Films at the Bleecker Street Cinema began with Robert Flaherty's *Nanook of the North* of 1922, and concluded with Andy Warhol's *Life of Juanita Castro* of 1966, a forty-five-year trajectory of decadence and depravity. Yet this too is a facile generalization. In his way, Warhol is more socially conscious than Flaherty, less exotic and romantic. The perverts and prostitutes in Warhol's world are no less real and sensitive for improperly flaunting their fey fantasies. Besides, there is still a great deal of conventional propaganda pouring out of the underground. Shirley Clarke's concern with Negroes in *The Connection* and *The Cool World* may be politically advanced, but hardly formally fancy. The real tip-off is the selection of Nelson's *Oh Dem Watermelons* and Preston's *Son of Dada* as short subjects in the Festival proper.

Both films feature unconventional techniques, particularly dizzying montage and surreal collage of paper cut-outs; but their big pitch is politics: *Watermelons* against racial condescension, *Son of Dada* against LBJ. Unfortunately, even viewers who endorsed the filmmakers' politics deplored their poetics. The point is that as much as we may talk about cinematic forms, most people are still obsessed by what a movie is actually about. Consequently, I think it was a mistake for the Festival to stress the relative respectability of the Independent Cinema by screening out the more outrageous filmmakers. Outrage is not only one of the historic functions of the avant-garde; it is the only advantage the outsider possesses against the superior resources of the insider. Ultimately the most insidious enemy of art is good taste.

In the realm of aesthetic distinctions, however, the Festival justified its special events section by presenting *Echoes of Silence* by Peter Goldman, a 26-year-old New York filmmaker on a $1,500 shoestring. Goldman's intuitive talent is indisputable. Yet many members of the critical establishment walked out of his film because of a lack of technical finesse. The anguished lyricism of lonely sensualists in New York counted for nothing with those for whom production polish is a *sine qua non*. But what does one expect for $1,500? *Breathless* or *L'Avventura*? Apparently. And this is the pitiful absurdity of audience expectations from a penniless American avant-garde. The Independent Cinema is thus caught in a vicious circle by becoming the victim of its exaggerated publicity, without which it would never attract any attention. It is simply sorrowful to watch Independent American filmmakers confronting the "art film" directors from abroad, not because the Americans are necessarily inferior in style and sensibility, but because the Godards, the Antonionis, the Resnaises, the Pasolinis are actually the Establishment with subtitles.

Therefore it is high time that the Independent Cinema be relegated to the limbo of journalistic jargon along with the "new wave." As Chabrol once remarked, "There are no waves; there is only the ocean." And in this ocean, there are good and bad directors, both above ground and under. Since facile generations thus are outlawed, the following observations are thrown out in no particularly set sequence.

• The Independent Film tends to subsist on its own rationales and exegeses. Peter Goldman one day may work in Hollywood. Stan Brakhage and Gregory Markopoulos probably never will. Goldman's film *Echoes of Silence* is embryonic fiction feature. Brakhage and Markopoulos are too subjective, too abstract, to concern themselves with standard conventions of movies. Does a filmmaker have to be an entertainer? Goldman probably would say yes. Brakhage and Markopoulos, no. Who is right? This depends entirely on where the cinema goes from here.

- As Independent Films become increasingly personal, audiences and critics should not be excessively disturbed that filmmakers do not reveal the decorous life patterns of mythical middle-class morality. To put it more bluntly, the facts of perversion and hypersexuality will become increasingly explicit.

- If the avant-garde faces any threat at all, it is simply that the squares are becoming more hip than the hipsters, that commercial movies are more salacious than underground movies, and that suburbia is more audacious than bohemia.

- Relaxed censorship is depriving the avant-garde of its *raison d'être*. So is the excessive gullibility of mass taste toward anything new. The bourgeois exploits the avant-garde artist simply to fulfill the fantasy of a daring, adventurous society. Actually the realities of mechanization and conformity are so overwhelming that the most superficial nonconformities are subsidized in a spirit of desperation. That is to say, if Jonas Mekas did not exist, the Establishment would have had to invent him.

- Mekas and his followers have succeeded in demystifying the medium. They have exposed some of the quasicriminal conspiracies that maintain movies as an industrial monopoly rather than as an individual art. By demonstrating that anyone can make a movie they make it possible for gifted individuals without relatives in Hollywood or the craft unions to enter cinema.

- Most Independent filmmakers lack the humility to be great artists. Their own personalities loom larger than either their art or their audience. Many are still overreacting against Hollywood.

- Academically and culturally speaking, the cinema is still the stepchild of the arts. The Ford Foundation gives millions to ballet companies and piddling amounts to filmmakers. The academic community still resists cinema in the curriculum. Consequently, there is a shortage of academic positions to provide some economic sanctuary for film poets.

• Many of the arguments of the avant-garde seem to presuppose either an unconditional subsidy or a commercially feasible captive audience. If to please an audience is invariably to compromise the artist's convictions, then art can never be either popular or accessible. But what possible motivation can society have to subsidize that which is denied it by definition? Again, without aesthetic distinctions or determinations of degrees, we are caught up in a Faustian fallacy of our time. Compromise and communication are not interchangeable terms, and self-expression is not sacred.

• The Independent Cinema serves a scholarly function simply by trying to be different. The outrageousness of Independent Films confirms the validity of some conventions and the arbitrariness of others. Independent Films serve a useful purpose through their parody, mockery, and general iconoclasm. Where the mystique of Independent Films was once realistic in seeking the reality beyond conventional movies, Independent Films are now more fanciful in tracing the fantasies of a culture oriented toward conventional movies.

• Independent Films overwhelmingly are Left-oriented though not as sacrilegious as the avant-garde blasphemies of the Buñuel-Dali era. Unfortunately, there is little shock mileage left in being "Left" in New York.

• Independent Films are developing a new breed of independent film critics of great sophistication and erudition, but there is little meaningful debate within the movement because skeptics seldom see enough Independent Films to qualify as experts.

• It is as fallacious to think that if you have seen three or four Independent Films, you have seen them all, as to think that if you have seen three or four commercial movies you have seen them all. Yet people keep asking me to show them "underground cinema" as if a few samples will suffice to define hundreds of separate spasms of creativity.

• Finally, the collectivity of Independent Cinema is not worth writing about. Only individual films. I have liked Kenneth Anger's *Scorpio Rising*, Andy Warhol's and Ronny Tavel's *The Life of Juanita Castro*, Adolfas Mekas's *Hallelujah the Hills*, Peter Goldman's *Echoes of Silence*, several works by Stan VanDerBeek, Carmen D'Avino, and Robert Breer in the more abstract categories. Martin Scorsese's short films reveal a wit capable of talking features. Robert Downey has his moments of hilarious satire. Shirley Clarke and Lionel Rogosin have given us some candid moments in the more depressed areas.

Add it all up and you have an interesting footnote to the history of world cinema. Much ado about nothing? Hardly. Someone has to man the outposts of culture, and the Independent Film is uniquely qualified to express the chaos and confusion of our time.

ART TODAY AND THE FILM
by Rudolf Arnheim

In his book Film as Art *(1957) Rudolf Arnheim writes: "The senses are useful when their contribution is not overestimated. In the culture we happen to live in, they teach us relatively little. The world of our century is a poor actor; it does show its variegated outside, but its true nature is not immediately apparent either to the eyes or to the ears."* *

The following paper was written as the initial presentation for a symposium on "Cinema and the Contemporary Arts" held at the Lincoln Center for the Performing Arts on the occasion of the Third New York Film Festival, September, 1965. Here Arnheim traces the historical procedure which has resulted in the new artist's view of time and space. He points out that "The destruction of the continuity of time and space is a nightmare when applied to the physical world, but it is a sensible order in the realm of the mind."

Rudolf Arnheim has also written a book on the "Guernica" mural by Picasso, and in 1954 published his classic Art and Visual Perception.

If the various arts of our time share certain traits and tendencies they probably do so in different ways, depending

* Berkeley, California: University of California Press, 1960, p. 196.

on the character of each medium. At first glance, the photographic image, technically committed to mechanical reproduction, might be expected to fit modern art badly—a theoretical prediction not borne out, however, by some of the recent work of photographers and film directors. In the following I shall choose a key notion to describe central aspects of today's art and then apply this notion to the film, thereby suggesting particular ways in which the photochemical picture responds to some aesthetic demands of our time.

In search of the most characteristic feature of our visual art, one can conclude that it is the attempt of getting away from the detached images by which artists have been portraying physical reality. In the course of our civilization we have come to use images as tools of contemplation. We have set them up as a world of their own, separate from the world they depict, so that they may have their own completeness and develop more freely their particular style. These virtues, however, are outweighed by the anxiety such a detachment arouses when the mind cannot afford it because its own hold on reality has loosened too much. Under such conditions, the footlights separating a world of make-believe from its counterpart and the frame which protects the picture from merging with its surroundings become a handicap.

In a broader sense, the very nature of a recognizable likeness suffices to produce the frightening dichotomy, even without any explicit detachment of the image. A marble statue points to a world of flesh and blood, to which, however, it confesses not to belong—which leaves it without a dwelling-place in that world. It can acquire such a dwelling-place only by insisting that it is more than an image, and the most radical way of accomplishing it is to abandon the portrayal of the things of nature altogether. This is, of course, what modern art has done. By renouncing portrayal, the work of art establishes itself clearly as an object possessing an independent existence of its own.

But once this radical step has been taken, another, even more decisive one, suggests itself forcefully. It consists in giving up image-making entirely. This can be illustrated by recent developments in painting. When the abstractionists had abandoned the portrayal of natural objects, their paintings were still representing colored shapes dwelling in pictorial space, that is, they were still pretending the presence of something that was not there. Painters tried various remedies. They resorted to collage, which introduced the "real object" into the world of visual illusion. They reverted to trompe l'oeil effects of the most humiliating dullness. They discredited picture-making by mimicking its most commercialized products. They fastened plumbing fixtures to their canvases. None of these attempts carries conviction, except one, which seems most promising, namely, the attachment of abstract painting to architecture. Abstract painting fits the wall as no representational painting ever has, and in doing so it relinquishes the illusion of pictorial space and becomes, instead, the surface-texture of the three-dimensional block of stone.

In this three-dimensional space of physical existence, to which painting thus escapes, sculpture has always been settled. Even so, sculpture, as much as painting, has felt the need to get away from image-making. It replaces imitative shape with the leftovers of industrial machinery, it uses plaster casts, and it presents real objects as artifacts. All these characteristic tendencies in the realm of object-making are overshadowed, however, by the spectacular aesthetic success of industrial design. The machines, the bridges, the tools and surgical instruments enjoy all the closeness to the practical needs of society which the fine arts have lost. These useful objects are bona fide inhabitants of the physical world, with no pretense of image-making, and yet they mirror the condition of modern man with a purity and intensity that is hard to match.

To complete our rapid survey, we glance at the performing arts and note that the mimetic theatre, in spite of an occasional excellent production in the traditional style, has sprouted few shoots that would qualify it as a living medium. Significantly, its most vital branch has been Brecht's epic theatre, which spurns illusionism in its language, its style of acting, and its stage setting, and uses its actors as story-tellers and demonstrators of ideas. Musical comedy, although so different from the epic theatre otherwise, owes its success also to the playing down of narrative illusion. The spectacle of graceful and rhythmical motion addresses the audience as directly as do Brecht's pedagogical expositions. And the modern dance can be said to have made its victorious entrance where the costumed pantomime left off. The most

drastic move toward undisguised actions seems to have been
made by the so-called Happenings. They dispense the raw
material of thrill, fear, curiosity, and prurience in a setting
that unites actors and spectators in a common adventure.

If we have read the signs of the times at all correctly, the
prospect of the cinema would seem to look dim—not because it lacks potential but because what it has to offer
might appear to be the opposite of what is wanted. The
film is mimetic by its very nature. As a branch of photography, it owes, its existence to the imprint of things upon
a sensitive surface. It is the image-maker *par excellence,* and
much of its success derives from the mechanical faithfulness
of its portrayals. What is such a medium to do when the
artificiality of the detached image makes the minds uneasy?

Ironically, the motion picture must be viewed by the his-
torian as a late product of a long development that began
as a reaction to a detachment from reality. The motion
picture is a grandchild of the Renaissance. It goes back to
the birth of natural science, the search for techniques by
which to reproduce and measure nature more reliably, back
to the camera obscura, which for centuries was used by
painters as a welcome crutch, back to the tracings of shadow
profiles, which created a vogue of objective portraiture shortly
before photography was invented. The moving photograph
was a late victory in the struggle for the grasp of concrete
reality.

But there are two ways of losing contact with the world
of perceivable objects, to which our senses and feelings are
attuned. One can move away from this world to find reality
in abstract speculation, as did the pre-Renaissance era of
the Middle Ages, or one can lose this world by piercing the
visible surface of things and finding reality in their inside,
as did post-Renaissance science—physics, chemistry, psychology. Thus our very concern with factual concreteness has
led up beyond the surfaces to which our eyes respond. At
the same time, a surfeit of pictures in magazines and news-
papers, in the movies and on television has blunted our reactions to the indiscretions and even the horrors of the journalistic snapshot and the Grand Guignol. Today's children look
at the tears of tragedy and at maimed corpses every day.

The cinema responded to the demand for concreteness
by making the photographic image look more and more

like reality. It added sound, it added color, and the latest developments of photography promise us a new technique that will not only produce genuine three-dimensionality but also abolish the fixed perspective, thus replacing the image with total illusion. The live television show got rid of the time gap between the picture and the pictured event. And as the painters took to large-size canvases in order to immerse the eye in an endless spectacle of color, blurring the border between the figment and the outer world, the cinema expanded the screen for similar purposes. This openness of form was supplemented by an openness of content: the short-story type of episode no longer presented a closed and detached entity but seemed to emerge briefly from real life only to vanish again in the continuum of everyday existence.

The extreme attempt of capturing the scenes of life unposed and unrehearsed by means of hidden cameras was received with no more than a mild, temporary stir—somewhere between the keyhole pleasures of the peeping Tom and those of the sidewalk superintendent. For the curious paradox in the nature of any image is, of course, that the more faithful it becomes, the more it loses the highest function of imagery, namely, that of synthesizing and interpreting what it represents. And thereby it loses interest. In this sense, even the original addition of motion to the still photograph was a risky step to take because the enormous enrichment gained by action in the time dimension had to be paid with the loss of the capacity to preserve the lasting character of things, safely removed from their constant changes in time.

Following the example of painting, the cinema has tried the remedy of abstraction. But the experiments, from Hans Richter and Viking Eggeling to Oskar Fischinger, Norman McLaren, and Len Lye, have amounted mainly to a museum's collection of venerable curiosities. This may seem surprising, considering the great aesthetic potential of colored shapes in motion. But since abstract painting is also on the decline, my guess is that once the artist abandons image-making he has no longer a good reason to cling to the two-dimensional surface, that is, to the twilight area between image-making and object-making. Hence the temporary or permanent desertion of so many artists from painting to sculpture and, as I said, the attempts to make painting three-dimensional or attach it to architecture.

The film cannot do this. There seems to be general agreement that the cinema has scored its most lasting and most specifically cinematic successes when it drew its interpretations of life from authentic realism. This has been true all the way from Lumière to Pudovkin, Eisenstein, and Robert Flaherty and more recently de Sica and Zavattini. And I would find it hard to argue with somebody who maintained that he would be willing to give the entire film production of the last few years for Jacques-Yves Cousteau's recent under-water documentary, *World Without Sun.*

However—and this brings me to the main point of my argument—Cousteau's film creates fascination not simply as an extension of our visual knowledge obtained by the documentary presentation of an unexplored area of our earth. These most authentically realistic pictures reveal a world of profound mystery, a darkness momentarily lifted by flashes of unnatural light, a complete suspension of the familiar vertical and horizontal coordinates of space. Spatial orientation is upset also by the weightlessness of these animals and dehumanized humans, floating up and down without effort, emerging from nowhere and disappearing into nothingness, constantly in motion without any recognizable purpose, and totally indifferent to each other. There is an overwhelming display of dazzling color and intricate motion, tied to no experience we ever had and performed for the discernible benefit of nobody. There are innumerable monstrous variations of faces and bodies as we know them, passing by with the matter-of-factness of herring or perch, in a profound silence, most unnatural for such visual commotion and rioting color, and interrupted only by noises nobody ever heard. What we have here, if a nasty pun is permissible, is the New Wave under water.

For it seems evident that what captures us in this documentary film is a most successful although surely unintentional display of what the most impressive films of the last few years have been trying to do, namely, to interpret the ghostliness of the visible world by means of authentic appearances drawn directly from that world. The cinema has been making its best contribution to the general trend I have tried to describe, not by withdrawing from imagery, as the other arts have, but by using imagery to describe reality as a ghostly figment. It thereby seizes and interprets the experience from which the other visual arts tend to escape and to which they are reacting.

In exploiting this opportunity, the cinema remains faithful to its nature. It derives its new nightmares from its old authenticity. Take the spell-binding opening of Fellini's 8½, the scene of the heart attack in the closed car, stared at without reaction by the other drivers, so nearby and yet so distant in their glass and steel containers; take the complete paralysis of motion, realistically justified by the traffic jam in the tunnel, and compare this frightening mystery with the immediately following escape of the soul, which has all the ludicrous clumsiness of the special-effects department. How much more truly unreal are the mosquito swarms of the reporters persecuting the widowed woman in *La Dolce Vita* than is the supposedly fantastic harem bath of the hero in 8½. And how unforgettable, on the other hand, is the gray nothingness of the steam bath in which the pathetic moviemakers do penitence and which transfigures the ancient cardinal.

The actors of Alain Robbe-Grillet move without reason like Cousteau's fishes and contemplate each other with a similar indifference. They practice absent-mindedness as a way of life and they cohabit across long distances of empty floor. In their editing technique, the directors of the *Nouvelle Vague* destroy the relations of time, which is the dimension of action, and of space, which is the dimension of human contact, by violating all the rules in the book—and some readers will guess what book I am referring to. Those rules, of course, presupposed that the filmmaker wished to portray the physical continuity of time and space by the discontinuity of the pictures.

The destruction of the continuity of time and space is a nightmare when applied to the physical world but it is a sensible order in the realm of the mind. The human mind, in fact, stores the experiences of the past as memory traces, and in a storage vault there are no time sequences or spatial connections, only affinities and associations based on similarity or contrast. It is this different but positive order of the mind that novelists and film directors of the last few years have presented as a new reality while demolishing the old. By eliminating the difference between what is presently perceived and what is only remembered from the past, they have created a new homogeneity and unity of all experience, independent of the order of physical things. When in Michael Butor's novel, *La Modification*, the sequence of the train voyage from Paris to Rome constantly interacts with a spray of atomized episodes of the past, the dismemberment of physical time and space creates a new time sequence and a new spatial continuum, namely, those of the mind.

It is the creation and exploitation of this new order of the mind in its independence of the order of physical things which, I believe, will keep the cinema busy while the other visual arts explore the other side of the dichotomy—the world of physical things from which the mind seems so pleasantly absent.

IS FILM CRITICISM ONLY PROPAGANDA?

by Parker Tyler

In the following lecture, which was delivered at the Fourth New York Film Festival (1966) at Lincoln Center, Parker Tyler takes a critical view of current independent filmmaking. He asserts that responsible criticism of these films is, in general, largely lacking. He observes that "freedom of expression is no guarantee of merit" and feels that the present generation of independent filmmakers do not offer value substantially above the level of current commercial movies. In his influential book The Three Faces of the Film *Mr. Tyler notes: "The one striking thing about the Experimental film is that its practitioners, if gifted and sincere, automatically acquire a unique aura. This aura is nothing but the INDE-PENDENT art of the film."* *

Parker Tyler was born in New Orleans in 1907. He has been an Editorial Associate and contributor to Art News *and in 1958 received the Longview Award for poetry. His other books include* Magic and Myth of the Movies, Chaplin, *and* Yesterday's Children.

* *The Three Faces of the Film,* New York: Thomas Yoseloff, 1960, p. 57.

Perhaps I am the most unpopular film critic in the world and maybe, despite my long record, I'm so unpopular because I'm not a very good propagandist for modern doctrines *in* film and *of* film. Let's look at the term propaganda. It means the systematic propagation of a special doctrine, religious, political, social, economic . . . artistic. . . . But what does the verb propagate signify? It merely means to multiply one's own kind, to reproduce, as do animals and, for that matter, vegetables. Is it that simple in regard to film? Perhaps, following the dictionary, it should be. But experience teaches us to suspect and examine the implications of dictionary definitions.

According to the dictionary, we might think that the duty of film criticism is to breed more film criticism of the same sort, the duty of films to breed more films of the same sort. From big Garbos, somehow, there should come little Garbos, who will grow up; from the avant-garde (apparently Garbo is still avant-garde) there should come more avant-garde, which will grow up. Surely it is clear that I'm being a little ironic, and that the whole point of film criticism viewed as propaganda is that it has a special doctrine, a viewpoint; that it is limited and exclusive, being for certain defined values and against other values, equally definable . . . that it can point, can divide the sheep from the goats, even within its own ranks; can develop theories of value, definition, analysis. Otherwise, it is no more than self-promotion, a variety of commercial advertising rigged up with gags, more or less refined and sophisticated. To cite an analogy: It is not the function of film criticism to choose between grapefruit and nectarines as commodities for the discriminating palate, but rather to help create the best nectarines and the best grapefruit.

I'm sure that we who are serious desire that *better film criticism* stand for values, that it should be able to point and distinguish, speak a coherent language, and espouse, at its best, a vigorous, high-level doctrine. In this same hall, last year, I solemnly questioned that better film criticism *as it exists* stands for this; I assumed that critics are very much behind-hand in their natural work of propaganda. For my pains, I was applauded and I was also contradicted and looked at askance. I was told in print—by an authority

who shall be nameless—that all the books that I saw as
lacking and needful *had* been written. Now this was a
childish admonition, based only on superstition and hearsay.
If we really inspected such books, we might see attempts at
the real thing, even near-successes, but widely recognized
theories, anything like a lucid and comprehensive body of
doctrine? No. Nothing like that save in the most limited
sense. At least, if such exists, it hasn't been announced in the
English language; nor, from what appears in *Cahiers du
Cinéma,* in the French language.

I'm devoting the rest of this talk to a series of propositions
that won't take too long. The remainder of our time I suggest be taken up with discussing and confirming or denying
my propositions, and with *evidence* rather than *rhetoric* and
prejudices. For simplicity's sake, I'll call the film criticism
that to me seems desirable Responsible Film Criticism.

FIRST PROPOSITION: *We cannot have responsible film
criticism so long as there exists the sentimental fetish of the
Good Old Days, both in Hollywood and European film
capitals.*

REMARKS: This attitude does not even represent "criticism"
but should be called smart antiquarianism. It cites master
directors and classic films by gauges and allusions whose
values are completely obscure, to me, and so far as I know,
untranslatable into any artistic or intellectual idiom known
to any of the other arts. Note that the habit of antiquarianism
does not rest chiefly on uniquely *filmic* values, on technical
quantities, but on total historic results, on so-called film
classics, whatever technical theories and assumptions the
said classics may have had.

SECOND PROPOSITION: *We cannot have responsible film
criticism so long as nominally serious critics (here I can
mention James Agee who was among the most talented)
imitate the habits of journalistic reviewers.*

REMARKS: What are the habits of journalistic reviewers
and why are they so bad? Because of the journalistic re-
viewer's job, he must, even at his best, and most sincere
and independent, assume that Hollywood (for example)
has a standard of The Best, and that this is authoritative at
any given time, by any given measure. But this rule of The
Best, alas, is vitiated by having been industrially determined.
Thus nothing could be more foolish than recognizing it. If

producers created artistic standards, the very occupation of
film critics would be superfluous and the discrimination of
the audience rendered quite meaningless. I have often been
asked: "Why aren't you writing criticism for one of the
New York dailies or weeklies?" The answer is simple: Because I like far too little that happens in film. To hold their
jobs, reviewers have to approve a minimum of the local
products and the imported products. Of course, a few
journalistic reviewers pretend not to accept Hollywood
standards and interests—these are the ones who lambaste one
day and laud the next—and perhaps they don't accept them,
consciously, but unconsciously they are occupational victims
of the same standards and interests. Moreover, most of even
the better journalistic reviewers are habitual fakers; they
vaunt having the know-how of a thing when actually their
gift of the gab has simply succeeded in dominating the professional competition of critics in their own class. True know-
how has very little to do with professional critical competence
as it is.

THIRD PROPOSITION: *Responsible film criticism has been
dealt a serious blow by the recent upsurge of the avant-garde
in the direction of Pop Art, which has substituted mere
qualities of smart novelty and unsmart impudence for creative meaning in film and represents a revolt of the amateurs
against the professionals.*

REMARKS: Here we are in focus with the theme of the
present forums. The state of the Independent Cinema touches
intimately the issue of film criticism as propaganda. We
may reserve argument as to just how good the current avant-
garde, or independent cinema, is. The avant-garde in theory,
I maintain, must be serious and positive, not simply active
and negative. It cannot be, with any growing profit, what
it now overwhelmingly tends to be: a sort of anti-commercial
demonstration protesting the segregation of small films from
large: by "small" and "large" I refer roughly to their professional scale, not their length. . . . The fact is that the whole
theory of the avant-garde has gradually, subtly, altered
within the framework of modern social and political protest,
and now proclaims itself as propaganda for a very loose and
inferior doctrine. Today, we have exponents of the nominal
Independent Cinema who welcome any creative-type manifestation, no matter what its artistic or nonartistic aims, no

matter what its technical or professional qualifications. Why is the wildest, willfullest daydream (which may be quite banal) no less than the most naive and flabby documentary welcomed, sometimes, with equal fervor?

Let me extend the remarks on this proposition because actually it leads to the summary proposition that will be the whole point of my argument. The source of all radical intelligence in the arts, accounting for all past revolutions of style and taste, has been the desire to see, to hear, to write with greater keenness or greater scope, with more depth, grace, or comprehensiveness. To "change the mode"— even as late as the first two decades of this century—did not mean to lower the standard of quality, to level off the average, to be more democratically inclusive.

Now, however, the avant-garde is making a popular front among the underprivileged element in the arts. That would be all right, it would be fine, if their number was only underprivileged in *opportunity*, but too often independent filmmakers are also underprivileged in *talent*. It is a classic radical quality, in art or politics, to be aggressive and also to be "different." But to be both is not enough for the avant-garde with a high standard. The avant-garde today is like the miniskirt. It's new and it shows things. But some knees are beautiful and some are not.

Unfortunately, being a "useful" critic of the Independent Cinema is to be one who obeys blindly, a propagandist rule of order. But this rule is as elementary and as dated as the old campaign for free speech. Take the element of censorship. Nowadays, sex in the films—all kinds of sex—is being stripped nude inch by inch. Freedom of visual speech, I grant, is a vital issue, and opens up fresh opportunities. But a film, as an artistic entity, is not necessarily improved by being bold or candid in its sex scenes—quite the contrary, it may get worse. . . . It should be tacit that freedom of expression is no guarantee of merit. But, apparently, it needs to be said.

Now, speaking of the critics who devote themselves mostly to the Independent Cinema, I grant that some of the appreciative little monographs that appear, for instance, in *Film Culture*, are intelligent and display insight into artistic and filmic values. But, more frequently, one finds in the little film magazines the abandoned outpourings of some

young or middle-aged enthusiast who wants to attract attention to himself or to a friend. If there is little discrimination
about the artistic quality of independent filmmakers, there is
almost as little about their critics. It strikes me very forcibly
that good film criticism, *responsible* film criticism, is impossible, when so high a degree of tolerance is exercised
toward manifestations of what roughly may still be termed
the avant-garde. The social and political cause of Integration is one thing, the "Integration" of all grades of noncom-
mercial film talent is . . . another.

I would say that today the reigning standard of the avant-
garde is a deliberately cultivated amateurism. And amateurism, as systematically, "critically" encouraged, can be just as
bad as its converse, professionalism. Certain kinds of "avant-
garde" amateurism are mere parodies of professionalism. It
is just as bad, this cult of amateurism, as the cult of professionalism propagated by the aforesaid journalistic reviewers.
The avant-garde, in trying to displace its two declared
enemies, the commercial film and the artistic academy, is
morally beginning to equate itself with them. Here the business angle comes in. Economic survival has always been a
major problem among ambitious artists who wished to change
or improve standards. Famous writers and artists, notoriously,
have starved during their lifetimes of neglect or uneven success. This, however, is a purely economic issue and its only
solution, of course, is patronage.

Patronage, admittedly, is a limited solution. But its dogmatic converse is universal subsidy. As to this, one can remark
that capitalism is a competitive system and that aspirants in
the film have to compete even for foundation grants. We find,
today, the avant-garde or Independent Cinema competing in
the open market. The Cinematheque, here in New York, exists
as a repertory theatre for the more radical filmmaking activities
in this country. One strongly doubts that, however long it has
been operating, the Cinematheque makes enough for itself or
its filmmakers to be self-supporting. Unhappily most of their
programs are very unfledged filmmaking and a good many
have the same "charm" as the commercial "nudie" films a
block away on 42nd Street. What does this mean? It means
that if what I call responsible critical standards were applied
to films shown at the Cinematheque, there would not be
enough films for a repertory house.

As I imply, the regular commercial houses are guilty of exactly this indiscriminateness, with ordinary financial profit as the only motive. There, it is true, lies a difference. . . . It is often repeated that serious young filmmakers want to make only enough money to make more films and keep a roof over their heads, etc. It is natural for the young, ambitious, and inexperienced to think like that—but suppose, miraculously, the degree of their public success were to soar? They might well sing another tune. Look what happened to the really talented John Cassavetes! Hollywood swallowed him whole, as the whale did Jonah, and after making a film or two of rather striped merit, he issues forth now as—a Hollywood *actor*. We remember that the same thing happened to that greatly promising but now long-ruined film talent Orson Welles.

What strikes me in this respect is that if commercialism doesn't suck gifted young filmmakers into its art-annihilating system, it creates what medical scientists call an "antibody," which, to be effective, it seems, has to be as all-encompassing, as uncritical, overtolerant, and fashion-mongering in its own way as Hollywood is in its way. This is the danger for the Independent Cinema.

Thus my FOURTH PROPOSITION: *The independent film as an outgrowth of the avant-garde film is basically the social and economic antibody of the commercial film and directly tends to substitute for the vices of its opponent its own peculiar vices.*

REMARKS: I argue that the context of this situation is the modern milieu of social–political–economic protest rather than any drive made by purely artistic protest; the implied logic: artists, too, ought to have jobs—it's too much the unionizing spirit of the old WPA on the rampage. . . . The fact is that a jaunty, more or less comic or campy, sort of nihilism has been spreading through the reels of a great number of 16mm film cameras. This has rightly been associated with certain radical movements in the arts, such as Dada, during the first quarter of this century. Very lately it has taken place in other arts—why not also in film? Why not, indeed? Yet what does it have to give? Very little that I can put a finger on. It often has mockery and spontaneity along with any number of faults. Mockery is feeble and infantile without real wit, and the current avant-garde, unlike the best Dadaists, has very little wit, and what it has is repetitious. In fact, underground and inde-

pendent cinema is so structured and mooded that it seldom
knows when it's being witty and pointed and when it's being
stupid and futile. The moral of my proposition: Just contra-
dicting a value or a form by giving it energy without intelligence is not in itself interesting, however much it rigs itself
out with a new vogue. As we see by glancing at the current
programs of New York's commercial houses, the cinema
wholly dependent on financial profits is far from reluctant to
take up the newest vogues in comedy and nudity. A few, but
a very few, independent filmmakers, I would add, are offering
substantial values above the level of current commercial
values.

And I come to my FIFTH PROPOSITION: *Film criticism can
be only propaganda for a naïve and gelatinous antibody of
the film so long as mere technical antics involving sensation
are deemed an adequate substitute for artistic, specifically
filmic merit—for cinematic form, for emotional and intellectual
values engendered through filmic means.*

REMARKS: I think it a poor general tactic, that before the
film itself has created a major body of superlative works of
its own, it begin contracting formal liaisons with other arts.
Mixed media may be amusing and modish; they certainly offer
"expanded" opportunities. But the expansion and complication
consequent on mixed media may be only distracting factors
that cloud the results even if the results are "different" and
more "amusing." I am sure there are great artistic possibilities
in merging theatre with film, and involving the audience too.
Though this is having an intensive revival just now, it isn't
quite new. Historically, the stage itself has already leaked into
the audience, assumed the audience as part of the theatrical
dimension. Obviously it is harder—in a sense, impossible—for
the film alone to do this; hence, the relevance of its joining
with the stage.

In many senses, one can say, film is acting up: the Independent Cinema, it seems, is not so independent as not to
want allies from other art media. I wonder, frankly, if the
drive behind this multimoded manifestation of energy is even
so artistic in character as to be called anti-art, as Dada used
to call itself. We are already familiar with what is known
as assemblage and collage in the plastic arts. The time has
come when it is hard to tell a "found object," or *objet trouvé,*
from an invented object because the invention tends so

strongly toward the found. An undercurrent of recent creations in such styles has been that it doesn't matter what is happening, just so "something" is happening or has happened; its degree of resemblance to art or just mere intelligibility is irrelevant. It doesn't even have to amuse. It doesn't even have to be a sick joke. It can be a dead joke. A dead joke, one might say, in which live people participate. Perhaps, the jokers seem to be hinting, that is just what civilization has come to be: a dead joke with live character–actors.

Of course, I speak of the extreme. Many imagine, I guess, that there's much live honest fun of a "different" kind in the Independent Cinema and its mixed media. If so, I gather that it's so spontaneous, different, and independent that it forms an antibody to everything but its own propaganda. Sometimes it is argued that criticism has always been too destructive and thus inhibiting, whereas the ideal of critical commentary is interpretive: it should explain virtues and leave faults alone. But this, I say, is proper only to *program notes* and explicit statements made by filmmakers themselves about their aims.

For sixteen years, the New York film society, Cinema 16, under the guidance of Amos Vogel, now director of these Festivals,* provided a showcase for radical and extraordinary films (sometimes feature length but usually short) and I myself often contributed—I hope helpfully—to the program notes. Certainly one can not be against the exhibition of the rare film that otherwise, because of various taboos, would not be available to interested audiences.

But the mere "cause" of the underdog element in some field of creative endeavor should not be glamorized and fetishized to the point where no critical discrimination, no knowledgeable analysis, can be applied to the said underdog. Right within the independent film movement has appeared a term that well describes a pivotal part of its activity: *fetish footage*. Well, "fetish" footage may have various subjects, may mean to be tentative or final, may even be poetically inspired, but often it is embarrassingly close to being Home Movies, and little more. I see no good reason why this neo-professional sort of home-movie making should be celebrated as a cause and its viewers expected to be blind to comparative values or

* New York Film Festivals.

why really criticizing them should be regarded as—well—dastardly. If, in the presence of fetish footage or related activities, one mentions some "principle" of art, one is apt to be rebutted by a partisan of the current independent modes saying that one simply isn't in step with what's happening. If one refers to last year's sensations, these are no longer, perhaps, *au courant*—they may have been replaced by newer ones. This seems to me the avant-garde attitude overasserted to the point of lunacy.

Now, for my final and SIXTH PROPOSITION: *In escaping from the Establishment in the arts, in the largest sense, the avant-garde as it exists is concentrating most of its energy on being radical and revolutionary for the sake of being radical and revolutionary alone and NOT in behalf of any known art form, however "mixed." By a kind of implosion and explosion it is homogenizing all protest elements to this end by using a language of signs that possesses no scale of values, no intelligible aims, and therefore is beyond criticism.*

REMARKS: It seems to me that this is not propaganda for anything at all like an art medium (say, the *film!*) but a propaganda of absolute parody. Nothing, I hasten to say, is to be excluded from parody. The old-fashioned silent film is parodied. Photographic skill is parodied. All human emotions and human dilemmas are subject to parody, presumably, and are parodied to the best ability of the parodist. It is not enough that old Hollywood films were naive and stereotyped and went in for the crudest human sentiment. This has to be expressed by the avant-garde over again to show that, as stupid and crude as it was, aesthetically and humanly speaking, one could really get some fun out of it. Oh, yes, I discovered that around 1940, and thereafter was called a surrealist film critic. But my purpose was to objectify and isolate the fun, which was ironic and satiric, not naive and credulous.

As for surrealism in film, we see what happened to a major filmmaker, Fellini, who made 8½ as a sort of parody of successful filmmaking; that is, the story of his failure is presumably more interesting and relevant than if he had succeeded in making the film he was supposedly trying to make. But Fellini already had a great deal of genuine know-how; I mean technical knowledge of all sorts. Nowadays, what is called the

Independent Cinema wishes to be independent of mere know-how: one parodies know-how itself by showing one doesn't know how!

Of course there are some exceptions, some small filmmakers who do concentrate on know-how and somehow have escaped the domination of the parody-mania. One of them, Ed Emshwiller, is to have a program in these special events. Several others have undeveloped poetic gifts and are floundering because of lack of means. Still others, because they have respect for form and the older avant-garde tradition are on the fringe of the Independent Cinema because they are considered too arty. Too straightforwardly arty, that is. But even the tongue-in-cheek arty, such as *Last Year at Marienbad,* is too straightforward for the latest movement in the avant-garde.

Here at the New York Film Festival, we can see just how far the colloquial designation of parody, which is "camp," has made an inroad on presumably serious big time film-making. We all know how James Bond has come to be rated. I just heard that his films are regarded by Willem de Kooning as superior to the small Independent Cinema. I wonder what De Kooning thinks of Morgan. But if we don't know, unless told by De Kooning, what he thinks of Morgan, we do know what Morgan thinks of King Kong. Morgan imagining himself as King Kong is a perfect realization of modern camp, however really entertaining the spectacle is.

I want to conclude with these remarks: Propaganda for the avant-garde, the underground, the independent cinema (mainly, I speak for America, of course) has been more effective than probably it is imagined by anyone, and actually has gotten quite out of the hands of those who wish to influence and determine the direction of the small cinema. When the avant-garde betrays its art, it betrays it into the hands of those to whom the dignity and the future of man, his glory and consciousness of godhead, the destiny of the great emotions and the great trials are all very incidental things. Nowadays we hear much talk of the power of communication systems, how all forms of human interchange, in their speed and multiplicity, affect the taste and the consciousness, and even the goals, of human society. Some speak for mass—and massive—communication, others against it. The reason I lament the state of propaganda in film criticism is that film critics have developed no means of dealing authoritatively and competently with this very complex, fluid, and all too universal situation. One potent factor in it is the modern shibboleth to which I already referred: that of democratic tolerance of everything—one might call it everything, for everybody, everywhere. But this, I argue, is a universal issue for human society and not the immediate or proper concern for the avant-garde as such. In short, even if art be considered a weapon of propaganda, it should succeed in being art, should insist on being art, otherwise it cannot make its own particular role effective. Propaganda for a social principle, a social truth, if it be cast in an art medium, must also be propaganda for art, and it cannot be propaganda for art if it is propaganda for anti-art. There are those who would insist that film is not primarily an art medium, or even an entertainment medium, but an informational medium. Obviously then it is an ideal vehicle for political information as well as other kinds. I should hate to think, personally, that the chief destiny of the Independent Cinema—if it is not just to be an absolute parody of absolutely everything—is, on the contrary, to be a bureau of general information. So I too wish to raise a slogan: THE INDEPENDENT CINEMA INDEPENDENT OF ITS INDEPENDENCE OF *CRITICISM*.

HAPPENINGS: THEATER BY PAINTERS *

by Henry Geldzahler

In this article Henry Geldzahler examines the reasons for the more or less simultaneous turn of a number of painters toward a theatrical medium. His remarks apply equally to the parallel trend toward filmmaking, which indeed, has involved many of these same painters. The author states the phenomenon to be the result of a need for a medium that allows representational content and as a solution to the momentary crises in the careers of a generation of artists—crises that may now have passed. He considers Jasper Johns and Robert

* Reprinted from *The Hudson Review*, Vol. XVIII, No. 4, Winter, 1965–66.

*Rauschenberg the major figures linking the Abstract-Expressionist view and the new aesthetic. Elsewhere, Mr. Geldzahler has written: "In the past eighty years or so the artist has been influenced not only by the advanced art of his own day and that immediately preceding, but by a new critical awareness of the entire history of art. If pictures lead to pictures, then the new availability of a much wider range of images and symbols from the art of all the world and all of history must have its effect." * According to Mr. Geldzahler, the new Happening and film art forms will make it possible to present the enlarged repertory of images demanded by the greater pictorial appetite of the new audience.*

Henry Geldzahler is Curator of the Department of Contemporary Arts at the Metropolitan Museum. Born in 1935, he was Commissioner of the American Pavilion at the Venice Biennale in 1966, and is Director of the Visual Arts of the National Council of the Arts.

Happenings are theater by artists. The emphasis is therefore quite naturally visual rather than verbal. The strength and interest of a Happening when it is successful is in the force of its imagery, the carrying power of its props, situations, costumes, and sequences. In this they relate, perhaps nostalgically, rather more to silent movies with their forceful visual nonsense, than to anything in the highly verbal Theater of the Absurd. If the Happenings are seen as an attempt on the part of painters to reintroduce recognizable, human content into our artistic life, and if the matrix from which they sprang can be seen as an involvement in Abstract Expressionism and a reaction by young artists against its persuasiveness, we are well into the generative processes that made it necessary for several artists in the same year to work out parallel solutions.

The situation in American art in the late 1950's made a way back to painting or representing the human figure in any new, contemporary, meaningful way seem impossible. After the tremendous energy and inventiveness of abstract painting, centered in New York in the forties and fifties, the reintroduction of recognizable content (objects, landscape, or the figure) appeared *rétardataire* and beside the point. The main issues that engaged the best and most mature artists were abstract man-

* *The Hudson Review*, Vol. XVIII, No. 1, Spring, 1965.

ners and imagery personally arrived at and subsequently staked out. These men left no room for the young artist who was not satisfied to choose between the manner of De Kooning and that of, let us say, Guston. There were, to be sure, still implications to be worked out by younger men in directions suggested by the relatively little known paintings of Newman and Reinhardt; these were to engage the sensibilities of the cool young nonromantics (Stella, Poons, Judd, Irwin, and others). But where could a richly romantic personality express itself in fresh terms after the license and extravagances of the most richly romantic artists in our history, the Abstract Expressionists?

Robert Rauschenberg pointed a way out of this dilemma by his inclusion of the real object in the work of art. Instead of representing a goat, that is, attempting to translate a goat into the two-dimensional terms of painting, Rauschenberg, shockingly, included the goat itself (stuffed but only slightly less a goat for that). There was ample precedent in kind for Rauschenberg's decision, if not in degree. His invention was to take collage, a staid and almost stately cubist technique, and push it radically, logically, and consciously to conclusions that were inherent some four decades earlier in the first gluing of a real newspaper, or swatch of wallpaper, to an oil painting. Thus one way out of the dilemma, how to represent the recognizable, was clearly not to represent it but to incorporate it.

It was in this atmosphere in 1959 that the Happenings were born, an atmosphere in which abstract art had been dominant for more than a decade, and in which the shock and invention were not only Rauschenberg's radical collage, but the younger artist Jasper Johns's targets and American flags, frankly two-dimensional subjects which did not so much have to be represented as presented. Thus, Johns and Rauschenberg stand as the major figures, transitional in retrospect, between Abstract Expressionism and Pop Art. Their work of the mid-fifties helped point to a way out of abstraction that had not been preempted by artists of the past. The crucial factor in innovational art is never newness or novelty as an end in itself. But, although repetition in modes already thoroughly occupied must be stale, we still had critics crying for a revival of the art they had liked in their earlier years. A new humanism was what they wanted. When they got Happenings and Pop Art, a new art with human content, it did not look exactly as they had expected, and they were disapproving—once again indi-

cating that art precedes criticism, an often strangely forget-
table truism.

Here we have an indication as to why the early practitioners of the Happening—Red Grooms, Allan Kaprow, Jim Dine,
Claes Oldenburg, and Bob Whitman—remain the interesting
ones, and also why their more recent work in this medium
has decreased in energy. The common solution to the apparently insoluble problem bound them together for several
years. But once this shared interest in theater was explored
and each created his several worlds of imagery, they turned to
the more lasting and traditional media of their art: painting,
collage, and sculpture. Only Allan Kaprow has remained
exclusively with Happenings. The men who did the first
Happenings have had no very convincing followers; just as
there have been no very convincing Pop artists after the first
wave broke in 1960 (Warhol, Lichtenstein, Rosenquist,
Wesselman, Oldenburg). The reasons are clear; both Happenings and Pop Art were vital solutions to the crisis of
artists, all between their early twenties and thirties, who were
searching for a way into suitable expression. Once they invented and staked out their ways, separate but related, those
who came after were no longer faced with the same type of
dilemma. A way had been worked out, a style invented, and
the result was too comfortable, too clearly marked, for those
that followed to feel the challenge. What resulted was what
might lightly be called second-generation art (in less than half
a decade); Pop Art and Happenings by minor talents who
poured their content, sometimes quite individual, into forms
that had been forged, ready-made for them, by the originators,
the first and only solvers of the problem. Thus also, when in
the spring of 1965 Dine, Whitman, and Oldenburg, themselves
the originators of the Happenings, mounted new works, there
was a staleness about their own continued efforts, which were
still fresher than those of any of their imitators, but not as
necessary or compelling as their Happenings of 1960–61.

Although John Cage's theoretical writings and ideas are
often cited as the single source, the sources of the Happenings
are complex. Cage writes in the Foreword to his remarkable
book *Silence* (Wesleyan University Press, 1961):

> At Black Mountain College in 1952, I organized an event
> that involved the paintings of Bob Rauschenberg, the
> dancing of Merce Cunningham, films, slides, phonograph

records, radios, the poetries of Charles Alson and M. C. Richards recited from the tops of ladders, and the pianism of David Tudor, together with my Julliard lecture, which ends: "A piece of string, a sunset, each acts." The audience was seated in the center of all this activity. Later that summer, vacationing in New England, I visited America's first synagogue, to discover that the congregation was there seated precisely the way I had arranged the audience at Black Mountain.

It is true that Allan Kaprow took a course in composition with Cage at the New School, an exposure which surely loosened and prepared him for his *Eighteen Happenings in Six Parts* (1959–the first use of the name Happening). However, the various theatrical forms and specific types of content that were the work of Oldenburg, Dine, Whitman, and even Kaprow had much less to do with the style and spirit of Cage than with German Expressionism, or our own Abstract Expressionism, which was an art of excess. What Cage stands for might be characterized as a neo-Dada flight from excess which resulted in compelling works that were only apparently simple-minded and absurd (Jasper Johns is in some measure their visual equivalent).

All the artists involved in Happenings from their inception were connected with the Reuben Gallery in downtown Manhattan. Much of the history of this movement and some valuable documents, statements by the artists and scripts of the Happenings, are brought together in the first book on the movement, *Happenings* by Michael Kirby (Dutton, 1965). He discusses possible antecedents of Happenings, among them Kurt Schwitters and his Merz poetry:

> In contrast to the drama or the opera, all parts of the Merz stage work are inseparably bound up together; it cannot be written, read, or listened to, it can only be produced in the theater. Up until now a distinction was made between stage-set, text, and score in theatrical performances. Each factor was separately enjoyed. The Merz stage knows only the fusing of all factors into a composite work. Materials for the stage-set are all solid, liquid, nongaseous bodies, such as white wall, man, barbed wire entanglement, blue distance.

This statement was first published (in German) in 1921. In

its breakdown of established categories and in its fusion of elements it must be considered a theoretical forerunner of the Happenings. Kirby also cites Tzara, Picabia, Satie, Cage, Schlemmer and the Bauhaus, Moholy-Nagy, Gropius, and Antonin Artaud as possible sources and forerunners, as well as certain of the more theatrical Surrealist manifestations (for example Duchamp's creating a room crossed by thousands of feet of string through which the spectator had to climb to view the 1942 New York Surrealist Exhibition).

The distinction must be made between a Happening, in which the audience is relatively fixed, and an Environment, in which the audience moves at will through a predetermined, structured space such as Duchamp's strings. The Environment is static in the tradition of the work of art; it is there and can be contemplated, experienced, and walked away from like a work of art. A Happening, on the other hand, exists in time as well as in space, and is therefore in composition related rather more to music and to theater than to painting and sculpture. Both Happenings and Environments are logical extensions of the work of the painter-sculptor mentality, the one in time and space, the other uniquely in space.

But the internal dilemma of painting was only one reason for the invention of an improvisational visual theater; there was also an impatience with the live theater, and with film that was still tied to the old forms. In 1961 (in an unpublished statement) Claes Oldenburg wrote:

> Test of film is what do you remember. Not the narrative but the images and in this sense the narrative is not important. I think it is so with theater too which I see not as a literary art primarily by a visual art . . . film has been dominated by theater and literature . . . it is a visual medium of course.

Film has fascinated and sometimes even preoccupied the recent generation of artists. The reason is surely, at least in part, the shifting forms on the large rectangle, which is the given shape of the movie screen as it is of the painting. It is also, conversely, for this reason that the traditional proscenium theater has seemed so tedious, so verbal and nonvisual. Here again we are faced with a rectangle, but with, even at best, relatively static sets. Whatever movement or eye-engagement there is is in the movement of the actors; actors who in a normal proscenium situation occupy about the lower fifth of their rectangular box. To a generation brought up to look and look hard at paintings and movies (both growing into over-size, in the past fifteen years), there is simply not enough to look at in the proscenium theater or, for that matter, in the concert hall. This has been a major reason for the fascination of the Happening, theater that surrounds the viewer immediately with an absolute minimum of distance, both physical and, when it works, psychological. Having actors on the spot and occupying the same space as the audience was a refreshing and involving visual experience after the coolness and distance of the theater.

Oldenburg again (unpublished):

> When sitting in a certified theater I find myself always watching what I am not supposed to; the peeling walls, the frayed rugs, the crossing and uncrossing legs of girls in the audience, etc. etc. and I see no reason for eliminating the power which place has over the audience.

Here we have a basic tenet of the Happening; the audience and the performance are surrounded by what happens; the action is never merely dead ahead but in several possible directions at once. The viewer must make choices, decide which action to follow if several are proceeding at once, or where the next event is likely to occur if nothing is going on for the moment. Thus each viewer or participant experiences a slightly different aspect of the multiplicity that occurs. This is particularly clear in the radically different photographs and film footage by different hands that are the only residue of each Happening. The viewer is not only in a position to make choices, he is forced to do so.

On the content of a Happening Oldenburg writes:

> It could be described as a short novel in which objects, rather than the description of objects, make up the language, a language which is necessarily more suggestive and on a more intuitive level. The composition as form is pre-arranged (that is, there are scripts) though rather freely— but the composition as meaning is not—that is a matter for the individual. . . . Needless to say the audience is also part of the event, which is not to be taken to mean that they are expected to contribute in any other way than has been determined by the arrangements made for their bodies.

A script exists, a series of impressions, possible working ideas, but the final determination is made by the cast reacting to Oldenburg's (or Dine's or Whitman's) formal vocabulary. Oldenburg, in his first working ideas, thinking on paper about a new Happening (*Washes,* 1965), notes:

> A cast will not be made up of actors or dancers, but of people I have come across or will come across in the remaining time, people whose use is suggested by some evident beauty or significant characteristics, for their suitability to the other parts and the themes as they develop; people whom I meet in the course of a day's events and who have the time to help me. They will not speak; they are my motors. My work with them will consist in finding out how to put them in natural motion by presenting them with a simple action or an object.

The description of a Happening can in no way replace the viewing of one. The types of props, characteristic space, extraordinary visual leaps from image to image do not lend themselves to verbal description. What do remain are films or photographs, memory cues to those who were present but rather formal and unrevealing of continuity to everyone else. The parallel may be made with Rubens's temporary triumphal arches in Antwerp, hung with hastily executed paintings, and with Bernini's plaster catafalque for a funeral, monumental efforts which were ephemeral by intent. From the Renaissance we have etchings and engravings which give us an idea of what these extravagances might have looked like. Today we have films and photographs, our contemporary print media and memorabilia, to record dead Happenings.

FILM AND THE RADICAL
ASPIRATION*

by Annette Michelson

Film as revolution and aesthetic subversion is the main concern of Miss Michelson in this essay. The European and American traditions are surveyed with a constant focus on the crux of cinematic development which the author believes ". . . lies . . . in the evaluation and re-definition of the nature and role of narrative structure." Annette Michelson was Paris correspondent for Arts *magazine and has written art and film criticism for many journals.*

For Noël Burch

The history of Cinema is, like that of Revolution in our time, a chronicle of hopes and expectations, aroused and suspended, tested and deceived. I came to know and care for film in a city which has traditionally sheltered and animated these hopes and expectations. It is not only the political and intellectual capital of its country, but that of filmmaking, as well. Quite simply, the distance between the Place de l'Opéra and the studios at Joinville is a matter of a subway ride, not of a transcontinental jet flight. I shall ask you to bear this elementary fact in mind because it has determined much of what I would ever have to say about most things. More than that, it provides the terms of a general, if somewhat crude, metaphor for my concern today. To speak of Film and the Radical Aspiration is necessarily to evoke instances of convergence and dissociation.

Two statements, first, however: not mine, but drawn from the writings of men of quite dissimilar sensibilities and voca-

* Read at the Special Events program of the Fourth New York Film Festival at Lincoln Center, September, 1966.

tions, living and working at a distance of almost two generations. The first, Benjamin Fondane, a writer and critic, a man of the left, died, when still young, in a German concentration camp. Writing in 1933, he said, "We are committed with all our strength to the denunciation of a world whose catastrophic end seems more than ever before inevitable. We demand its rightful liquidation, whether that liquidation produce an irremediable vacuum of nothingness or a sovereign renewal through revolutionary means. Such should be—and this regardless of the deep inner wounds inevitably involved in such an aspiration—the aims of will and consciousness today. . . . As for film, the curve of its development has rapidly ascended, only to sink into an immediate decline. Stuffed to bursting, tricked out with an absurd and meretricious pomp, with every kind of frill imaginable, it has hypertrophied into a monstrous industry. The attraction was merely potential, the magic contained . . . the seeds of an unpardonable decay until, with the abruptness of a volcanic eruption, the huge shambles collapsed beneath the weight of its own emptiness. And yet, the cinema continues to interest us for that which it is not, for that which it failed to become, for its ultimate possibilities. . . . It may be that film is the expression of a society unable to sustain a world . . . of the mind. It may be that this tardily conceived art, child of an aged continent, will perish in its infancy. It may be, too, that the Revolution is not utterly to be despaired of."

The second statement—just one sentence—was written by a Movie Star and published in *Film Culture* a year or two ago. The Movie Star in question, a performer of quite extraordinary charm and originality, is Taylor Mead, and I presume that some of you have seen him in independently produced films. Taylor Mead has said, "The movies are a Revolution."

Film, our most vivacious art, is young enough to remember its first dreams, its limitless promise, and it is haunted, scarred, by a central, ineradicable trauma of dissociation. The attendant guilt and ambivalence, their repressive effects, the manner above all, in which a dissociative principle has been alternately resisted or assumed, converted into an aesthetic principle, the manner in which this resistance or conversion modifies or redefines cinematic aspirations are, like everything concerning film, unique in the history of Western culture.

A dream, a presentiment of the medium inhabits and traversed the nineteenth century. Almost every form of popular diversion characteristic of the era—the family album, the wax museum, the novel itself, the panopticon in all its forms—can be read as an obscure, wistful prefiguration of cinema. My own revelation of the wax museum as prefiguration came a year or so ago when I chose, as a Christmas treat, to accompany a bright little American, French-educated boy to the Musée Grevin. It struck me, as we went slowly through the long, dark, labyrinthine corridors, punctuated by the rather grand and spectacular tableaux which chronicle the whole of French history, from the early Gauls until the Gaullist régime, that the wax museum in its very special, hallucinatory darkness, its spatial ambiguity, its forcing of movement upon the spectator, its mixture of diversion and didacticism, is a kind of proto-cinema.[1] And of course the historical mode of discourse is, above all, that of the earliest films which celebrated state occasions, public festivities, followed monarchs to christenings and assassinations. The extraordinary rapidity of the cinema's growth seemed to confirm this vision of a century's wistful fantasy (only seventy years have passed since Méliès witnessed the Lumières' demonstration and produced his own first reel). So too, did the general climate of anticipatory enthusiasm and accord which animated filmmaking and criticism in their early, heroic period. That climate seems, in retrospect, Edenic.

Consider the atmosphere surrounding the early theoretical discussions: the Eisenstein-Pudovkin debate on the nature

---

[1] For this reason, Erwin Panofsky's remarks on the waxworks in *Style and Medium in the Moving Pictures* (*TRANSITION Magazine*, No. 26, New York, 1937) would seem to misinterpret the order and reverse the intention and significance of things. I would argue that film, rather than "adding movement to stationary works of art," fulfilled the desire for movement which informs the conception of the wax museum. This becomes apparent, of course, only when one considers the experience, both kinetic and visual, within the whole space and sequence of the spectacle, rather than the aspect of the individual tableau as such. This aspiration toward movement and the heightened immediacy which it confers upon the experience is, I believe, borne out by the additional spectacle provided by the Musée Grevin in "The Chamber of Transformations," a remarkable early instance of an "environmental" fusion of changing light, sound, and *décor*.

of montage, involving the conception of images as "cells, not elements" engaged in dialectical conflicts, as opposed to the "linkage of chains." Or the discussion, somewhat less familiar to historians, of the function of the subtitle as it crystallized during the 1920's in France: Kirsanov's elimination of the title in the interest of visual explicitness, René Clair's reduction of the title's role to the strictest minimum, the stress placed by Desnos and the Surrealists on its exclusively poetic use, on the subversion of "sense in the interests of poetry." While the controversy developed—and with the unique intensity and inventiveness which characterize critical discourse in France—technology was preparing to transcend the problem. The claim that the "shriek" or "grinding of brakes" was no less real or "present" for being understood rather than heard was rendered comically irrelevant; the problem was simply canceled by the arrival of sound.

Generally speaking, however, discussion, fruitful or academic, took place within a context of broad agreement as to the probable or desirable directions of the medium. Styles, forms, inventions, and theoretical preoccupations were largely complementary, not contradictory. A spectrum rather than a polarity of possibilities was involved. The Surrealists' admiration of American silent comedy, reflected in the work of Artaud and Dulac among others, the universal excitement over the achievements of Russian film, Eisenstein's openly acknowledged debt to Griffith and that of the young Dreyer to both, testify to a certain community of aspiration. Eisenstein, in the very beautiful essay on *Griffith, Dickens, and the Film Today* said that "what enthralled us was not only these films, it was also their possibilities." And speaking of montage: "Its foundation had been laid by American film-culture, but its full, completed, conscious use and world recognition was established by our films."

The excitement, the exhilaration of artists and intellectuals not directly involved in the medium was enormous. Indeed, a certain euphoria enveloped the early filmmaking and theory. For there was, ultimately, a very real sense in which the revolutionary aspirations of the modernist movement in literature and the arts, on the one hand, and of a Marxist or Utopian tradition, on the other, could converge in the hopes and promises, as yet undefined, of the new medium.

There was, among the intellectuals concerned with cinema's

revolutionary potential, both social and formal, a general and touching reverence for an idea of its specificity. There was, above all, an immediate apprehension, cutting quite across theoretical differences, of its privileged status, its unique destiny.

In an essay on "The Work of Art in the Era of Reproduction Techniques," whose influence is so strongly evident in Malraux's aesthetics, Walter Benjamin attacked reactionaries, such as Werfel, who, by relegating the movie to the articulation of fantasy and faery, were engaged in a reduction of its scope, a tactics of repression. The most intensely euphoric expression of the new passion, of the convergence of modernist aesthetics and an Utopian ideology is Élie Faure's "Art of Cineplastics," really an essay in aesthetics-as-science-fiction which predicts the cinema's radical transformation of the very nature of spatio-temporal perception, of historical consciousness and process.

Anticipations and speculations and, more significantly still, the inventions and achievements of the Americans, Russians, French, Germans, and Scandinavians were predicated, then, upon complementary apprehensions of the morphological and syntactical possibilities of the medium evolving within a framework of concord and mutual recognition, shattered, ultimately, by the growing, the traumatic, awareness of a principle of dissociation inherent in the art and its situation.

The point of shock is easily located in history: that moment, at the end of the 1920's, in which the "hermaphroditic" nature of a craft, which had already expanded and hardened into an industry, could no longer be ignored. The classical instrument of industrial revolution being division of labor, a generation of hardy adventurers, artist-entrepreneurs, director-producers, such as Griffith, were replaced by paid employees. The ultimate consequences involved something analogous to a dissociation of sensibility. This, in turn, rapidly engendered a register of limits and conventions which have acted to inhibit, divert, and reshape cinematic effort.

We are dealing with a Fall from Grace. For men like Griffith, Eisenstein, Von Stroheim, Welles, and many more of the most brilliant and radical talents, it created, as we know, in the gardens of California an irrespirable atmosphere, a corruption which was to impair much of the best work done anywhere.

Intellectuals and filmmakers alike, here and abroad, reacted with an immediate tension of distrust and, in many instances, withdrawal. The widespread resistance to the introduction of the sound track, for example, could certainly be shown to mask or reflect a hostility to the prospect of the medium's accelerated development into an instrument of mass culture. A French philosopher of my acquaintance claims to have stopped going to the movies in 1929. For Fondane, "the sound film is good only in so far as it is dumb." And for Artaud, "cinematic truth lies within the image, not beyond it." The resistance to sound—and it was a resistance to the Word, not ever to music, which had, from the beginning, found a place in cinematic convention—expressed a nostalgia for an era of mute innocence and untested hope. It was, in short, a pastoral attitude.

The disenchantment, the sense of moral and aesthetic frustration expressed by Fondane were general. The history of modern cinema is, nevertheless, to a large degree, that of its accommodations to those very repressive and corrupting forces of the post-1929 situation. A complex register of limits and conventions engendered by that situation has been *productively* used. Historical precedents abound, but few or none have attained a comparable degree of dialectical paradox, intricacy, and scandalousness.

It is the acceptance of the dissociative principle, its sublimation and ultimate conversion to aesthetic purposes which characterize recent, advanced filmmaking in France and elsewhere in Europe. It is the almost categorical rejection of that principle and the aspiration to an innocence and organicity which animates the efforts of the "independent" filmmakers who compose something of an American avant-garde. All discussion of the nature and possibilities of advanced filmmaking today, of film aesthetics, and of future possibilities must, I believe, take this divergence of radicalisms into account. It must also take into account the fact that the question is, as Walter Benjamin remarked, "not whether we are dealing with an art" (and some, apparently, still ask that question), "but whether or not the emergence of this medium has not transformed the naure of all art."

The general resistance in this country to the notion of this transformation assumes its most crucial aspect, not in circles unconcerned with film, but rather in those presumably animated by a commitment to its development. The discomfort and hostility of many, indeed most, film critics to those aspects of contemporary cinema which bypass, contradict, or transcend the modes and values of psycho-social observation is familiar; they provide, in fact, both context and target for this series of occasions known as a "festival." Certainly it is true that the generally *rétardataire* character of our film criticism reflects an anxiety about the manner in which post-war cinema, in Europe and America alike, has, at its best, transcended the conventions of a sensibility formed by the premodernist canon of a primarily literary nineteenth century. Both Amos Vogel and Richard Roud have quite rightly called attention to this fact in texts published on the occasion of the Festival's opening. Sadder and more disturbing still, I think, is the revelation, through this fact, that critical rejection of the formal principles and techniques of disjunctiveness involving sound, cutting, or any of the other parameters of film as represented in the work of Bresson, Resnais, or Godard, on the one hand, or in that of Anger, Breer, and Peter Emanuel Goldman, on the other, is part of a more general, basic, powerful contradiction or regression. One simply has to face the fact that a great part of a generation who came to maturity in the twenties, who were nourished by, and committed to, the formal radicalism of a Pound, a Stein, or a Joyce, are these days concerned—absurd and incredible as it seems—with, let us say, the novels of Saul Bellow and Norman Mailer! If the crux of cinematic development lies—as I think it does—in the evaluation and redefinition of the nature and role of narrative structure, we may say that the history of academicism in filmmaking and film criticism has been that of the substitution of novelistic forms and values for theatrical ones—and this in a century which saw a flowering of American poetry.

Critical malaise and contradictions, therefore, quite logically, focused last season on two films of Jean-Luc Godard: *Le Petit Soldat* and *Alphaville*, first presented in New York within the context of the Lincoln Center Festival. I say "logically" because it is precisely in so far as *Alphaville* constitutes a really remarkable instance of a reconsideration of the nature and possibilities of certain narrative conventions that I wish to consider it ever so briefly at this point.

Alphaville is an anxious meditation, in the form of a suspense story, on the agony and death of love, liberty, and language in a society which is trapped in the self-perpetuating dialectic of technological progress. It is about feeling in deep freeze. Now, to argue or contest the validity of that idea as a theme of discourse seems to me somewhat questionable in itself, but to attack the "story" except insofar as it served as a support for a cinematic structure was, above all, to betray insensitivity to the film's central "statement."

The violent rehearsal of the content-versus-style liturgies which greeted *Alphaville* only testified, in a negative fashion, to Godard's central importance. Together with a few of his European contemporaries he does dominate cinema now and much of what is done anywhere has to be situated in relation to the work of these men. Above all, however, the complex *statement* of the film in regard to the possibilities of narrative convention transcends, in interest and importance, the nature of its *discourse*, and the hostility displayed toward that *discourse*, I take to represent simply a displacement (or dislocation) of hostility to its formal, cinematic *statement*.

François Truffaut, reflecting somewhat casually on the history of film, once divided its protagonists into two sorts: the creators of "spectacle" or entertainment, such as Méliès, and the experimenters or inventors, such as Lumière. To this Godard replied that he had always tried to make "experimental" films in the guise of entertainments. *Alphaville* is such a film. Its conceptual and formal complexities fuse into an elaborate and precisely articulated metaphor of Immanence, of the ambiguity of location and dis-location, in both their spatial and temporal modes.

Paris now, her public buildings, offices, hotels, garages, corridors, staircases, and escalators are revealed to those on intimate terms with her landscape, as invaded by the Future. Frontiers between past, present, and future are—like the distinctions between invention and entertainment—abolished through a series of formal strategies: a *prise de conscience* secured through a *prise de vues*, or revelation through imagination. This film, shot entirely on location, is the film of *Dis-location*. And as narrative structure, lighting, cutting produce a visual, temporal, or situational transformation, so a continual play with language transforms things known and seen. Thus, the low-income housing developments of post-1945 Paris, known as *Habitations à Loyers Modiques* are the clinics and insane asylums of the future: *les Hôpitaux des Longues Maladies.* The city's peripheral avenues, *les boulevards extérieurs,* shift and expand into an irrevocably disquieting suggestion of the routes of interplanetary space. Function and scale of object and place are continuously altered, as image and sound converge upon site and situation in the exploration of the cinematic figuration of dislocation, of the ambiguities of time and history. As Gertrude Stein said, "Composition is not there, it is going to be there and we are here. *This is some time ago for us naturally.*" The shifting—within—simultaneity of sameness and difference, of being and going-to-be, while we *are,* "some time ago, naturally," structures the time–space within which the mind (and *Alphaville* is *about* the birth of mind and sensibility, the rebirth of language *as* a rebirth of love) is constrained to function: that of a dislocation with respect to time. The "past–future" tense of which Godard speaks is our *present situation.*

The progress or plot of *Alphaville* is, therefore, the passage from one revelation to another; its peripeties are perceptions, structured by the pace and tension of a detective story, of "finding truth." In the face of this, the accusations of "triviality" or "pretentiousness" became embarrassingly irrelevant. The film "states" its concern with the creation of a morphology; the concentration is on pace, tension, weight, and syntactic coherence through narration—narration being in this instance a form of "relating" in the fullest possible sense of the word: a manner of creating *relational* strategies through *telling.*

Alphaville stands, then, as a remarkable instance of a *critical* allegiance, shared by the major European filmmakers, to the conventions of Hollywood's commercial cinema, and of the conversion of those conventions to the uses of advanced cinema. For the allegiance *has* acted as context and precondition of formal radicalism. [And it is interesting to consider that Godard's attachment to the Monogram film, the "B series" production, is paralleled, or anticipated, by Eisenstein's lifelong affection for the early films that began to come to Russia when he was a boy. He speaks with tenderness of films like *The House of Hate* and *The Mark of Zorro.*] The importance of the suspense story, as refined by Hitchcock for the further use of men such as Resnais and Godard, lies in its paradigmatic character as narrative form, as a "vehicle" of dramatic and formal invention. Perfected in the Hollywood of an era following upon the Fall it was adopted and refined, sublimated in the interests of a formal radicalism.

The earliest, and certainly the most sumptuous, anticipation of this strategy is Feuillade's *Vampires*, shown in its entirety here for the first time during last year's festival. Together with *Alphaville*, it dominated the occasion. Made by a man of utterly intrepid imagination, its formal inventiveness is supported by a firm commitment to a notion of film as a technique of narrative for a mass public. I have discussed elsewhere the manner in which *Vampires* not only sets forth the themes developed in *Alphaville*, and the way in which the cinema of Méliès and Feuillade adumbrated, within the context of the medium's earliest stages, the principles and strategies of which Surrealist art and film provided a subsequent résumé.

"Please believe me," said Feuillade, "when I tell you that it is not the experimenters who will eventually obtain film's rightful recognition, but rather the makers of melodrama—and I count myself among the most devoted of their number ... I won't in the least attempt to excuse [this view] ... I believe I come closer to the truth." It was strict adherence to the logic of this view which guaranteed, for Feuillade, a margin of improbability, of open-ness, of that oneiric intensity which gives *Vampires* its place among the masterworks of cinema.

Predicated on the development of a narrative convention both strict and elastic enough to accommodate a tension between dramatic probability and fantasy, between the continuity of suspense and the discontinuity of structure—between discourse and poetry, in short—Feuillade's work relates more to the future of film than to its past. Which is to say, as Robbe-Grillet has said, that "Imagination, when really alive, is always of the present." Alain Resnais's fascination with Feuillade might partly confirm this. Resnais's work, like that of his European contemporaries, perpetuates the commitment to the constraints and stimuli of a given form; above all, in its straining of the limits of that form, it exemplifies a commitment to the value of Form as such which animates the best of advanced European cinema today.

Now, if we assume, as I shall, that the radical or revolutionary aspiration, both *formal and political*, achieved a moment of consummation in the Russian film of the twenties and early thirties, we know, too, that the paradigmatic fusion was dissolved by the counterrevolution of Stalinism. As this happened (and the installation of Stalinism in its more or less definitive form dates from 1927, the year of Trotsky's expulsion from the Soviet Union, only two years before the introduction of sound into film), European cinema, and European art as a whole, abandoned a certain totality of aspiration. The process of dissociation, the split between formal and political aspects of radical or revolutionary efforts was created, irremediably so—at least through our time. The result was either reaction, or a sublimation of the revolutionary aspiration into a purely formal radicalism. The vestiges of the politically revolutionary experience and tradition are henceforth expressed in the form of nostalgia and frustration. Politically oriented art at its best became a chronicle of absence, of negation, an analysis of dissociation, and, in the best modernist tradition, a *formal statement of the impossibility of discourse.*

The nostalgia and frustration are explicitly stated in Godard's *Le Petit Soldat* by Michael, the hero: "In the early thirties, young people had the revolution. Malraux, for example, Drieu la Rochelle, and Aragon. We don't have anything any more. They had the Spanish Civil War. We don't even have a war of our own." The formal articulation of this nostalgia for a revolutionary impulse and hope involves a succession of fascinating paradoxes and failures. The case of Resnais, who almost alone of his particular generation has attempted to articulate a strong personal political commitment, is particularly fascinating. I have in mind not only *Hiroshima* but *Muriel*. In both films he has visible difficulty in *situating* the commitment within the total structure of his work, in finding a visual trope that will not inflect the style or distend the structure. The result is a rhythmical, dramatic, and visual caesura, the stylistic articulation of aphony.

The two explicitly political passages in these films are both distanced, bracketed as spectacles or diversions. In

Hiroshima the anti-war demonstration is inserted as a film sequence enacted within the film, while in *Muriel*, the Algerian war is evoked, not shown, in an amateur movie, by an agonized verbal commentary (the account of a young girl's torture by French soldiers), in counterpoint to the series of innocuous amateur shots which parody the myth of bar-racks'-life hilarity.

This sequence constitutes the most brilliant, the definitive articulation of the disintegration of a cinematic arena for political discourse. The despair over that disintegration is the film's central political "statement." The "statement's" intensity, however, is further amplified through the further distancing of bracketed statement from *itself* (the distance between image and commentary). Its isolation within the texture of the total work, its particular, stylistic disjunctive-ness, its own colorless color, are slightly at odds with the disjunctiveness and invented color of the whole. Through a speculative and stylistic refraction Resnais proposes an image of the failure of nerve which generated the Fifth Republic. His trope is that of the caesura. The crack, the flaw, the rhythmic, visual gap or caesura created by this interlude or "diversion" is the *form* of Resnais's declaration of aphony. It declares his nostalgia for the film which could *not* be made; it incarnates the artist's struggle with the dissociative principle and the politics of dissociation.

And it is fascinating, but distressing beyond telling, to see, in *La Guerre Est Finie*, Resnais's ultimate attempt to assume what he obviously regards as the discursive responsibility of his position, the diabolical logic of that principle in operation. Like *Alexander Nevsky*, *La Guerre Est Finie* is the chronicle of an artist's defeat; it represents a total inversion, the most concrete negation, of a form and a style. In this film, it is the erotic sequences which assume the aspect of interludes or diversions within the total structure and the bracketing or distancing is achieved through a reversion to a hieraticism of style we have, of course, known and loved: that of *Hiroshima* and, above all, of *Marienbad*. These passages now produce the caesuras which arouse our nostalgia. Far more painfully, however, they declare Resnais's *own* nostalgia for his past achievements. *Vivement Harry Dickson!*

Lucien Goldmann, writing a few years ago in *Les Temps Modernes* of the supposed atrophy of historical and social consciousness in the New Wave directors, remarked with a sigh that political energy and vitality seemed concentrated in the Left, while cinematic talent was reserved for the Right. Goldmann's characteristically Marxist conservative taste and aesthetics aside, the problem needs to be restated— and far more explicitly than is possible on this particular occasion. Most briefly put, however, one might formulate it in the following manner: if, for the young Russians of the immediately post-Revolutionary period, the problem was, as Eisenstein said, "to advance toward new and as yet un- realized qualities and means of expression, to raise form once more to the level of ideological content," the problem for Resnais and his peers is to raise, or rather accommodate ideological content to, the formal exigencies of a modernist sensibility. Ultimately, ideology of any kind—whether that of Surrealism, Marxism, or the anti-humanism of the New Novel—provides, at best, a fruitful working hypothesis for the artist. Eisenstein's conception of montage, derived from the orthodoxy of the Dialectic, is not really so theoretically convincing as it was aesthetically regenerative. The energy, courage, and intellectual passion which sustained both theory and work were, of course, among the noblest of our cen- tury. Eisenstein is a model of the culture of our era—in his defeat as in his achievement, and down to the very frag- mentary quality of his work!

One's sense of his defeat, visible in *Alexander Nevsky*, is so particularly agonizing because it constitutes a unique example of what one might call the pathos of dissociation pushed to an extremity of academic style. This pathos, writers like Babel and Mayakovsky were spared—through death or suicide. What remained of the aspiration toward a revolutionary art in the Soviet Union after the defeat of Eisenstein had thenceforth to capitulate. In Europe, that aspiration was eventually, in the cinema which interests us, to be sublimated into a concentrated formal radicalism; elsewhere, it assumed the aspect of subversion. This brings us to American film of the "independent" persuasion.

Though generalization about American film is subject to the usual objections, one must, as I briefly indicated at the beginning of this talk, begin one's consideration of this film- making with a recognition of its almost categorical rejection

of the aesthetic grounded in the conventions hitherto discussed. The filmmakers with which we are concerned have,
in fact, been led to abandon the tactics of reconciliation
basic to European films as a whole. Most important, this rejection is in turn predicated on a negation, critical or apocalyp-
tic, of the middle-class society which supported Hollywood,
its aesthetic, industry, and art, and which *continues* to
sustain—however precariously and capriciously—the activity
of most major European directors. This basic dissimilarity of
commitment is beginning, moreover, to make itself felt in
discussions between French and American filmmakers and
critics. When Louis Marcorelles of the *Cahiers du Cinéma*
claims, as he did this last spring while addressing a group
of independent filmmakers and critics, that American films
are unprofessional, unconcerned with the problems of mass
communication, and therefore negligible, he betrays, of course,
a certain polemical self-indulgence. Ignoring the immense
difficulties confronted by artists who, working in a society
which, unlike that of many European countries (and especially his own), preserves the sanctity of "free enterprise"
by withholding the state subsidies which create a more
open situation for the young European, he betrays, above all,
an extraordinary insensitivity to the pressures which force
artists into an artisanal relationship to a powerful industry
and to the steadfastness with which they have undertaken
to re-create cinematic language for themselves and their contemporaries.

Many of our best independent filmmakers, such as Kenneth
Anger, Robert Breer, Peter Emanuel Goldman, Jonas Mekas,
and Shirley Clarke, are committed to an aesthetic of autonomy that by no means violates or excludes their critical view
of the society in which they manage, as they can, to work.

There is within "independent" circles another direction
or style of effort which I now want to consider, as it
represents a militant aspect of radical aspiration in American
film. It is postulated on a conception of film as being, in
the very broadest sense, redemptive of the human condition itself. This quiet attitude, however estimable, generates
the most difficult and inhibiting contradictions for contemporary radicals. Beneath the burden of Redemption, the
formal integrity which safeguards that radicalism must, and
does, ultimately dissolve. I am referring to a cinema rep-

resented by the work of Stan Brakhage, and, to some extent, by the criticism of Jonas Mekas—who is sitting in the first row with a tape recorder. I would have wanted, of course, to screen some films or sequences to illustrate this consideration, but must content myself with some quotations from critical writings—and from Brakhage's voluminous correspondence.

"What's the use of cinema if man's soul goes rotten?" says Mekas. "It is not a question of film being good or bad artistically. It is a question of . . . a new understanding of Life."

Brakhage, speaking before a gathering in Berlin in December, 1965 (and this passage, somewhat longer, is extracted, unlike the preceding ones, not from *Film Culture*, but from a report on that Berlin occasion in an article published, according to my recollection, last year in *The Village Voice*).

"This camera," said Brakhage, "I take with me everywhere now . . . I took it last night into East Berlin. I was, from the very entrance, in a state of terror that I had not imagined existed before. Finally the tension mounted till I felt compelled to take an image, which is the only time when I do work, when that compulsion or need arises directly from something in living. I had nothing to work with but empty streets and a few lights, and as I worked with those, with a fast-speed color film, and I tried to make an impression of my feelings from just those lights as I was there, inside, that which was an incredible experience for me. I have always taken seeing to be anything that comes to me in the form of an image, whether it be closed-eye vision, the dots and whirls and shapes that come when the eyes are closed and that can be seen when the eyes are open; memory, the remembering of images or the in-gathering of light in the immediacy of the eyes opening. I took images as I could, according to feeling. So that as I've trained myself to hold this camera so that it will reflect the trembling or the feeling of any part of the body; so that it is an extension, so that it becomes a thing to in-gather the light . . . I do not know what I will need to do when I get home in editing to capture the quality of that feeling and to say something of that experience."

Now for many of us, I imagine, and particularly for those

who, like myself, have been for some time concerned with contemporary painting and sculpture and the problems of critical method deriving from this development, this statement has a very familiar ring indeed—and highly problematic implications. If, for men like Anger and Breer, or for Resnais and Godard, art and the radical aspiration supplies a ground for an ethos, art does literally become, for Brakhage, "nothing but a construction in ethics" as Baudelaire suggested, and the artist a tintype of the "moral hero." The rhetoric is that of Abstract Expressionism, and I dare say that the pages of *Film Culture* represent in the New York of 1966 the last precinct of the action-painter's active authority.

As a prelude to a brief consideration of the nature and consequences of this authority, here is a passage from an essay on De Kooning by Harold Rosenberg:

"Since, for De Kooning, art must discover its form in the actuality of the artist's life, it cannot impose itself upon its practitioner as other professions do upon theirs. Art becomes a way by which the artist can avoid a way. . . .

"By a mutual indetermination, art and the artists support each other's openness to the multiplicity of experience. Both resist stylization and absorption into a type. The aesthetic aim to which De Kooning applied the label, 'no style,' derives from and is the experience of this philosophy of art and of the self.

"In conceiving of art as a way of life, De Kooning makes his engagement in his profession total in the sense of the absorption of a priest or saint in his vocation. The idea is faulty. Painting lacks the structure of values by which ethical or religious systems can sustain the individual."

This unusually lucid expression of reserve from the theoretician of action-painting with regard to an aesthetic-as-morality is ultimately not surprising; it expresses the inevitable recognition of the perils and limits of a certain radicalism and its rhetoric.

Here, however, are Godard's thoughts on the matter (and we must have some day a "Wit and Wisdom of J.-L. Godard"; he is an aphorist in the grand tradition of Chamfort): "Between aesthetics and ethics, a choice must be made, of course. However it also goes without saying that each word contains a bit of the other." "Trusting to luck means listening to *voices*." "If the ways of art are unpredictable, this is be-

cause the ways of chance are not." And finally, "Making
films resembles modern philosophy, Husserl, let's say ... an
adventure, plus the philosophy of that adventure, life, and
reflecting on life."

Painters, sculptors, and their critics are involved, at this very
moment, in a kind of chastening reappraisal of a rhetoric
which passed for the thought of action-painting, in a critical
surveyal of the arena whose space measures the relation of
its philosophical assumptions to its metaphors. It may be
premature to demand from the independent or underground
filmmaker (confined, as he is, to an even more marginal
position in society) the critical stringency now beginning to
inform the reassessment of action-painting and its aesthetics.
   To return, briefly but more specifically, to the work and
thinking of Brakhage: I would argue that the notion of the
camera as an extension of the body or its nervous system
seems to me highly questionable, and that, ultimately, it
limits and violates the camera's function. Certainly, this way
of thinking calls into question the instrument's fundamental
power as expressed in the metaphor of the camera as eye,
a marvelously sensitive and flexible one to be sure, that
supreme instrument of *mediation* which is also the "mind's
eye," whose possibilities infinitely transcend the limitations
of crude automatism. If cinema is to embody, as according
to this aesthetic it does, the drama and pathos of creation
itself, then one may ask whether the history of academicism
in film—which, as I have already suggested, proposed the
substitution of novelistic forms for theatrical ones—is not
thereby simply extended by the uncritical parody of Abstract
Expressionist orthodoxy.
   My own feeling is that the work of Resnais and Varda
(to mention only artists represented at this festival) constitute renderings of the agonistic dimension which are
infinitely more radical and powerful; their "statements"
proclaim the recognition of the dynamics of the medium—
and this in the most open and least prescriptive manner possible.
   These "statements" by no means necessarily exclude the
possibility of stimulus or nourishment from other, developing
arts. In America, the work of Robert Breer, for example, has
an immediacy produced by the elimination of narrative as

plot, or plot reconceived as progress, involving a complex visual logic, high speed of images, the use of subliminal vision. All these factors articulate a cinematic aspiration toward the condition of the "object" instantly apprehended, an aspiration shared by our most advanced painting today. Rather than fusing in a con-fusion, this work proposes a situation in which film and painting may converge within a tradition of formal radicalism. Breer's films, in their intransigent autonomy, make an almost wholly plastic use of reference and allusion, by no means excluding extra-plastic resonances, but animated by a sense of structure as progress-in-time so absolute and compelling that very little else has room or time enough in which to "happen."

The extraordinary advantage of American cinema and its situation today does lie partly in the possibilities of these convergences and cross-fertilizations. It may be that American film is unique in its access to a multiplicity of vital efforts unprecedented since the immediately-post-Revolutionary situation in Russia. One thinks of its already established, though still embryonic, contacts with a new music, dance, theatre, painting, and sculpture. And all these are in turn, of course, heightened, and perhaps somewhat endangered, by a forced confrontation with technology in its most paroxysmic and pervasive form.

It is precisely at this point that one may anticipate the difficulties that may soon confront the great figures of European cinema, most particularly in France. If cinema and literature have so wonderfully nourished and sustained each other in postwar France (and this within the context of an anti-literary ontology of film), this is, I believe, in so far as they were both involved in a refining of their *respective* ontologies: the Robbe-Grillet–Resnais collaboration is, of course, a supreme instance of this kind of intimacy of independent forces.

Interestingly enough, however—and disquietingly too— the extra-cinematic, the intellectual context of French film has been (with the exception of Resnais and Bresson) and continues to be, almost exclusively those of Romanticism and Surrealism. In the entire corpus of postwar film I would cite offhand only four examples of the really significantly composed musical or sound track, and this during France's remarkable post-Webernian renewal of music: Michel Fano's serially composed sound track for *L'Immortelle*, Henze's score for *Muriel*, Barbaud's interestingly conceived, though questionable, score for Varda's *Les Créatures*, and above all, the utterly remarkable spoken sound track of Jacques Tati's *Les Vacances de Monsieur Hulot*—certainly, the most deeply Webernian of all in its exquisite economy, in its inventive use of silence!

In our country, the questioning of the values of formal autonomy has led to an attempted dissolution of distinctions or barriers between media. Perhaps, however, this is because our social and economic hierarchies and distinctions remain pretty well impervious to the radical aspiration of filmmakers and of artists in general. The hierarchical distinctions, the barriers between forms are, of course, infinitely more vulnerable. Cinema, on the verge of winning the battle for the recognition of its specificity—and every major filmmaker and critic of the last half-century has fought that battle—is now engaged in a reconsideration of its aims. The Victor now questions his Victory. The emergence of new "intermedia," the revival of the old dream of synaesthesia, the cross-fertilization of dance, theatre, and film, as in the theatre pieces of Robert Whitman, the work of Ken Dewey (and both are, significantly, represented in this year's festival), constitute a syndrome of that radicalism's crisis, both formal and social.

In a country whose power and affluence are maintained by the dialectic of a war economy, in a country whose dream of revolution has been sublimated in reformism and frustrated by an equivocal prosperity, cinematic radicalism is condemned to a politics and strategy of social and aesthetic subversion.

"To live," as Webern, quoting Hölderlin, said, "is to defend a form." It is from the strength of its forms that cinema's essential power of negation, its "liquidation of traditional elements in our culture," as Benjamin put it, will derive and sustain its cathartic power.

Within the structure of our culture, ten-year-olds are now filming eight millimeter serials—mostly science fiction, I am told—in their own backyards. This, perhaps, is the *single most interesting fact* about cinema in our time, and the real source of hope for "independent" cinema. Given this new accessibility of the medium, anything can happen. Astruc's dream of the camera as fountain pen is transcended, the camera becomes a toy, and the element of play is restored to cinematic enterprise. One thinks of Méliès, both Child and Father of cinema, and one rejoices in the promise of his reincarnation in the generation of little Americans making science fiction films after school in those backyards. Here, I do believe, lies the excitement of cinema's future, its ultimate radical potential. And as André Breton, now a very venerable radical, has said, "The work of art is valid if, and only if, it is aquiver with a sense of the future."

THE REALITY OF NEW CINEMA
by Ken Kelman

In this essay Ken Kelman discusses the contributions of the New Cinema to a definition of film reality.

Traditional cinema made clear distinctions between the "real" and "subjective" (content) on the one hand, and between the "real" and "abstract" (form) on the other. Perception—the seeing or hearing of things—came through either the "filter" of characters who were understood as sharing their experience with the audience; or through the "impersonal" camera which was understood as presenting phenomena "objectively," with mechanical fidelity (that is, in recognized customary ways, the machine itself having been invented and developed to reproduce our *standard* perceptions). Psychological states were generally shown from the outside looking in. But when the converse treatment was attempted, when the material was presented to indicate mental processes directly, as most classically in *The Cabinet of Dr. Caligari*, it was "framed" by "reality" (standardized *par excellence* in Hollywood's "dream sequence" technique) so there would be no confusion, no misunderstanding that the world of dream, vision, or hallucination could be accepted as a "real" one. Similarly, abstraction was very clearly "abstract," distanced from "reality" by the use of geometric shapes (Richter,

Fischinger), or, when "real" objects were edited in "abstract" patterns, by the marked fantasy and whimsy of their treatment (Man Ray, McLaren).

What has been occurring with increasing clarity in recent years, chiefly in the New American Cinema, is the crossing of these well-established and confining boundaries. The stages of this revolutionary process follow, not in their strictly chronological development, but in order of departure, more and more radical, from conventions of old cinema.

(1) A breakthrough of prime importance is implicit in the conscious articulation and exposure of filmic illusion. This is exemplified in the work of Bruce Conner, with his use of scratchy old newsreel and cartoon footage, and numbered "leader" (the "10-9-8-7 . . ." that begins reels of film) at various places in his movies, as well as repetition of the same shots until they seem more *film* than illusion. Such devices have sporadically cropped up in other avant-gardes and Nouvelles Vagues, but never before were united to such purposeful and concentrated effect. The most full-fledged instance yet of the anti-illusion film is Stanton Kaye's feature *Georg*, in mock *cinéma-vérité style*, where the "reality" (or illusion) of cinema ironically interplays with that of life itself (or the subject); during the course of which various fancy film techniques are subtly mishandled to call attention to themselves, the camera's shadow appears in the picture, lettering appears between reels, etc.

(2) An even more striking change is implicit in the way in which some of today's film artists handle the concept of reality. Conventional film has established traditions of "reality" which, even in documentary, preclude its being too "real." Sheer undiluted "reality" has always been associated with "primitive" style, and a maxim of popular art has been that too much "reality" will bore, stupefy, cease indeed to have the impact of the "real." The *effect* of "reality," or rather, the use of "realistic" materials to entertain or make points, has been the traditional goal of filmmakers. To show life in all its nuance and detail (with no arrangement or abridgement for purposes of theme or drama) is to show life in its infinite richness *and* poverty, with all its surprise *and* dullness. This is what Andy Warhol has done in his unedited, "straight" versions of sleeping (*Sleep*), eating (*Eat*), and more complex matters (*Screen Test, The*

Chelsea Girls). Warhol's approach is the denial of contrivance, of spurious appeals, the presentation of "reality" for its own sake and no other. And the very fact that no "realistic" *effects* are striven for gives to Warhol's hyperrealism an illusionistic quality, that which life itself gives when contemplated with absolute unwavering focus; an undeviating concentration that old cinema never conceived, since such purity is indeed a negation of the "reality" (illusion) principle. In short, the border between illusion and "reality" is not clear enough either in life or in the cinema of absolute realism to satisfy the old standards.

(3) The converse of the ultimate "objectivity" of Warhol is the "subjectivity" of Stan Brakhage or Carl Linder, a yet more extreme departure from normal movies. Here perceptions and mental states *are* the norm, the "reality"—as validly as conventional images (with the *customary* focus, perspective, angle, of "recognizable" objects) themselves only externalize *ideas* of "reality." Brakhage is aware of "reality" as conditional, as dependent on, indeed existing, in the mind and its eye. His world is not constructed of the rigid preconceived "truths" without which standard movies would be lost (e.g., for him a mountain may be a breast, a blood corpuscle, a creature struggling up a mountain); and, rather, consists of images correlative to immediate personal perceptions (e.g., he has handpainted patterns over the birth of his child, patterns which he actually did see, does see at times of emotional stress, visions which were an absolute "reality" for him at the time, and which thus complete the truth of the situation—what the conventionally trained eye perceives *plus* what the inner ancient eye experiences). The visionary and hallucinatory worlds of Brakhage and Linder are not "framed" in another, more conventional world (as in *Caligari* or *Dead of Night*, or even, more subtly, in *Un Chien Andalou*), but are projected directly, immediately and unmediated, without any "explanatory notes," seeking no justification in the eyes of the "regular" world.

(4) Finally, and most recently, there has emerged film dispensing entirely with figurative imagery, whether "real" or "abstract"; film consisting absolutely of light: black-and-white in Tony Conrad's *The Flicker*, pure basic colors plus white in a remarkable section of John Cavanaugh's *Acid Man*. Here there is hardly even any question of "real," "illusory,"

"abstract," "subjective," "objective"; there are no images to interpret. The vision shown is that of sheer light, light as the medium and power, light as the substance and subject. And traditional realism is made practically absurd (in its assumption of verisimilitude as basic truth) by the stark undeniable "reality" of perception itself—not of preconceived images we have been taught to see in certain ways, as "real," as "abstract," as "fantastic"—of nothing more than the very light, the light upon the eye.

The four new ways of handling cinematic illusion that are noted above display a progressive tendency toward richness and flexibility of meaning, away from the calculations of specific emotional effect, toward liberation of the senses, away from insistence on the credibility or "reality" of a particular illusion. The art, not of anti-illusion or anti-realism, but of conscious illusion and conscious realism, is hardly out of its infancy in film, compared to other media; but by the same token, in film it is growing at the greatest rate of all.

THE CAMERA AS A GOD *

by Charles Boultenhouse

In these notes the filmmaker Charles Boultenhouse provides a salutary corrective for the easy acceptance of Hollywood movies as conscious or unconscious art, reminding us that "the significance of such a cinema is centered entirely upon the sensibility of the person experiencing it." While today's art can incorporate all aspects of mass culture, mass culture continues nonetheless to pursue its independent existence.

In ancient times anything from trees to the wind was thought to be inhabited by spirits. Many of these spirits ultimately became gods. This metamorphosis was the result of the ministrations of priests, magicians, and sorcerers (the artists of those times) who discovered the potential of the spirits by intuition and perfected them through ritual. Robert

* Reprinted from *Film Culture*, No. 29, Summer, 1963.

Graves has reminded us that Phoebus Apollo began as a mouse demon.

The good filmmaker is he who is engaged (consciously or unconsciously) in preserving and perfecting the demon in the camera; the very best filmmaker is he who is engaged in transforming the demon into the god. I am sure you will see that an idea so theological as this will probably make out experimental film to be positively sacred in character and commercial film rather blasphemous. You will be right.

The commercial film, however, is being well spoken of these days. An effort is being made to bestow on it a kind of authenticity which, I believe, is an absurd thing to try to do. There are two assertions which I think are particularly wrong: one is that commercial film is a natural kind of Pop art, the other is that commercial film conceals a director of such creative intensity that he can be regarded as an Author (in the higher sense).

I Snap, Crackle, and Pop

Let us first consider movies as Pop art. Said without sneers, this means that Hollywood is the Original Pop Art and is GREAT because IT IS what IT IS. Gorgeous flesh and mostly terrible acting! Divine! Campy dialogue and preposterous plots! Divine! Sexy fantasy and unorgasmic tedium! Divine!

Now the significance of such a cinema is centered entirely upon the sensibility of the person experiencing it. When Parker Tyler wrote about basically bad films that were also basically fantastic, he transformed them into something more than they appeared on the surface. As Paul Goodman said, "Parker Tyler reacting to a Hollywood movie is a better movie than they ever dreamed of there. . . ." Furthermore, Mr. Tyler wrote playfully and consciously. He never regressed to the teen-age responses that now appear in serious magazines.

The question of Hollywood in relation to all of us was clearly raised at the 1961 Creative Film Foundation evening at Cinema 16 when the painter and filmmaker Alfred Leslie, taking issue with the derogatory remarks made about Hollywood went to the microphone to announce that he liked Hollywood films and always had. Although the late Maya Deren, chairman of the evening, rose in full and splendid fury and offered rebuttal (as did Shirley Clarke), neither pointed out the following: that, even though Alfred Leslie enjoyed Hollywood films, when it came to making a film (*Pull My Daisy*) neither the standards nor methods of Hollywood were used. In a sense, we all grew up on Hollywood, and for many of us, our first experiences of the Marvelous are enshrined in the tacky trappings of Hollywood glamor. But at the same time that these films aroused, they also failed to satisfy. Hollywood is the tease of all time. See how its seething teen-age adorers long for the corny fantasy to turn into pornography. Reflect that it never will. Think how pornography would fulfill Hollywood. Remember that it never will. No ritual orgy will be set off by a modern King and Queen of the May. The gods of the teen-agers will not strip and copulate. Thus the only thing that could save the Pop art of Hollywood is precisely what will not occur. The teen-agers of all ages who worship its fetishes will never be satisfied: nor will the Demon of the Camera, bored almost cross-eyed by the miles of Nothing passing before it into Oblivion.

II *"Author Author!"*

Another strategy to give prestige to the commercial film is the claim that directors can be artists and indeed, unbeknownst, actually have been artists all along; that in developing their craft, they have been developing style, and in discovering their own styles and methods, have developed the art of the film as a whole. I find this a particularly depressing idea because, originating in France, where it has a certain plausibility, it has been applied to Hollywood, where it has very, very little. The Hollywood director is usually surprised to discover that his "art" has been taken seriously; this is because he had never been serious about "art" as such. His first concern has been to make his film as exciting as possible in order to keep the customers coming to see it, so that the investment would be protected—yield a profit.

A Hollywood director, plainly speaking, is a craftsman using all his skills to protect an investment by making as large a profit as possible. If his skills and devices are repeated and developed to the point where they can be identified, this does not make him into an artist; I must say, though I have never invested in a commercial film, were I to do so, I would absolutely insist that the director protect my investment to the utmost of his abilities. It is not surprising that if many successful Hollywood directors are terribly, terribly old, it is because the banks trust them, and clearly the banks are correct. One cannot help sympathizing with those men who now spend what euphemistically are known as the Golden Years out in the hot sun, still directing Westerns in some godforsaken spot on the planet.

When it comes to the total work of these efficient, imaginative craftsmen, one must simply face the facts. Their films cannot be studied as a developing revelation of artistic intention, not because their skills did not develop, but because they never had a single artistic intention, and it is pointless to pretend that they did. In a recent issue of *Film Culture*, a preposterous comparison was made between the anonymity of the Hollywood craftsmen and the anonymity of the creators of the great cathedrals. The comparison is absurd because the intentions of the cathedral builders and the Hollywood directors are opposed. The great cathedrals were dedicated to the glory of God, which (it is my pleasure to remind those whose minds it has escaped) is an exalted and exalting thing to have done. It is no matter that the burghers of the medieval towns were enthusiastic supporters of those enormous and expensive enterprises since they knew the cathedrals meant pilgrims and pilgrims meant business; the point is, the vast cathedrals in themselves, *for* themselves, were vast and vibrant with their dedication to the great idea of immortality. Hollywood, on the other hand, becomes aware of exaltation only in the last few moments of a picture—where it takes on the form of a particularly repellent musical climax—and is dedicated to a particularly empty idea: entertainment must be superficial distraction.

In the world of Hollywood, it would be a waste of time to study the techniques of the best directors—barring the exceptional aforementioned case where one's living depends on one's sound investments. Critical analysis is therefore quite irrelevant. For the critic, the study of film style ought to be restricted to those directors who are genuine "authors" (it is no accident that the greatest of them have written scripts of their own:

Eisenstein, Welles, Pagnol, Cocteau, Fellini, Antonioni, etc.).
The truth is that the commercial director should have the
proper and honest reward of being credited with a job well
done rather than wear the dubious appellation of "artist."

The demon in the camera, however, likes the so-called
"auteur" theory because the demon wishes it were true. When
this theory is applied to the films of those to whom it is usually
applied, it is confused because it doesn't remember those cases,
or remembers them only vaguely, as in an interminable daydream. Even after seeing such film works anew, the demon
does not remember them because they have merged so hopelessly with the endless miles of other commercial films that all
seem interchangeable and unchanging—indistinguishable and
undistinguished.

III   Not Just an Experiment

The experimental film has a wonderful way of persisting.
Someone or other always seems interested in looking at them.
Always there seems someone new who wants to decipher the
enigmas and blazons of Cocteau; to analyze the dreams of
Maya Deren; to soar into the flying signs and symbols of Stan
Brakhage; to—but rather than seem to promote all this, I prefer to analyze. The experimental film is not just an experiment
in the scientific sense, but it does resemble science in that each
of its films is a stage in the study of the Being of the Camera.
Since Poe, all the arts have tended to evolve an almost scientific attitude toward the given Nature and Being of their own
materials. All the arts are thus engaged in testing; film especially so. All the arts are also engaged, in Wallace Stevens's
phrase, in making "Notes Toward a Supreme Fiction." Film
especially so. I advocate, in an analytical spirit, that the Supreme Fiction wants the Camera to be a God.

SHORTCOMINGS OF THE SEXUAL METAPHOR IN NEW YORK'S INDEPENDENT FILMS

by Ronald Tavel

Ronald Tavel was born in Brooklyn. He was Playwright-in-Residence for the Playhouse of the Ridiculous in New York, where his works included Shower, The Life of Juanita Castro, The Life of Lady Godiva, Screen Test, *and* Kitchenette. *He has written and directed numerous films for Andy Warhol Films Incorporated, among them* Screen Test, Vinyl, Suicide, Space, Hedy, Withering Sights, Hanoi Hannah, *and parts of* The Chelsea Girls. *He is the author of the Off-Broadway play* Gorilla Queen.

> Little flower—but *if* I could understand
> What you are, root and all, and all in all,
> I should know what God and man is.
> —Tennyson

If you hold that eternity is in a second and infinity in a grain of sand, it follows that any arbitrary moment or haphazardly chosen object, properly handled, contains within it the possibility of unveiling the face of final truth. Up from Aristophanes and down to Mae West (probably America's best playwright), the sexual metaphor has proved a singularly rewarding approach to a vision of man and his relation to the firmament. A child develops within the bonds of his dependency on others and is later compulsively motivated by his sex drives to reclaim the lost union of his childhood. For the artist, understanding of this urge toward re-union with the race of mankind may illuminate an individual's re-union with conceptual reality. Among "underground" filmmakers the sexual metaphor is used with great frequency, yet the movies they produce all convey

110

a sense of incompletion. Perhaps the reason for this is that none of these young Americans can satisfactorily be termed either classical or romantic. All slip into a third category, variously defined as fragmentary, decadent, mannerist, or fractional, and so, unhappily, their works join the bulk of our nation's creative output and seriously fall short of the ultimate standards raised in continental Europe as far back as Homer. If we ask why these movies are incomplete, we invariably are led to the conclusion that their makers are as fractured as the visions they produce.

Clearly, the general creative temperament of our age is romantic. With certain notable exceptions (classicists like Jasper Johns and William Burroughs), nearly everything about our contemporary avant-garde interests bespeaks romanticism. One may note especially the attention paid to mysticism,[1] transcendentalism, psychedelics, astrology, minority sexualism, obscurity of form, mixed media, iconoclasm, and expansion of acceptable subject material. The fractionalism of the moviemen in question, then, would seem to be a result of degeneration from the romantic mode. How and why did it take place?

One of the earliest exponents of underground cinema was the singularly aptly-named Kenneth Anger. Mr. Anger's major metaphors are sex and astrology. His first important film, *Fireworks*, remains his most successful. In this opus he presents with disarming honesty and innocence the sexual fantasies of a youth decidedly past the security that can be gained from a delicately balanced love-union and now well on his way to responding only to a parental protector so ominous in his ability to defend that he is virtually a sadist in the most dramatic sense of the word. Anger's nonfluid and unimaginatively focused commercial venture, *Scorpio Rising*, conveys a distrust of human beings so overwhelming that the life of the entire

[1] Mysticism in Western art (Oriental art is another matter) is almost entirely romantic. Shakespeare's mystical mythology in *The Tempest* would be enough in itself to qualify him as a romantic did not the unmitigated passion that is the totality of *Lear* definitively place him in that category. Sidney, Blake, Coleridge, Whitman, Ginsberg, Cézanne, Giacometti, etc., are all unreservedly romantic. W.B. Yeats, a genuine classicist who spent all his life studying mysticism, left a body of work from which his occult concerns may easily be dismissed despite the fact that few scholars have had the courage to note as much.

race is defined as little more than a sadomasochistic orgy—
and not the most authentic of orgies, at that. (Anyone harboring reservations about Anger's suspicions of mankind is urged
to read his book, *Hollywood Babylon*, which is extraordinarily
paranoid in its interpretation.) Astrology, the second ingredi-
ent in *Scorpio Rising*, enables Anger to celebrate his birth and
the position of his major stars in what is traditionally the most
evil of all the signs of the zodiac—that is, supposedly, the
most paranoid, the most jealous, and the most sexual in that it
governs the genitals themselves. To make art depend on astrology in itself implies failure, since the determinations of
astrology preclude the numberless possibilities which lie open
to us, pre-establish a fixed vision, and deter the artist from
an organic substantiation.

Gregory Markopoulos, too, appears to use sexuality as a
metaphor. Many of this filmmaker's early works, like *Du Sang
de la Volupté et de la Mort,* remind one of Cocteau. Greek
myths have certain drawbacks as movie subjects since they are
wholly verbal, and literature has not as yet mixed well with
visual revelation. For example, Antonioni proved rather disappointing in *Red Desert* when, after an observationally accurate
and painstaking buildup, he relegated his pronouncement
(*"Tutto canti"*) to the narration in the little allegorical beach-
and-sea scene: for nothing in the bathing girl, the rocks, the
beach, or the waves innately invests the consciousness with
such a conclusion. At the showdown, he cannot make the eyes
convince. Markopoulos shares this shortcoming. The viewer
must bring to his films a wealth of extracurricular knowledge
and is then obliged to play games with Markopoulos's use or
abuse of such information. The obscurity is excessive, self-
indulgent, and extreme; but it fails to intimidate since it
usually merely distracts the viewer from what he is seeing by
substituting concern for what the filmmaker is referring to.
Sexuality appears to be the subject of the myths, but it continually eludes us inasmuch as the sneaky peeks at nudes are as
much of the sexual union as we are going to get. I'd feel much
healthier if that expert editing were to pause for five full
seconds and let me look at that most natural of attractions, the
unadorned human. (As a footnote, I must add that Markopoulos's newest film, a compilation of three-minute portraits,
is his purest visual achievement and a tour de force in pro-

viding unending interest in something that could easily have proved unmitigated tedium.)

Jack Smith takes Aristotle to task by propounding the theory that pornography can be art. If by pornography is meant anything that moves the audience to action, the present writer would have to reassert Aristotle's rejection of it, since to pornograph a viewer is to make him aware of himself as separation and his physicalness as incompletion, and to move him to action is to demote him from the level of free contemplation. The problem is, however, more complex than it might seem, and I believe Smith may have made, or at least inaugurated, an important contribution to cinema. For if you can accept sexual *desire* as the initial involving factor, that which sucks the audience into the forthcoming experience and, once that audience is firmly enmeshed, proceeds to raise it to inactive and ever-broadening speculation, then it may be possible to consider turning pornography into art or, to be precise, letting pornography lead the spectator into art. But having allowed this much to Smith, we are then confronted with where his work takes us: for far from rounding out into reunion with the human race, it leads us into a highly forsaken and pitiful isolation where sexual ecstasy is re-enacted at the earliest stages of childhood fixation, where fantasies protect us from an inordinately hard-to-attain reality, and where identification with a sensationally psychotic mother is the only means to channel the crucified libido. It is quite possible that *Flaming Creatures* (one of the best examples of cinematography on record) does not bring us nearer to sexual comprehension through its point-blank confrontations with genitals, but rather encourages us to the celibate annihilation of which it is so innocent an exposé, allowing us to breathe easy and rest deceptively securely on the first and most frustrating rung of concupiscent defeat. Smith's subject matter is Hollywood, his method sexual hyperbole, and his product a confection that might well be labeled "The Epic of Infancy"; he is as exacting in detail as any mannerist, and we have from him the most obviously fragmented concept of life to be offered by an important contemporary creator.

Andy Warhol Films Inc. (a company name covering a multitude of sins and virtually an army of cooperative artists) is dominated by its eponymous founder, most significantly

Mike Sullivan: From *Tarzan Finds a Mate*, 1965

when the films defend an unmoving camera. Here one is given a very persistent and precise point of view: all objects and changes in the universe relate to the central and unblinking, absolutely fixed eye. It is the most boring and least entertaining position of vision, but it is the most exact that ever challenged a movie audience. It is the telescope of the voyeur, the sexual participation that never surmounts the starting stage, and, on further consideration, it comes dangerously close to necrophilia: for the motionless camera eye does not seem to achieve its end until the beholden object also ceases to move. Sometimes the object fails to budge for six hours. Herein all sexual activity is defined as too problematic, and nothing short of death can reduce interpersonal difficulties to a level at which they can be coped with. When the camera pans (and Warhol himself is usually behind the abruptions) one has the opportunity to study the personality of this eye, and more often than not the foregoing assertion is confirmed: for the camera wanders indiscriminately over the situation, sensation, and character of what is performed before it, resting for a moment on some specific or other, but wholly ignorant or repressive of the events taking place. As Warhol's scenarist, I struggled to reassert the human jurisdiction in the graphic, until our dichotomy of intention finally tore the films in two. For when one is positive about saying nothing one can still say nothing with fascinating conviction.

Turning to a still younger generation of filmmakers, we discover that the works of William Vehr are often confessedly little more than the statement of their own fractionalism. Each begins electrifyingly, forcefully, with a grandiose and exotic sexual phantasm, builds up with delicious visual taste, to a towering center, and then brusquely ends. It is as if Mr. Vehr, all decked out in his sex delirium, has nowhere to go.

In the films of Michael Sullivan, sexual connection is so arduous to cement that when it is finally within grasp it immediately degenerates into that finality of self-imprisoned despair called cannibalism. At the end of the film *Tarzan Finds a Mate* he does so only to devour her.

In summation, if we accept these underground practitioners of cinema as capable commentators on our culture, we must conclude that America is as sexually distressed and conceptually schismatic a society as any in the history of civilization.

23 TOWARD RE:PROGRAMMING *NATURE* WITH MIRRORS: FILM, THEATER &

by Kenneth King

Kenneth King is a dancer/choreographer and graduate in philosophy who has presented a number of dance-theater works at The Bridge and elsewhere in New York. The most recent of these, the full-length m-o-o-n-b-r-a-i-n *with* SuperLecture *incorporates film, dance, sculptured objects, and programmed tapes in expressing King's concept of a new, programmed art for the cybernetic age—an art that will transcend the conventional boundaries between separate art forms, and at the same time provide a legitimate communicative medium.*

1.
THE SUPER-CONCENTRATED TRADITION OF THE FILM FORM, INCLUDING THE NUMEROUS AND DIVERSE SOURCES OF FILM INFORMATION (histories, technique manuals, autobiographical data, formal criticism, scenarios, popularizations, etc.) MAY NOW BE UNDERSTOOD IN ULTRAMODERN *CYBERNETIC* TERMS, CORRELATIVE WITH INFORMATION THEORY.

2.
LIBRARIES AND OTHER VAST SOURCES, INCLUDING ALL FILMS THEMSELVES, AS WELL AS ADDED SOCIO-CULTURAL *DATA*, CONSTITUTE A *CORE* OF INFORMATION, OR *CONTENT* OF A *MASS MEMORY* OF, FOR EXAMPLE, AN IBM 7044, PROGRAMMED FOR INSTANT RETRIEVAL, PROJECTION.

3.
THE NATURE OF THE *PROGRAM* IS SUGGESTED IN PART BY THE NATURE OF THE FILM MEDIUM AND IMPLICIT IN THE FORMAL INNOVATIONS OF MOD-

ERN ADVERTISING, JOURNALISM AND TELEVISION;
IN META-CYBERNETIC TERMS THE PROGRAM IS A
TECHNICAL ASSEMBLAGE OF PROCESSED MONADS,
OR *BITS* OF INFORMATION.

4.
THE PROCESS OF PROGRAMMING AND THE PRO-
GRAM ITSELF NOW SUGGEST REVISING THE USUAL
FORMS OF OUR THINKING, NAMELY BY ABANDON-
ING THE USUAL PLATONIC/ARISTOTELIAN DUAL-
ISMS SUCH AS FORM–CONTENT, ABSTRACT–REAL,
SUBJECT–OBJECT, DIRECTOR–FILMMAKER, DANCER–
CHOREOGRAPHER, ETC.

5.
THE TWENTIETH CENTURY PSEUDO-AESTHETIC IS
ONE OBSERVING THE DISSOLUTION OF MECHANI-
CALLY SPECIALIZED ART FORMS *AS FORMS* (EX.
THEATER AS PLAY OR DANCE, LITERATURE AS
NOVEL, POEM, PAINTING AS PAINT ON CANVAS,
ETC.) RENDERING THEM INCREASINGLY REDUN-
DANT AND DEMODED (BUT MORE POSITIVELY, IN-
CORPORATING THEM INTO MORE EXPANSIVE
PROGRAMS) BECAUSE A FORM AS A DISCRETE
PHENOMENON IS NO LONGER INCLUSIVE NOR
PLASTIC ENOUGH OF/FOR "NATURE" AND HUMAN
EXPERIENCE IN THE TOTALLY-VIBRATING CIR-
CUITRY/ENVIRONMENT.

6.
AN ANALYTIC COMPARISON OF THE FILM FORM
WITH OTHER ARTS SUGGESTS GENERAL RELA-
TIONS, FOR EXAMPLE: EDITING TECHNIQUES, JUX-
TAPOSITION OF SERIAL MATERIAL, DEVELOPMENT
AND COHESION/UNITY AS A LINEAR WORK–THE
NOVEL; VISUAL AWARENESS OF GRAPHIC AND
COMPOSITIONAL ELEMENTS, PLASTICITY, FLEXI-
BILITY–PAINTING; MOVEMENT AND RELATION-
SHIPS OF CHANGING FORMAL PATTERNS AND
IMAGES–CHOREOGRAPHY; PRESENTATION AND
PRESENCE-ATION OF OBJECTS, IMAGES, PEOPLE–
THEATER; ETC.

7.
PERHAPS IN GENERAL TERMS FILM, AT PRESENT,
IS A SYNTHESIS OF WESTERN ARTISTIC TECH-
NIQUES WHICH HITHERTO HAVE BEEN EXPRESSED,
SEPARATELY, AS FORMS.

8.
IT IS THE "NATURE" OF MODERN ADVERTISING,
JOURNALISM, TELEVISION, AND FILM TO COMBINE
VISUAL AND DISCURSIVE MATERIAL (DATA), I.E.,
A SERIES OF ELECTRONS, POINTS, AND BITS INTO
A PROGRAM, MORE ARTICULATELY UNDERSTOOD
AS A MOSIAC/COLLAGE OF DATA, PATTERNS,
INTERCONNECTING TEXTURES (ORAL, AURAL, VI-
SUAL), IDEAS, SENSATIONS, ETC., ALL AS INFOR-
MATION.

9.
THUS PROGRAMMING AND THE STRUCTURE OF
THE PROGRAM ITSELF ABSORB AND INCORPORATE
WHAT HAVE BEEN TRADITIONALLY DEFINED AS
FORM AND CONTENT—AN INTELLECTUAL ISSUE—
JUST AS THE PROGRAM (*AS PROGRAM*) CAN SIMUL-
TANEOUSLY SYNTHESIZE SEVERAL DIFFERENT
ARTISTIC/TECHNICAL/COMMERCIAL OPERATIONS
(TECHNIQUES) ON A PRACTICAL LEVEL. FOR EX-
AMPLE, THE PRODUCTION/PRESENTATION OF A
TELEVISION PROGRAM, A COMMERCIAL MOVIE, OR
AN EDITION OF A POPULAR MAGAZINE COMBINE
MULTI-SPECIALIZED PROCESSES SUCH AS WRITING,
EDITING, DIRECTION, LAY-OUT OR COMPOSITION,
PRODUCTION, GRAPHICS, ETC.

10.
THUS OUR THINKING CAN EXPAND OUR ACTIONS
JUST AS DIFFERENT ABSTRACT OR CONCEPTUAL
PLANS CAN AUGMENT ARTISTIC/SCIENTIFIC OP-
ERATIONS.

11.
ONE POSSIBLE PREMISE FOR A DIFFERENT PRO-
GRAM *IN TOTAL* IS REALIZING THAT THE "NATURE"

OF OUR CONTEMPORARY "LANDSCAPE" IS NOW
COMPOSED OF CHEMICAL, ELECTRICAL, MECHAN-
ICAL, ETC., TECHNOLOGIES. WHAT IS SOCIALLY AND
ELECTRICALLY CHARACTERISTIC OF TECHNOLOGY
IS A CONSTANT PROCESS OF EXCHANGING ACCESSI-
BLE INFORMATION AS WELL AS A SYNCHRONICITY
AND TRANS-PENETRATION BETWEEN (ARTISTIC/
SCIENTIFIC) FIELDS, THE DATA SERVICING A SE-
RIES OF RELATED ISSUES AND TASKS.

12.
IN THE ARTS, FOR EXAMPLE, SPECIALIZATION HAS
CREATED A TRADITION OF FORMS. THE PRESENT
CHALLENGE TO SPECIALIZATION, WHICH HAS RE-
SULTED IN THE FORMS, FOR THE MOST PART,
LOOSING THEIR SOCIAL EFFECTIVENESS, ARE "MU-
TATIONS" CURRENTLY MISLABELED AND LUMPED
UNDER THE TERM "MIXED-MEDIA." THESE PRO-
GRAMS ARE AS YET, UNTETHERED, OPEN-ENDED
AREAS OF ARTISTIC EXPLORATION WHICH ARE,
WITH REGARD TO TRADITION, "EXTRA" OR "POST"
FORMAL, YET SEEN EXPANSIVELY AS A *COAGULA-
TION* OF PAINTING, GRAPHICS, ELECTRONICS, MU-
SIC, RADIO, FILM, DANCE, LITERATURE, ETC.

13.
THE POWERFUL FUTURE IMPLICATIONS OF FILM,
LIKE TELEVISION, LIE NOT SO MUCH IN THE PER-
FECTION OF THE FORM NOR IN "IMPROVING" THE
CONTENT, BUT IN SIMPLY DESIGNING NEW PRO-
GRAMS. UNDERSTANDING THE FILM MEDIUM
MEANS UTILIZING THE POWER-POTENTIAL OF A
PIECE OF TRANSPARENT CELLULOID, A POWER
COMPARABLE TO THAT OF CHEMISTRY AND CHEM-
ICAL TECHNOLOGY (GRASS, HASH, ACID, A., DMT,
ETC.) AS A *MEANS* FOR REPROGRAMMING HUMAN
PERCEPTION, INTELLIGENCE, SOCIAL ORIENTA-
TION AS WELL AS (PLEASURABLY) HEIGHTENING
SENSE OPERATIONS. A GOOD HISTORICAL EXAM-
PLE OF A CHEMICALLY CLAIRVOYANT, AND STILL
EXTREMELY "FAR-OUT" FILM IS FRANCIS PICABIA'S
AND RENÉ CLAIR'S *ENTR'ACTE*, MADE IN 1924. THIS

FILM NOT ONLY INTRODUCED A VITAL NEW SENSE
AND PENETRATION OF VISUAL SPACE, BUT ALSO
PRESENTED A RADICALLY NEW APPROACH TO ED-
ITING THROUGH THE JUXTAPOSITION OF DISPAR-
ATE TEXTURES (AURAL, ORAL, TACTILE, VISUAL),
AND SIMULTANEOUSLY UN(DER)COVERING A PRO-
GRAMMED *SENSE* OF POETRY—AN "UNDERGROUND"
POETRY, A SENSE CULTIVATED BY THE TECHNICAL
IMPLICATIONS OF "SPACING OUT" AN IMAGE.

14.
FILM AND TELEVISION HAVE A SEVERE, BUT VITAL
SIGNIFICANCE FOR THEATER, JUST AS RADIO DOES
FOR MUSIC. ANALOGOUS TO THE STRUCTURE OF
PROGRAMMING (MOSIAC/COLLAGE) IS THE POWER-
POTENTIAL OF FILM AND MAGNETIC RECORDING
TAPE TO *STORE* (VISUAL, AURAL, ORAL) BITS OF
INFORMATION (OR, *PREPARED* SENSATIONS) WHICH
CAN BE INSTANTLY RETRIEVED TO RECIRCUIT ANY
COMBINATION OF AESTHETIC RESPONSES (PLEA-
SURE, DISGUST, EUPHORIA, HORROR, ETC.). THIS
CYBERNETIC VIEWPOINT AND CHEMICAL COUN-
TERPOINT—*SEEING* THE HISTORY OF FORMAL ART
AS A CORE OF CODIFIABLE INFORMATION IS AN
IMPORTANT IDEA WITH VARIOUS IMPRE(PLICATE)-
ATIONS WHICH COULD POT(ENT)ION(ABLE)LY
CLARIFY THE PRESENT LINGOguisM (YSTIC) CON-
FUSION OF/BETWEEN ART FORMS.

15.
FOR EXAMPLE, IN CHOREOGRAPHIC TERMS, OUR
SENSE OF MOTION, OUR KNOWLEDGE AND UNDER-
STANDING OF SPACE AND PERSPECTIVE HAVE BEEN
RADICALLY REVISED NOT ONLY BY THE TRADITION
OF TWENTIETH-CENTURY EUROPEAN AND AMERI-
CAN PAINTERS WORKING OUT FORMAL, ARTISTIC
ISSUES, BUT BY PHYSICISTS AS WELL, WORKING
OUT THE ISSUES OF QUANTUM MECHANICS AND
THE IMPLICATIONS OF RELATIVITY THEORY, AND
ALSO BY FILM AND TELEVISION. ALL FORMALLY
RECIRCUIT OUR NOTIONS OF SPACE, e-MOTION
AND PERSPECTIVE BY QUALIFYING THREE-DIMEN-

SIONALITY IN PSYCHIC AND PHYSICAL TERMS. AND IN OLD TERMS: MOVEMENT CAN NO LONGER EXPRESS OR CONTAIN THIS NEW INFORMATION.

16.
IN THEATRICAL TERMS—THE EXPLOSION OF VISUAL DETAIL AS A PHENOMENON IN ART, RESULTING IN THE CROSSING OF CIRCUITS OF MICROSCOPE AND MOVIE SCREEN, IS A PROCESS WHEREBY ILLUSION BECOMES IMAGE AND GESTURE BECOMES OBJECT, BRINGING ABOUT THE DISSOLUTION OF THE ACTOR'S "PRIVATE" PSYCHOLOGY. INSTEAD OF THE AUDIENCE LOOKING *INTO* (IN ON) THE PERFORMING AREA AS IF THE FAKE FOURTH WALL HAD BEEN REMOVED, THEY ARE NOW CONFRONTED WITH AN ELECTRIC, THEATER-ART OR MIRROR-LIKE EXEORCISE WHEREIN VISION IS FUSED TO MEANS. THAT IS, THE AUDIENCE IS NO LONGER PASSIVE, NOR ARE THE SPECTATORS PROGRAMMED FOR "CHAOS," AS AT A HAPPENING, BUT RATHER ARE BLOWN-OUT ON A PUBLIC SCREEN, SENSING IN SOME PSYCHIC FUSION THAT THEIR PRIVATE "SELF" *IS* THAT PUBLIC SCREEN, NOW A COLLECTIVE, MYTHIC DISASTER.

17.
. . . THE EMERGING CITIZEN, IT APPEARS TO ME, SEEKS MORE AND MORE INFORMATION: NOT ONLY FACTUAL DATA BUT ALSO THE WORK OF IMAGINATIVE KNOWING. TO HIM, INFORMATION SERVES AS A FIELD OF CONSCIOUSNESS, FOR TO POSSESS INFORMATION OF WHATEVER LEVEL OF IMPORTANCE, OF WHATEVER GRADATION OF TASTE, IS TO ENTER MIND OUTSIDE ONESELF. TECHNOLOGY TYPICALLY CHANGES AND EXTENDS SENSIBILITY. THE NEW MEDIA ENABLE YOUNG PEOPLE, PARTICULARLY, TO ENTER THE CONSCIOUSNESS OF PEOPLE THEY HAVE NEVER KNOWN IN "REAL" LIFE.
(William Jovanovich, "Aspects of the Present," *The American Scholar,* Vol. 36, No. 1, Winter 1966–67, p. 39.)

18.
. . . AND WE DO NOT THROW AWAY THE GOOD
GRAIN JUST BECAUSE THE RATS OFTEN GET INTO
IT. —MEISTER ECKHART

19.
WITH CULTURE, TASTE, SENSIBILITY: FORMS AND
VALUES FOR SEEING. WITH OPEN EYES: THE MOON
IS ONE'S HEAD, THE SKY IS (ONE'S) SKIN. IN PLACE
OF SPECIALIZATION: SECULARIZATION—BEING
SPACED OUT. AND FROM THE JAZZ MUSICIANS, A
LINGOguisM(YSTIC)AL GIFT: "I DON'T UNDERSTAND
IT, BUT LET'S GO AND DIG WHAT THE CAT'S INTO."

20.
BY THE EXPLOSION OR BLOWING-OUT OF DETAIL
ON THE MOVIE SCREEN, AS NOTED PRIVATE PA-
THOLOGY BECOMES A PUBLIC'S MYTH—A PUB-
LIC'SILL(I)NESS. A FORMAL EXAMPLE: CARL
DREYER'S *JOAN OF ARC*—THE CAMERA'S FOCUS ON
THE ACTRESS' FACE MAKES THE FACE A PLASTIC
OBJECT. BUT IT IS THE PLASTICITY, THE PATHOS,
THE TENSIONS ON THE FACE WHICH MAKE IT THE
"SUBJECT" OF THE FILM.

FILM CREATES ITS OWN MYTHOLOGY—EVEN AD-
VERTISEMENTS ARE PRODUCTS OF A COMMER-
CIALLY-BLOATED AND OVER-BLOWN FREUDIANISM.
ON STAGE THE FOCUS AND PENETRATION OF
SPACE DISLOCATES GESTURE AS 2-D IN FAVOR OF
A LENGTHENED CONTEMPLATION OF OBJECTS,
AND RELATIONSHIPS EXTENDING *BEYOND* 3-D and
SPACE. WITH THE ILLUSORY FOURTH WALL OF THE
THEATER REMOVED THE AUDIENCE NO LONGER
CONFRONTS AN ACTOR, SOMEBODY ELSE'S HANG-
UPS. THEY CONFRONT THEMSELVES AND THEIR
LIFE IN A PUBLIC MIRROR (THE SCREEN) IN WHICH
THE REFLECTION, DISTORTION IS A HALLUCINA-
TION, CORPORATELY "REAL" (IMMEDIATE) AND
PENETRATING PSYCHIC DIMENSIONALITY—
THROUGH THE HISTORICAL, THE MYTHIC, THE
GENETIC, THE PATHOGENIC.

21.
NATURE BLOWN-UP IS NATURE BLOWN-OUT. THE
EXPLOSION OF NATURE IS SYNONYMOUS WITH
INTENSIFYING SENSE EXPERIENCE—METAPHORI-
CALLY BY ZOOMING INTO VISIONS AND PHENOM-
ENA, INTO AND THROUGH OBJECTS ONCE POSITED
BY PAINTERS ON EASELS AND PLAYWRIGHTS ON
STAGES. IN MUSIC: LA MONTE YOUNG'S USE OF
ELECTRONIC SOUND EQUIPMENT, EMPLOYING,
SPECIFICALLY, "DRONES" AND HIGHLY AMPLIFIED
"MIXED" SOUNDS AND SOUND PATTERNS TO AB-
SORB, GET THE AUDIENCE *INSIDE* THE PERFORM-
ANCE, ALSO A NEW VIRTUE OF ELECTRONIFIED
DISCOTHEQUES WHERE "UNDERSTANDING THE
MEANS" MEANS LIBERATION FROM THE BODY
THROUGH THE BODY'S SENSE-NETWORK. PRODUC-
ING A NEW LINEAGE OF MUSICIANS BEGINNING,
MAYBE WITH THE BEATLES, INCLUDING THE SU-
PREMES, SIMON AND GARFUNKLE, DONOVAN, AND
NOW, BOBBY DYLAN. IN MODERN THEATER:
"DANCER" MEREDITH MONK'S TRANSCENDANT
THEATER-WORK "8 MILLIMETER EARRINGS."

22.
IT IS NOT THE DESTRUCTION OF THEATER, THE
DEATH OF THE NOVEL OR PAINTING NOR BROADER
ISSUES OF "COMMUNICATION," LANGUAGE, NOR
"ALIENATION" WHICH ARE ISSUES AT HAND, BE-
CAUSE THOSE SOUR CRITICISMS ARE ROOTED IN
NEWTONIANISM AND THE LINGER(INEAGE) OF
PLATOtudes; THE NOTION OF INVENTION LIMITED
TO A FORM AND FORM-ULA.

23.
THE PENETRATION OF FILM, *THROUGH* THE ME-
DIUM, IS A PROCESS SYNCHRONISTIC WITH THE
MIXING OF "FORMAL" AND "POPULAR" ARTS AS WELL
AS WITH OTHER EVENTS SUCH AS THE OVERHAUL-
ING OF FORMAL SEXUAL VALUES AND PRACTICES IN
A REVOLUTION EXTENDING ART BEYOND LIFE AND
LIFE BEYOND HISTORY INTO THE PRESENT, I.E.,
INTO THE MYTHIC. FOR THE ISSUE AT HAND IS,

BA(SICK)LY DESPERATION WITH THE ALL-PERVAD-
ING, STINKING MEDIOCRITY, CONDITIONED À LA
AMERICANA VALUES—SO THAT REVISING AN ART
FORM HERE AND A CIVIL RIGHTS PROTEST THERE,
EXPANDING CONSCIOUSNESS ON THE HOME FRONT
AND GETTING-THE-FUCK-OUT OF VIETNAM
INSIDE OF SOUNDS, VISIONS, TOTAL ART ARE PART
OF A *TOTAL PROGRAM*, DRASTICALLY SELF-AWARE,
PLEADING, EXTREME, BUT NEVERTHELESS HUMAN,
SENSUAL, AND AGAIN, NATURAL. NATCH—ORALLY.

THIRTEEN CONFUSIONS *
by Amos Vogel

*In this article, Amos Vogel claims to represent " . . . criticism
from within." There will be those from "within" who may
find Mr. Vogel's criticism actually comes from outside and to
the right. Though the author claims the " . . . highest and most
necessary loyalty to the movement," he cannot be accused of
harboring great sympathy for it, especially when he deals with
it under headings such as "Confusing Freedom with Formless-
ness" and "Confusing Good with Bad." Mr. Vogel challenges
the frequently lauded policy of open screenings for all filmmakers currently allowed at the Film-Maker's Cinematheque—
he feels that we " . . . coddle the experimenters with misplaced
tolerance." The author thinks the new film movement will
profit by the emergence of the new type of film critic with
primarily visual rather than literary orientation—these critics
come largely from the ranks of art history and criticism.*

*Amos Vogel is Director of New York Film Festival at Lin-
coln Center and Director of the Film Department at Lincoln
Center. He is well known as the founder of Cinema 16 and
has lectured on film history and aesthetics at Columbia University, Hunter College, New York University, and the Museum of Modern Art, as well as abroad.*

* This article has appeared in *Evergreen Review*.

After two decades of obscurity, poverty, ignorant rejection, and dogged persistence, the American film avant-garde suffers today, for the first time in its history, from an ominous new ailment: over-attention without understanding, over-acceptance without discrimination. Crime of crimes, it has become fashionable. Its gurus and artists are in danger of becoming the avant-garde establishment; its growing fame hides only imperfectly an inner weakness. The following observations, aimed at the removal of confusions, represent a criticism from within, fully cognizant of the movement's many achievements.

These lie not merely in the many talents and works it has discovered and championed, but in its continuing creative "desecration" of the medium, leaving nothing undisturbed, taking nothing for granted. In the hands of the movement's foremost practitioners, film is sacked, atomized, caressed, and possessed in a frenzy of passionate love; neither emulsion, exposure, lighting, film speeds, developing, nor rules of editing, camera movement, composition, or sound are safe from the onslaught of these poetic experimentalists who have irrevocably invaded the medium. While most commercial films can safely be followed with one's eyes closed, these works force spectators to open them wide, thereby rendering them defenseless against the magic powers of the medium.

The American avant-garde is part of a strong international trend toward a more visually-oriented, freer, more personal cinema. This movement expresses a revolt against the ossifications of institutions and the conservatism of the old. It represents a cinema of passion.

By restoring the primacy of the visual element, this movement brings us face to face with the essence of the medium, the profound and inexplicable mystery of the image.

Thematically, stylistically, and ideologically, the films belonging to this tendency reflect and prefigure an era of social change, disorientation, and decline, and are suffused with an existentialist humanism devoid of certainty or illusion. Liberated from nineteenth-century art, they increasingly displace realistic narrative structures, clearly defined plots, and well-delineated characters by visual ambiguity and poetic complexity, exploring ideas and forms vertically instead of illustrating events horizontally. There are strong influences of surrealism, neo-Dadaism, Pop Art, the "absurd" theatre and the Theatre of Cruelty, Robbe-Grillet and the new novel. Textbook rules of filmmaking have been abandoned. Editing is explosive, elliptic, unpredictable; camera movements fluid, frequent, and free; time and space are telescoped, destroyed, or obliterated and memory, reality, and illusion fused, until, in a flash of revelation, we realize that the totality of these uncertainties and discontinuities reflect nothing less than the modern world view in philosophy, science, art, and politics. These questioning, white-hot filmmakers—themselves anguished configurations of the anxieties and limited wisdoms they portray—are the committed artists of the sixties, the true explorers of our day.

But the American avant-garde seems to have arrived at a crossroads. On the one hand, the seeds planted by Frank Stauffacher's "Art in Cinema" series and Maya Deren's screenings in the forties, as well as Cinema 16's programs of 1947–1963, have been transformed into a full-blown, highly visible movement. There are unceasing, voluminous productions; new exhibition outlets; schools, art centers, and civic groups clamoring for the "underground"; discotheques and coffeehouses utilizing film-oriented mixed-media techniques; mass circulation magazines and television providing widespread publicity. This new stage remains the undeniable achievement of Jonas Mekas and the "New American Cinema" Group.

On the other hand, however, there now exists a certain wariness concerning the movement even among its friends and supporters. Too many of the films are unsatisfactory, even with the greatest of efforts at a sympathetic magnification of their small virtues. In film circles, it is no secret that, after all the growth and publicity, audiences at the Film-Makers Cinematheque in New York are leveling off. To this must be added the paradox of voluminous productivity and little new talent; the growing credibility gap between the movement's house organs and observed filmic quality; the absence, despite new and laudable attempts, of any real resolution to the crucial distribution and exhibition problem. As the faint odor of trouble becomes more noticeable, the evangelical ardor of the movement's leaders becomes more insistent, the manifestos and exorcisms less circumspect.

To begin the process of an informed critique of the American avant-garde (and more specifically, the ideology and style of the New American Cinema tendency within it) is an act of the highest and most necessary loyalty to the movement. The time has come to rescue it from the blind rejection of commercial reviewers and the blind acceptance of its own apostles; both posing as critics and neither subjecting it to dispassionate, informed analysis.

1. Confusing Times Square with Manhattan

The New American Cinema (NAC) and the American film avant-garde are *not* synonymous. The NAC group is the dominant, but not the only factor within the American independent film movement today. Because of its vociferousness and quantity of production, it impresses its values and style on the entire movement, and is frequently and erroneously equated with it. This leads to the convenient omission of Bruce Baillie and the Canyon Cinema Cooperative, other West coast filmmakers; George Manupelli and Richard Myers in the Midwest; and Hilary Harris, Carmen D'Avino, Francis Thompson, Len Lye, and others in New York.

2. Confusing a Producers' Cooperative with a School

The New American Cinema is neither ideologically, stylistically, nor otherwise a unified movement or tendency. In its manifestos, it elevates eclectic aestheticism and undifferentiated enthusiasm into a principle, instead of admitting that the group—ranging the spectrum from Anger to Breer to Warhol to Brakhage—is an economic and not an aesthetic unit.

3. Confusing Historical Continuity with Immaculate Conception

It is necessary to situate the NAC within history—the past, the present, the speculative future. As to the past, the American film avant-garde has its roots in the European surrealist and expressionist avant-garde of the twenties and the American experimentalists of the forties and fifties. The current NAC leaders, for obvious and indefensible reasons, prefer to draw a veil of silence and disregard over the past, thereby contributing to the provincialism of its adherents. It is only recently and because of internal criticism of the kind perpetrated here in public that a few of the works or writings of the "forerunners" have begun to appear on some Cinematheque programs or in *Film Culture*. Nevertheless, it is safe to say that the crucial importance of such filmmakers as Sidney Peterson, the Whitney Brothers, Ralph Steiner, Oscar Fischinger, Watson-Webber, Maya Deren, Curtis Harrington, and James Broughton remain unknown or unanalyzed trivia in the ideological development of the new generation. A resemblance to a certain type of history rewriting is not entirely out-of-place. It evinces the customary narrowness and demagoguery, but it fortunately unaccompanied by effective control over the information media. One shudders at what might happen if some of our present-day proponents of total liberty became Commissars of Film Culture.

As to the present, the NAC is undeniably and inevitably part of the worldwide movement toward a more visual cinema, all their protestations to the contrary. It is impossible to remain neutral when confronted with the astonishing provincialism of the NAC's ideologues in dismissing, disregarding, or exorcising Antonioni, Godard, Resnais, Skolimowski, Bellocchio, and Lester; and as their field of vision narrows, magnifying every object in it, until pygmies loom like giants.

The NAC will transcend its present dilemmas only by studying carefully the techniques and achievements of these experimenters; and by fully acknowledging that this international "pro-visual" movement is neither an exclusive club nor a dogmatic sect, but includes both Emshwiller and Antonioni, VanDerBeek and Godard. No film or filmmaker can be read out of this movement by papal decree.

Jonas Mekas's statement at the recent Museum of Modern Art "New Cinema" symposium ("Old cinema, even when it is successful. is horrible; New Cinema, even when it fails, is beautiful") is provocative and untenable. Bertolucci's *Before the Revolution*, Rivette's *Paris Belongs to Us*, Dreyer's *Gertrud*, Skolimowski's *Walkover*, Schorm's *Courage for Every Day*, Teshigahara's *Woman in the Dunes*, Rocha's *Black God and Blond Devil*, Jancso's *The Round-Up*, Paradjhanov's *Shadows of Forgotten Ancestors*, Antonioni from *L'Avventura* to *Blow-Up*, Resnais from *Hiroshima* to *La Guerre Est Finie*, Godard's *Breathless* to whatever his latest—*all of these were*

Bernardo Bertolucci: From *Before the Revolution,* 1964

created within what Mekas calls the "old" cinema—are avant-garde works. They are not merely more important than the failures, but often more important than even the *successes* of the independent avant-garde. Some day soon an interesting discussion will be begun as to the relative degree of experimentation, achievement, subversion, and political or artistic daring in these works on the one hand and the NAC films on the other. In any case, the creations of these so-called "commercial" directors can be disregarded only by hopeless dogmatists.

4. Confusing Freedom with Formlessness

Lack, failure, and disregard of form is the over-riding weakness of today's avant-garde. Current tendencies in all the arts toward improvisation, fluidity, and chance are mistaken for a total absence of form, and the temptation is to disregard the fact that it is precisely the achieved works of this kind that reveal an inner structure and logic.

This inner coherence is "felt" rather than explicable. It is totally lacking in so many current efforts, which could go on equally well for fifteen minutes or for fifty, and in which the succession or duration of shots remains totally irrelevant or mutable in terms of the total construct of the work. They lack surprise, mystery, and that inexorable form and flow that are the characteristics of all great art.

Film, both as a plastic and time art, involves considerations of tempo, length, progression, editing, camera positioning. These considerations, even in experimental works, are not and can never be suspended. They operate quite independently of the artist's announced intentions on the deepest psychological levels, and they determine the work's value as art. A strong sense of form, structure, and tempo are inevitably present in the best works of the American avant-garde movement, quite regardless of their specific and differing aesthetic commitments.

5. Confusing Content with Quality

Thematic liberation is no guarantee of quality. Nor is the use of five simultaneously-operating projectors, extreme nudity, unexceptionable anti-Vietnam sentiments, hand-held cameras, portrayals of transvestism. Said Cocteau ironically, when first confronted with Cinemascope: "The next time I write a poem, I shall use a larger piece of paper."

6. Confusing Non-Selectivity with Art

The NAC's proudly proclaimed policy of showing, distributing, and praising every scrap of film is self-defeating. Every new person who gets a camera and thereupon "completes" a "work," immediately obtains a public showing and distribution. In this manner several hundred titles are added to the yearly "oeuvre" of the American avant-garde. Under the circumstances, it is easier to discover epigones of Brakhage than new Brakhages.

It may be essential to show every single film to filmmakers at internal, workshop screenings so that they can see each other's work; it is suicidal if this is done with general audiences. Given the present volume and level of "production" —miles of new films—this gluts the market and inundates the viewer in a morass of mediocrity or worse. Sooner or later, the audience refuses to accept the frequent ratio of five minutes of promising footage to two hours of tedium. Unable to judge the works in advance or to rely on somebody else's judgment (since no selection takes place), they ultimately decide to stay away or to stop renting films, their frustrated interest supplanted by hostile irritation. How could they have known, amidst the welter of unknown new productions and a total absence of critical writing, that *Metanomen, Lost in Cuddahy, Oh Dem Watermelons,* and *Relativity* were most eminently worth seeing and four hundred other recent films were not?

There is therefore a need for a new showcase for the avant-garde, not under the control of one faction within the movement, however important, but presenting the best new avant-garde films, as carefully selected by a group of avant-garde— including NAC—critics and writers. Selectivity is a function of taste and of proper growth.

Any criticism of this method of selection as an impermissible "directing" of public taste is hypocritical. First, wherever there is exhibition, there is prior exercise of judgment. Second, this criticism applies, if anywhere, to the *present* system of control by one faction.

7. Confusing Good with Bad

It is time for the NAC to admit that there is such a thing as a bad avant-garde film; that in fact there are more bad avant-garde films than good ones; that at least half of the films presently exhibited or distributed are bad; that one must be able to point out why some are bad or why others are good; and that to do so, it is necessary to establish critical standards and to develop critical writing and taste.

It is time to admit that not all that is good is avant-garde; that not all that is avant-garde is good; and that even a good avant-garde filmmaker can make a bad film.

Ultimately, there is only good and bad art, within the framework of one's particular value system. Our real interest in avant-garde art resides not in its being avant-garde, but in its implicit promise of quality as against the exhaustion of the commercial cinema. There is nothing inherently superior or automatically supportable in the concept of avant-garde cinema as against the "old" cinema, unless it proves its superiority in practice.

8. Confusing Propagandists with Critics

It is quite correct to say that publicists and propagandists were eminently essential to the creation of this so often unjustly maligned and disregarded movement. No one will deny their success in contributing to the creation and visibility of the movement.

In the process, however, they have unperceptively blurred all distinction between propaganda and criticism, until their "reviews" and house organs have begun to resemble the literary vanity presses, with an appropriately hallucinatory inflection.

Today, when the avant-garde is entering a dangerous new stage, analysis must take precedence over publicity and the two must be clearly distinguished from each other.

Publicists are hyperbolical, particularly where the client's products are concerned. For this reason, the following formulations, continually posing as critical evaluations in published articles and essays, should properly be labeled publicity or advertising copy: "A work of beauty," "a beautiful

Maya Deren: From *Ritual in Transfigured Time*, 1946

work," "it is beautiful." Particular care must be taken with such phrases as "One of the . . . " (e.g., "This is one of the most beautiful works of the American avant-garde"). Finally, the continuous procession, week after week, of new masters, geniuses, and giants quickly becomes an object of suspicion or ridicule.

We need proponents, not fetishists, of avant-garde cinema. We must rigorously insist on the same standards of judgment for avant-garde films as we apply to any other works of art. This concern with standards must not be equated with authoritarian strictures regarding style or content. On the contrary, it is when we coddle the experimenters with misplaced tolerance, when we talk of "achievement" where there are only attempts, of "attempts" where there is nothing, of "retrospectives" after two years of production, that we profoundly weaken the movement.

9. Confusing Publicity with Achievement

Publicity is no proof of quality; large-scale attention by the mass media is no guarantee of achievement. It merely denotes that the avant-garde film has reached the level of a marketable commodity; it has become "copy." This is because the avant-garde's aggressively antiestablishment stance expresses itself frequently in well-advertised taboo subjects: eroticism, "deviations," drugs; charmingly offbeat acts and disturbances; publicizable new techniques (mixed media, "creative" tedium); and interesting visual gestures of a vaguely oppositional nature.

Since this limited radicalism is, by virtue of nonselective programming, drowned in endless reams of innocuous films, it is the more easily subsumed by the establishment, which, by publicizing it, robs the underground of its cult appeal while simultaneously deriding it ideologically. In this sense, the latitude granted to these isolated showcases for exhibiting whatever they wish implies that they serve as a safety valve for the draining off of radical impulses and that the avant-garde, at the very moment of its acceptance by the establishment, is faced with the possibility of imminent emasculation or absorption.

10. Confusing One Swallow with a Summer

The commercial success of a single film, *The Chelsea Girls*, must not blind us to the realization that the distribution and exhibition problems of the avant-garde remain unresolved. The reviews and word-of-mouth publicity regarding this film's presumed depravity and sexual daring automatically provide a ready-made audience for it. No pejorative comment is intended; the saleability of sex in a sexually repressed society is inevitable.

11. Confusing One Generation with Another

It is a significant comment on the stagnation of the American avant-garde that most of those who are by common consent considered today's best directors are members of the middle generation first seen at Cinema 16: Anger, Brakhage, Breer, Clarke, Conner, D'Avino, Emshwiller, Harris, Frank, Markopoulos, Menken, Maas, Rice, VanDerBeek. Of the younger generation, among the few to approach the above in promise or interest are Warhol, Bruce Baillie, Peter Goldman, and, possibly, Tony Conrad and Sheldon Rochlin.

Among the welter of new works and new directors there will undeniably be found new talents, and, in this sense, the present explosion of filmmaking is to be welcomed. But after more than six years of this activity, it is today equally legitimate to speculate as to the paucity of significant new talents and to wonder, when they do arise, about the influence of unquestioning acceptance and the dismissal of world cinema on the later development of such new talents.

To this query must be added the threatening- or already-accomplished exhaustion of some of the middle generation talents and their inability to progress beyond earlier achievement.

12. Confusing Literary with Visual Critics

The movement needs not merely critics as such; it needs visually-oriented critics. Most of the current reviewers and critics come out of a literary or journalistic tradition. Their

Sidney Peterson: From *The Cage*, 1947

commitments are to clear narratives, realism or naturalism, noble and identifiable sentiments, with the visual serving as illustration of an underlying literary thesis. This is criticism oriented toward sociology, literature, psychology, not toward the visual essence of cinema.

Art critics and historians, such as Amberg, Arnheim, Hauser, Langer, Panofsky, Read, Richter, Schapiro, and Tyler, have always concerned themselves with the aesthetics of film; and the recent incursion of new art critics and historians into film criticism (Battcock, Cohen, Geldzahler, Kepes, Kirby, Meyer, Michelson, O'Doherty, Sontag) is therefore to be welcomed and encouraged. Visually oriented, their special sensibilities and commitments, their opennesss to the techniques and philosophy of modern art, could significantly contribute to the elaboration of an aesthetic for the visual cinema. This new aesthetic must include an investigation of the differences between film and the other plastic arts (the element of time, the illusionary portrayal of motion and reality on a two-dimensional surface, the use of sound, the cinema as a palace of dreams). These "filmic" characteristics, at least in the case of Happenings, Environments, and mixed-media works, are now, in any case, becoming more closely related to the other arts.

The NAC could do worse than to concern itself with these questions and to study the writings of these new critics, as well as the works of Balázs, Nilsen, Cocteau, Eisenstein, and Pudovkin.

13. Confusing Popes with Free Men

Ultimately, the growing ability to "see" implies the ability to see oneself. Growth occurs through mistakes recognized as such, criticism realized as valid, the exposure of the self to new and alien influences, interaction with a hostile yet changing world. Blind adulation and hermeticism are the enemies of growth and lead to the repetition of what has already been achieved; the rise of epigones and mediocrities; the progressive narrowing of vision and the cumulative deterioration of taste. What the American avant-garde is confronted with is sectarianism parading as freedom, flattery as criticism, sterile eclecticism as artistic philosophy, anti-intellectual know-nothingness as liberation. Dogmas, myths, and popes are inevitable stages in human pre-history; a higher stage will be reached when they are superseded by men of free will.

A LETTER TO
GREGORY BATTCOCK*

by John Bernard Myers

"Time" as an element of film can be interpreted in a variety of ways. In this letter (dated 1967) John Bernard Myers is critical of the treatment accorded "time" by the new film artist.

Mr. Myers is a director of the Tibor De Nagy Gallery in New York City, and a former film critic, who claims to have given up film criticism some time ago. He writes for various journals on many different topics, including criticism of the recent New York World's Fair, which included apt observations on the vulgarity of that event.†

How kind of you to send me your essay on the Andy Warhol film, *Empire*. I read it with care and was particularly struck by a sentence in which you indicate that the purpose of *Empire* was "to present the essential character of the medium." Yet you go on to ask why it "was not simply a blank or exposed film run through the projector." Later in your essay you write that time is perhaps the most important single element to distinguish film from other visual art forms.

Now "time," as it happens, is precisely the reason why I have not cared for the work of the so-called underground filmmakers. They completely misapprehend the problem. I believe it was Cocteau who had the notion that the main difference between photography and cinematography was the presence of time in the latter. He proposed comparing the

* The essay on *Empire* referred to in this article is included at the end of this book under the title *Four Films by Andy Warhol.*

† "Junkdump Fair Surveyed," *Art and Literature,* No. 3, Autumn-Winter, 1964.

photograph of any still object with an identical movie of the same object. Cocteau said he was sure that in the movie he would feel the element of time running *through* the object. But knowing the metaphysical hijinks of which Cocteau was capable, I suspect that he was really stressing here the importance of time as an element to be manipulated in film art. I think that Cocteau's *Blood of a Poet* is the perfect example of his cinema aesthetic.

The basic aesthetic for contemporary painting, I believe, continues to derive from 1910–1912 Cubism. So too I am convinced that the film that matters today derives from Eisenstein's great insight during the period of the twenties. For him the art of the moving picture consisted in the juxtaposition of pieces of film placed in the order most appropriate to the director's feeling or idea. Eisenstein called this process of art *montage*. The underground filmmakers have put their noses up into the air, it seems to me, in regard to this basic aesthetic theory. The very essence of film, that which makes film unique even when the photography isn't very good, is the rhythm, or intuitive putting-together of the pieces of film. I have never yet seen a movie that I enjoyed that was ineptly or crudely cut. This enjoyment is not simply a question of speed or slickness. Rather I should compare good montage with good style—as in, for instance, a poem where the style evolves from the choice of words in relation to the poem's music or meter. "Pet him, pink her, play games with them" (Joyce), "Toasted Suzie is my ice-cream" (Stein), are quotes which easily identify the authors since the words and the music of the words constitute their style, a very good style indeed.

In a way one must praise Warhol for raising the question, "What do you mean by time in a movie?" He places a camera before the Empire State Building for several hours. The time in which it took to make the film is the time it also takes to unreel it. This supposedly is real time, not a depiction of time. To him it would seem, in other words, that time is exactly like the unreeling of a film; for me, a highly simplistic concept. If I were the camera, I would faint with boredom staring that long at one thing, the Empire State Building. Two hours would seem like two years. My legs would buckle, my eyes would bulge.

In an interview in *The New York Times* Warhol remarked

that he wished he could get enough money together to be able to cut and edit his movies. But this struck me as strange, since the cutting of a film is the least expensive aspect of filmmaking. Actually, I believe that Warhol prefers to sense his films as a totally realistic flow of time. Certain critics have seemed to endorse his vision by insisting that any film, cut or uncut, is the experience of the flow of actual time. For example, the critic Annette Michelson feels that Warhol's *Kiss* increases the erotic impact (in this case, voyeurism) by using as the time to unreel the film the actual time it takes to kiss. At this point I quite lose my bearings, since I have always believed that the experience of time—whether in a kiss or in the drilling of a tooth—is primarily psychological and that the passage of time in human affairs is unmeasurable except in subjective terms.

About "time," now, I have really said more than enough. A more correct understanding of film art, as already indicated, relates to the juxtaposition of images to create tension. In his book, *Film Form*, Eisenstein discourses at length on the possibilities inherent in montage—not only the juggling of time—but the changing of visual meaning through the combinations and contrasts of images. Eisenstein demonstrated this infinite visual and dramatic range in his own work. Both in his theories and his movies he has demonstrated the fundamental importance of meter and rhythm—in short, a good style.

The cinema of Carl Dreyer must certainly stem from this tradition. In *Gertrud* we have an authentic existentialist vision. Here the movement of the images depends on very slow cutting. Dreyer holds a scene for long periods, for instance the heroine singing an entire aria, the camera moving not at all while we are saturated in the vision of her beauty. Dreyer's point of view is exquisitely stated by the *lentissimo* rhythms of his editing.

In complete contrast to Dreyer are the choppy, syncopated rhythms of Resnais's *Muriel*—a film of great merit and in the direct tradition of Eisenstein's film aesthetic. The images sometimes remain on view for only a few seconds—a hand on a door, a glimpse of a room, a vista of a street. The frames pile up, always suggestive in their meaning, but only decodable in relationship to each other. Resnais's strange concept of life—the confusion in his characters about what once

Alain Resnais: From *Muriel*, 1963

Peter Moore

Yvonne Rainer: From *The Mind Is a Muscle,* a ballet, 1966

happened to them in the past, and even about what is happening to them in the present moment—is alternately comic and pathetic. And so the cutting alternates between lingering shots and instantaneous impressions—an appropriate meter to the time flux of the characters, the images, the story.

Film is not painting, nor is it theatre, nor is it a form of "happening." Perhaps, in another art, Yvonne Rainer has come closest to what film is, in her ballet, *The Mind Is a Muscle*, where she has "cut" movement into patterns and shapes as though she were editing a movie. This basic apprehension of film form is antipathetic to critics like Pauline Kael and Dwight Macdonald, which is why they write largely as though film were a side-product of sociology. But then many moviemakers and movie directors have just as little understanding as Miss Kael or Mr. Macdonald and use only the tried-and-true clichés of film montage to produce their entertainments. No one much cares. But I tend to be less permissive with the avant-garde, who are called that, after all, because energy should be their chief capital; energy, resourcefulness, and invention.

So you see, my dear Gregory, it is not simply contrariness on my part to reject many of the so-called avant-garde movies which are now in fashion. I really see the film and feel it quite differently. I cannot be convinced that anyone has yet discovered an aesthetic which goes beyond Eisenstein. And so also you must see why I say "no" to your invitation to contribute to your anthology.

As always, cordially,

JOHN BERNARD MYERS

PART III

FILMS AND FILMMAKERS

MARCEL DUCHAMP'S
ANEMIC CINEMA

by Toby Mussman

The several branches of art today acknowledge the influence of Marcel Duchamp. In this article Toby Mussman discusses Duchamps films and points out their relevance to new works by experimental artists in New York today.

In her essay "One Culture and the New Sensibility," Susan Sontag remarks: "The primary feature of the new sensibility is that its model product is not the literary work, above all, the novel. A new, non-literary culture exists today, of whose very existence, not to mention significance, most literary intellectuals are entirely unaware." * Cage, McLuhan, and Whitman are commonly considered the prophets of this new culture, and the notes that follow the article on Duchamp consider Whitman's role.

Toby Mussman was born in 1940, graduated from Yale University, and has done graduate work in art history at New York University. He has written for Artforum, Film Culture, *and* Art and Artists. *The article that follows is a revised version of one that originally appeared in* Art and Artists, *July, 1966.*

Near the end of an hour-long interview with Marcel Duchamp in December, 1965, I asked what validity there was to a statement I have read in a university arts journal claiming that the title *Anemic Cinema*, which Duchamp gave to his only extant filmmaking effort, should be taken as a proclamation of the film's generally anti-cinema attitude. In his tone which is both familiar and polite yet always comfortably aloof, he replied that not in any way had he intended anything which could be construed as a Dada anti-cinema joke. Then almost

* *Against Interpretation*, New York: Farrar, Straus & Giroux, 1966, p. 298.

in the same instant as though recoiling from too comfortable a
position, he said, "But you know, I really should have had
a placard with the word 'anti' forever imprinted right across
my forehead." Shortly afterward I related this event to an
acquaintance whose response was, "Anti-what? What exactly
was his 'anti' directed against?" My reply of the moment was,
"Everything"; but upon reflection, I see that the answer
would have been more accurate had it been, "Anything."
Anything, that is, which presented itself to Duchamp in the
form of tradition or dogmatic formula.

Gleizes and the Cubist theorists refused Duchamp's *Nude
Descending a Staircase* entry into the Salon des Indépendants
of 1912, and within three years Duchamp came to America to
live and work for most of the rest of his life. He was refused
by dogma because he had refused to paint a picture according
to dogma's rules. He left what was already old in its own
time and reached for the new which had yet to come of age.

Duchamp's "anti" cannot be looked at simply as a reaction,
but must be understood more in terms of a recoil, which
sought an entirely independent fruition in previously un-
trammeled areas of visual and mental investigation. I mention
areas of mental investigation not only because, of course, they
are fully documented in the *Green Box* but also to refer to
Duchamp's early and far-reaching investigations into the idea
of art. He provided a dramatic point of departure and inspiration for the later business of questioning what art's limits are
and the recognition of the significance of decision-making
amidst indeterminacy to be extended by Cage, Rauschenberg,
Johns, Warhol, and Kaprow. Andy Warhol's twenty-minute
movie of Duchamp, where he sits closed-mouthed for the
duration while a "cuddly little actress" rubs herself up
against him, is the perfect homage paid by the younger
artist for the aesthetic affinities he feels toward the man who
knocked on the door first.[1]

One of the results of Duchamp's recoil-like attitude was to
be in the direction of an infant, and up to his time only timidly
explored, medium—the cinema. Even though Robert Lebel[2]
feels that the movies must have had some influence, if only

[1] "Passport No. G255300"—An interview with Marcel Duchamp
conducted by Otto Hahn—*Art and Artists Magazine*, July 1966.
[2] *Marcel Duchamp*, Robert Lebel, New York, 1959.

indirect, on the sequential configuration of *Nude Descending a Staircase* and Duchamp himself used the term "cinematic blossoming" as early as 1912 to describe the apogee–combination of the stripping of the Bachelors and the imaginative stripping by the desirous Bride, his ambitions to make a film do not seem to have been a direct descent from the ideas around the *Nude Descending a Staircase–The Bride Stripped Bare by Her Bachelors, Even* works.[3]

Duchamp has explained in the interview I conducted with him that *Anemic Cinema* came out of investigations which he said had begun to take on obsessive proportions, something of an *idée fixe*. For some time he had been interested in creating abstract, whirlpool-like illusions of three-dimensionality using a kinetic device. As early as 1920, while in New York, he attempted with the assistance of Man Ray to make an abstract 3-D movie by employing two cameras. Man Ray has described what they were trying to produce as "a double, stereoscopic film of a globe with a spiral painted on it." [4] Unfortunately, owing to a mishap in developing, most of the work was lost except for two short strips, which when viewed through an old stereopticon would produce the desired effect of relief out into the viewer's space.

It was also in 1920 that Duchamp, in a parallel pursuit of the same goal, built his first machine, *Revolving Glass* (which, as is well known by now, nearly maimed Man Ray when it flew apart in a trial run). Constructed of five graduated lengths of black and white striped glass attached to a re-

[3] The development from the *Nude* through the *Bride* to the *The Bride Stripped* paintings is a long and complex one. It is bound up in movement, change, sexuality, and finally a very unique sort of transcendence. Grossly stated, the Nude or Virgin becomes the Bride (Woman) who is the embodiment of human desire and who is activated or "sparked" by the Bachelors (Man). The Bride, as the principal subject of these paintings, takes as her model the design of machine gears, but the way in which she operates is quite different from anything that could be called a mechanism. Just as human reason always calls for something beyond what it already understands, so too does the Bride reach out for a new realization beyond her own capabilities. Her action is directly analogous to the sexual act. The sexual act becomes a metaphor for the human metaphysical vision.

[4] Man Ray, *Self-Portrait*, Little, Brown and Company, New York, 1966, p. 99.

volving metal rod, it could successfully create the appearance
of concentric circles forming a low relief. From a photograph
of the way *Revolving Glass* appeared in motion, we can compare it to Duchamp's later, more sophisticated use of concentric circles placed in a pattern off the central axis to form
a spiral in the *Rotative Demi-Sphere* (1925) or the undulating,
coil-like effects of *Anemic Cinema.*

Before arriving at the final technique employed in *Anemic
Cinema,* Duchamp also experimented briefly with the ana-
glyphic process in 1920–21. (Within recent years we have
seen this technique exploited to achieve a limited popular
success in 3-D movies and comic books.) Duchamp filmed a
specially prepared revolving sphere, so that when the resulting footage was projected and looked at through glasses with
one red and one green lens, an adequate effect of a spiral
receding into depth was obtained. This short film, which according to Ado Kyrou's recollection in his book *Le Surréalisme
au Cinéma* was titled *Moustiques Domestiques Demi-Stock,*
fell out of Duchamp's possession and was apparently lost
sometime during the thirties.

In 1921 Duchamp began working on the optical discs,
which would eventually accumulate through several modifications to twelve in number by 1935, when they were published
in an edition of 500 sets under the collective title of *Rotoreliefs.*
The discs were originally designed to be recorded on film, but
later when they became the *Rotoreliefs,* they could be placed
on any turntable device with 33 revolutions per minute and
observed as long as desired. In *Anemic Cinema,* with its total
running time of seven minutes, each of the ten separate discs
is made available to the viewer for only about thirty seconds.
When looked at statically, a disc is made up of a flat pattern
of black and white concentric circles placed in various off-
center arrangements. When in motion, one is no longer aware
of the disc as such, but rather an independent and ambiguously
defined spiral or series of cones weaving into spatial depth
one minute and then projecting forward out from the surface
in the next.

Duchamp found the exploitation of this kind of optical illusion intriguing, because given a limited viewing time, the be-
holder's eye does not have sufficient opportunity to categorize
the optical play. Nor does the viewer have time to adjust himself physically to the ambivalence his eye is experiencing.

Duchamp liked the idea that any two different people watching a disc at the same time would not be subject to the same simultaneous perceptual experience. One's perception of the film would oscillate according to one's optical faculties, which we can assume are as widely variable as any of the other physical characteristics. The discs are similar in principle to the fluctuating play in Josef Albers's drawings of the fifties or the spatial contradictions in Analytic Cubist works (i.e., Braque's *La Portuguaise*). Duchamp, by putting his discs in motion and strictly limiting their exposure time added a new kind of complexity and indeterminacy, which, he hoped, would leave his viewer unsettled and comfortably on edge. He stated emphatically that thirty seconds is the optimum amount of time to look at the discs, and I take this as an implication that to study them for any appreciably longer period would lessen his intended effect of imprecise perception, resulting in an off-balanced sense of mystification in the viewer.

To act as rests and counterbalances, Duchamp inserted one of nine alliterative puns, also on rotating discs, between each pairing of the optical discs. The words and sense of the puns are revealed as they revolve at what seems a normal reading speed. The puns provide a curious complement to the experience of following the spirals of the optical discs around and into depth at the center only to have the eye thrown back out to a peripheral circle or to realize that the center is also the foremost tip of a cone projecting outward. In both the optical and the verbal discs, the eye is lead into the center only to be laughed at for being there. The puns, unlike ordinary sentences, do not attempt to make a definite statement, but rather they cast ironic doubt on the ability of any written sentence to make ultimate and absolutely conclusive sense. Aphorism is rendered invalid, or at the very least always open to question.

The puns, because of their alliterative nature, are untranslatable. Here is a sampling in French:

"*On demande des moustiques domestiques (demi-stock) pour la cure d'azote sur la côte d'azure.*"

"*Avez-vous déjà mis la moelle de l'épée dans la poêle de l'aimée?*"

"*Esquivons les ecchymoses des esquimaux aux mots exquis.*"

At a superficial glance they resemble any other typical sentence, but then as we read them for meaning, their sense begins to double back on themselves, forcing us to take a second look. It is in the second look that the abstract play on similarity of sound and letter becomes a counterpart to the spirals and cones of the optical discs. That is, they are founded on a circular sort of reasoning, ultimately leading nowhere. The title itself, *Anemic Cinema,* suggests initially the stylized play of inversions that we find through the main part of the film. It is an anagram of the word "cinema," "anemic" being not quite the reverse spelling of cinema and the two words together forming something of an inside-out rendition.

Duchamp's experiments with kinetic optical illusions are, in several ways, related to his better-known work. During his long career, he has frequently demonstrated a propensity to make analyses of actions through sequential time. Duchamp's preoccupation with a literal movement in *Nude Descending a Staircase* may have been what made his work seem so ungracious to Gleizes. In *Sad Young Man on a Train* (1911), an important step toward his more accomplished statements, Duchamp attempted to portray various sensations experienced by a man passing through an isolated and somber mood. A man on a train is within an environment that is actually moving; a mood is neither static nor precisely definable, mood is always flux. Duchamp's Nude comes down the stairs, his Virgin is transcendentally transformed into a Bride, and his paintings are states of action, not merely extracted moments. The development of his painting passed through higher and higher degrees of activity until we reach *The Bride Stripped Bare by Her Bachelors, Even* (also known as *The Large Glass*), which projects a very special state of self-transcendence. The fusion of the Bride being stripped bare by her Bachelors and her concomitant "imaginative desiring" is an event impossible to realize in normal cause-and-effect time relationships. This totally mysterious, unstable state of *The Bride Stripped Bare by Her Bachelors, Even* can be likened to the physically perceived state of ambivalence produced for the viewer of *Anemic Cinema.* If *The Bride Stripped* painting represented a culmination of his depictions in a static medium of states of action, it is not in the least bit surprising that Duchamp's next field of investigation should focus on the manipulation of objects actually in motion.

The metaphorical mechanizations of desire, female sexuality, and the sexual act realized in *Nude Descending a Staircase* through *The Bride Stripped Bare by Her Bachelors, Even* find an equivalent via allusion in *Anemic Cinema's* spirals and cones. The fact that the cones are placed just off center establishes immediately an undulating sensation, while at the same time contributing to a more general, if elusive, seductive tone. In two of the discs, the concentric circles are more regular and only slightly off the central axis which allows easily for the suggestion of a female breast. The focal points here act as and exaggerate the nipple. In other discs, the indication is one of focusing through the convolutions of the spirals, and thus suggesting penetration into vagina–womb. To take the metaphor of penetration a bit further, I turn to Norman O. Brown who says: "The woman penetrated is a labyrinth. You emerge into another world inside the woman. To explore is to penetrate the world in the insides of the mother. The penis is the bridge; the passage to another world is coitus; the other world is the womb–cave.' [5] The discs of *Anemic Cinema* delight the eye by pulling it into depth, by demanding that it penetrate. But once the eye does do as asked, it is inevitably frustrated, confused by the never-ending swirl, and finally thrown back out to try again. The ambivalent perception Duchamp has forced on the eye is the penis-bridge. The way that the eye reads the optical illusion as both going in and coming out—that is, the eye goes back, and forth, reading it first as penetration and then as a protrusion—makes an abstracted allusion to the sexual act. The element of spatial ambiguity in *Anemic Cinema* is taken into an entirely ecstatic realm when we consider that Duchamp constructed specially for the first showing of the film a projection screen of translucent glass, like that used in bathroom windows, with a reflective mirror-silver backing.

After *Anemic Cinema* was shown in 1924–25 and assembled in 1926 in France, Duchamp made no further ventures in film until Maya Deren came to him in 1943 for advice on an idea to capture in a movie the magic of Surrealist objects. She shot several scenes which included the Surrealist painter Matta and Duchamp sipping drinks at a Fifth Avenue café, but the work, called *Witch's Candle,* was never completed. Her in-

[5] Norman O. Brown, *Love's Body*, Random House, New York, 1966, pp. 36 and 48.

tention was to adapt the Surrealist aesthetic to make a film
promoting open defiance of normal time and space relationships—a goal she achieved with distinction under a dream
format in *Meshes of the Afternoon*.

The spatial ambiguities of *Anemic Cinema's* optical discs
and the verbal ambiguities of the pun discs have a tendency to
create a limbo-like atmosphere, comparable to that of dream.
Hans Richter was particularly aware of this when he used the
Rotoreliefs in one of the six sequences of his surrealistic film,
Dreams That Money Can Buy, in 1944–46. Using color filters,
Richter allowed his camera to glide softly by the turning
discs, enveloped them in kaleidoscopic effects with prism
lenses, and arranged the discs in various fragmented views,
thus nullifying the purely optical effects Duchamp had intended in *Anemic Cinema*. It is entirely to their credit that
even when adapted in a fashion considerably removed from
the original intention, the optical discs lend themselves without duress to another, equally significant beauty. One could
imagine the *Rotoreliefs* being adapted still further under new
conditions to exploit their extraordinary properties of ambiguity
and intangibility.

In film, at least, Duchamp has spawned no immediate followers. The *Rotoreliefs* were too pure and special a sort of
experiment, and the puns, always a Duchamp trademark, were
too personal. What is most significant about his work today
is the way in which his ideas, partially in reaction to the
nearsighted theories and practices of a formalist art, have
been taken up and extended by a large number of contemporary painters and sculptors (most prominently Robert
Rauschenberg, Jasper Johns, Robert Morris, Richard Hamilton,
and Andy Warhol).

Duchamp's early turn to film in order to confront questions
arising out of his experience of painting comments on the
general breakdown of aesthetic categories encountered by
artists in the twentieth century. Underground filmmakers,
many of them originally painters, currently working in New
York and elsewhere, take considerable encouragement and
inspiration from the pioneering efforts of artist–filmmakers
like Richter, Léger, Man Ray, and Duchamp. Recognizing
the potential expressive values of two of the cinema's principal
faculties—motion and the orchestration of temporal relationships, younger artists—such as Bruce Conner, Robert Whit-

man, Andy Warhol, Robert Breer, or Stan VanDerBeek—have become increasingly less concerned with the literally static confines of the canvas. Just as for hundreds of years painters have taken up sculptural investigations to complement those encountered two-dimensionally, these contemporary artists have seen, like Duchamp, that a logical way to handle questions implied in their more traditional work on a flat canvas is to move into the relatively undeveloped dimensions of time and motion.

THE IMAGES OF
ROBERT WHITMAN

by Toby Mussman

In many ways the new movie/theatre performances in New York are the purest realizations of McLuhan's theory that art adapts a new medium as soon as it has fallen out of front-line usage as a conduit of information. After a technological advance has been thoroughly absorbed by its immediate function, it becomes an artistic tool as, for example, fluorescent light tubes have done for Dan Flavin.

People like Andy Warhol, Robert Whitman, Stan VanDerBeek, Ken Dewey, the USCO Group, and others have created a sensation in the last year with their movie environments and performances using multiple projectors and lighting systems. Their efforts represent a digging into and ultimately an expansion of the mechanics of the film medium and its accompanying atmosphere. Like some mad alchemist in the projection booth conjuring up visions with his magic shaft of light exploring an old, womblike hall, they are finding new dimensions of that fantasy world we have all known as "the Movies."

In December 1965, Claes Oldenburg constructed a literal replica of the experience of watching movies in a happening performance called *Moviehouse,* at the Film-Makers' Cinematheque. Oldenburg simulated, in his ironic and sublimely surreal manner, an audience sitting through a late afternoon film. A comparison with the numerous film-watching scenes in the movies of Jean-Luc Godard ought to be noted here. Godard's characters are always going to the movies. By this he says that man cannot and will not escape his mirror, echoing the ideas of Artaud and Cocteau. In an existential world man draws sustenance from his mirror. It is his psychic nourishment because self-awareness is his only redemption. Man can only be responsible if he is self-aware, and he can only be self-aware if he is willing to look at a reflection of himself and question it.

The concept of an ambivalent play as embodied in the mirror-image metaphor is helpful when looking at the "theatre pieces" of Robert Whitman. On the same nights as the Oldenburg event at Film-Makers' Cinematheque, Whitman introduced a new work called *Prune Flat,* which was also performed regularly on weekends from May to August 1966. That Whitman set up a work to run for three months is a distinguishing characteristic of his conception of a Happening; terming his works "theatre pieces," he certainly does not think of them as exercises in impermanence.

In 1960, Whitman was much impressed by *The Burning Building,* by Red Grooms. Of it Whitman says, "That performance of Red's was so flamboyant and beautiful. It had a great influence on everyone at the time. It convinced many people, who perhaps were undecided about Happenings as a medium, of the expressive power available to them." [1]

Whitman did his first work, *Small Cannon,* later in the same year, already using movie projection combined with painted and constructed objects to make what he terms an "expressionistic" production. From the beginning his intention has been to create a theatre experience which is at total variance with more traditional verbal theatre. In this light his aesthetic comes proximate to Artaud's vision of a theatre "that is addressed first of all to our senses" and abides by "the visual language of objects, movements, attitudes, and gestures." [2]

To realize this vision Whitman posed the following question,

[1] Mr. Whitman's comments are taken from an interview conducted with him by the author on June 21, 1966. Unless otherwise indicated, all terms and descriptions appearing in quotes were taken from that interview.

[2] *The Theater and Its Double* by Antonin Artaud, Grove Press, Inc,. New York, 1958, pp. 38 and 44.

"How do you paint cold air?" It is an old question, but Happenings provided a new solution. What Whitman saw was that he could work directly with the sense impressions of a physical thing like cold air or a movie projection beam. They could, in fact, become the suggestive elements, the raw materials, of the images he constructed.

In April 1961 Whitman did *Mouth,* and in 1963 *Flower* and *Mouth,* among others, all of which exhibited his tendency to build an interior, womblike space as an action center for both audience and performers. *Water,* which Whitman marks as an important breakthrough to his mature work, housed its audience in vinyl cubicles sheltering them from artificial rain while a number of identity-altering acts went on before them. A film was projected onto a sheet in the middle of the performing area so that part of the audience saw it from the front while others witnessed it from the back; a girl wearing a simple print dress wandered into the projection beam and found, to her bewilderment, that a film image of her in a solid color dress was being projected both onto the screen and onto her person.[3]

For *The Night Time Sky,* in last year's New York Theatre Rally, Whitman began with an idea of a theatre work "with itself as its own subject" using what he believes must have been "the first theatrical things, when the sun goes down, night falls, the stars come out, and people imagine what the constellations are." [4] Audience members, entering through a tunnel endowed with mixed noises of a crowd, band music, and a steamship whistle, were greeted with a movie and their own shadow-image cast onto the screen as they made their way into a large, domelike space. Once there, the spectators observed through skylight holes in the ceiling the images and events taking place above them. The last scene, one of the tours de force in Happenings, was of a film projected onto the ceiling in huge close-up showing through a glass-bottom toilet someone defecating and urinating into it and the several flushings of it. Of this piece Whitman says, "I thought of people thinking things, digesting them, defecating them, a work fertilizing something. The audience, fertilized by the

[3] *Happenings* by Michael Kirby, E. P. Dutton & Co., Inc., New York, 1965, pp. 172–183.

[4] The "Happenings" issue of the *Tulane Drama Review,* Winter 1965, carried Whitman's description of the performance.

experience, leaving, taking the experience of the work out into the street with them." [5]

What we begin to see in looking at several of Whitman's works is that he is intrigued by turning the mechanics of a subject or a medium inside out in order to arrive at an extensive and intricate play of imagery among various levels of illusion. *Prune Flat* opens with a sustained close-up of a movie projector mechanism in operation, a sequence which as Whitman says "acts as a clue" to what follows. Next we see full-screen images of individual fruits and vegetables being sliced open and out of which pour such disconcerting items as small steel balls, feathers, or simply the insides of a persimmon. What is revealed to us is a labyrinthine world of surprise and mystery.

In the main, *Prune Flat* consists of a play of images (foliage, landscapes, and cityscapes) projected on a screen and onto girls who move about the stage dressed in plain white frocks and caps. In this way, the girls become a living, moving screen and are given the option of being absorbed into whatever is being projected, or moving about in order to contradict or oppose it. One of the girls finds an isolated image of herself being projected onto a shadowed portion of the screen in the midst of the foliage, etc. The physical ambivalence confronting the audience is astonishing. Are we seeing, at any given moment, the actual girl standing there or her film image? Here we have cinema as a hall of mirrors, pointing to life's multiple layers of illusion, which Whitman peels back one by one before our eyes.

Whitman, who made a film in 1962 that concentrated solely on a person rolling about in bed for twenty minutes, believes that motion pictures magnify and give a new reality to the object seen. Long duration shots provide the viewer with a special kind of "comprehending detachment," so that the object can take on a "mystical significance, a chance for it to begin to breath." In its reverence for the object, his view resembles that of Fernand Léger; and there is little doubt that the latter would welcome the advances Whitman has made to his thesis that "motion pictures should concentrate on bringing out the values of the object" and that various attention-focusing devices, including "enormous enlargement," can give

[5] *Op. cit.*, 1.

the object "a personality it never had before." [6]

About the use of film in general, Whitman feels that, "even though it has its own artificial limits, that is, it is not a natural phenomenon like cold air, it can be used to bring out a ghostlike record of an actual event. Films represent the ghosts of actuality, something like the memory of things past. In addition, movie projection can become an image in itself, and therein have a tremendous impact."

This brings us to a consideration of just how Whitman works out a satisfactory flow between separate images. He is concerned with being able to present a "sense of order which develops out of the practical nature of the situation (image)." This means being acutely responsive to whatever associations the particular image elicits in its own right, or as Whitman says, "the image itself" will tell him how it can best be treated. His responsiveness and willingness to work directly with the concrete nature of an individual image or object significantly lie parallel to the attitude Robert Rauschenberg has expressed so eloquently in painting.

Above all, Whitman is aware that his performances use time and that interrelationships depend in large measure on the demands of an individual image's duration and where accordingly it best fits into the articulation of the whole piece. His conscious intention is to work with time as though it were a plastic element. As he has said, "Time for me is something material . . . it can be used in the same way as paint, or plaster, or any other material . . . it can describe other natural events. . . . If I am making an object, and I want to find the story of that object, one way to do it is to see what people do when they are involved with it. . . . The images make real the experiences of the time."[7]

[6] From an article by Léger entitled "A New Realism—The Object," which first appeared in *The Little Review*, Winter 1926.

[7] This comment was distributed to the audience as an introduction before the performance of Whitman's latest piece, *Midsummer*, which was first given in a field near Easthampton, Long Island, in August 1966.

HARRY SMITH INTERVIEW *

by P. Adams Sitney

*Harry Smith has only recently become widely known in ex-
perimental cinema circles, although he has been making films
for some twenty years. He is particularly admired for his
inventive experiments with ways of working directly on film
without the use of a camera. In 1965 he was awarded the
Seventh Independent Film Award by* Film Culture *with
these words: "His abstract works, both in color and black
and white are among the most complex and rich, among the
most beautiful, yet to come out of cinema. The modulations
of color and form are so certain and subtle, delicate and
bold, that these films rank among the very few where attempt is absolutely realized in attainment."*

P. Adams Sitney is an editor of Filmwise *and has written
articles on film for many publications, including* Film Culture
and The Yale Literary *Magazine.*

The dating of my films is difficult because I had made
the first one, or part of that, in 1939. It was about twenty-
five years ago, although it says forty years in the *Catalogue*,
because at different times I have posed as different ages.

PAS: *When were you born?*

I never give that information out. I would like to say
that I'm the Czar of Russia. My mother always claimed to
be Anastasia. That's how I got Mr. R. interested in these
things. This interview has to be severely cut down. Like
no names, Mr. R., you know, or something.

I had drawn on film for quite a while, but exactly which
one is number one I don't know. It was made something
between 1939 and, I would say, 1942 at the latest. Later I

* This material is excerpted from a longer version which appeared in *Film Culture*, No. 37, Summer, 1965.

was very disappointed to find out that Len Lye had done it. Naturally I was horrified when either Dick Foster or Frank Stauffacher showed up with a book one day and told me that not only had Len made hand painted films, but he had done 16mm ones. Then later somebody in San Francisco whose name I forget (he was the Harley-Davidson agent) got like stimulated by me and made 8mm hand painted films.

#1 was made by taking impressions of various things, like cutting up erasers or the lid of a Higgins ink bottle. That's where I derived all the circular shapes. There's a kind of cork on the top of it. I dipped it in the ink and squashed it down on the film; then later I went over the thing with a crow-quill pen. However the colors aren't too good in that film. I can't remember how long it took to make it, because I'd made a number of others. I had a considerable number of films that have not been printed at all. Undoubtedly less than half of my stuff is in my possession now.

PAS: *Were the early films made on 16mm?*

No, on 35 mm. After I made #1 I met the Whitney brothers through Frank Stauffacher and Dick Foster. Foster was the one who had really started the Art in Cinema Society because he had been in New York and had met filmmakers there. But later he and Stauffacher fell out; so I took over Foster's position. They sent me down to Los Angeles to look for films. That's when I met Kenneth Anger, who sort of remembered me when he was up here last month. It must have been 1944, maybe, when I made that trip.

PAS: *He made* Fireworks *in 1947.*

1947? He definitely remembered me when I brought up the situation during which our meeting occurred. How old was he at that time?

PAS: *About seventeen.*

Everybody was very embarrassed at his films at that point. It was a horrible thing! He was embarrassed, I was embarrassed. I went to his house and he was afraid his mother was going to find out that I was there; she was upstairs. He looks today almost identical to the way he looked then; that's the amazing thing! It was a small bungalow type place . . . I didn't realize the artistic quality of *Fireworks* until seeing it this year; then it seemed like some kind of homosexual exercise. When Kenneth sat down in something like a golden chair from Versailles of his mother's, the chair's leg fell off. He was very embarrassed. "My mother might hear me." Then in order to get the leg back on the chair he raised the venetian blind and the cord broke and the thing fell all over the floor. However I did manage to get the film for the Art in Cinema Society, which I think was its first large showing. The auditorium of the San Francisco Museum of Art seated at least, I suppose, three hundred people. He came up to the showing and embarrassed everyone. After the clapping at the end of the film I thought he was putting his hands up like a prize fighter. But when he was here a month or so ago he explained that that was a sign having something to do with the Aleister Crowley cult—I forget what—perhaps Shu holding up the sky.

Originally, I was mainly a painter. The films are minor accessories to my paintings; it just happened that I had the films with me when everything else was destroyed. My paintings were infinitely better than my films because much more time was spent on them. I can show you slides of them. I don't have any slides that were made since about 1950. That's a painting that was made of the score for one of the films that were shown. That's like the scenario for the last movement of one of those color films.

My first film was made by imprinting of the cork off an ink bottle and all that sort of thing, as I said before. The second one was made with come-clean gum dots, automatic adhesive dots that Dick Foster got for me. It's like a paper dot with gum on the back. The film was painted over with a brush to make it wet, then with a mouth-type spray gun dye was sprayed onto the film. When that dried the whole film was greased with Vaseline. Of course this was in short sections—maybe six-foot-long sections. Anyway they would be tacked down. With a tweezers the dots were pulled off. That's where those colored balls drop and that sort of stuff. Being as it was pulled off, it was naturally dry where the dot had been and that part which had been colored was protected by the Vaseline coating at this point. Then color was sprayed into where the dot had been. After that dried, the whole film was cleaned with carbon tetrachloride.

The next one was made by putting masking tape onto the film and slitting the tape lightly with a razor blade and a ruler, and then picking off all those little squares that are revolving around. I worked off and on on that film for about five years pretty consistently; I worked on it every day at least. I may have abandoned it at one point for three months at the most.

#1 took a very short time. Either a day or a week. Then *#2*—which was much longer than the form it is in now: it was actually at least a half an hour long—it was cut down to match a recording by Dizzy Gillespie, which I believe is called "Guacha Guero." It took maybe a year to make. Then the next one I worked on about five years, then I gave up that particular style. There were maybe eight years of it. I developed certain really complicated hand painting techniques of which I made only short versions. For example, painting the whole film a certain color and then smearing Vaseline on it; and then taking a stylus and scraping designs off. It is possible to get a lot of spirals and curvilinear designs which I was never able to get by cutting off the masking tape; then spraying bleach into the place that had been scraped off, I think Clorox, which would then remove the background material where it had been scraped off; washing the Clorox out; and then spraying another color into the place where the groove was. I made short samples of that sort of material. As I say, less than half of all that stuff is in my possession at this point. I also made alternate versions of a great number of scenes. Sometimes in order to demonstrate how it was done I made up special reels that partially had the masking tape still left on, and partially the first . . . Anyway there are thousands of feet that were never printed, and several entire very long films. Many of those films are missing totally. I never edited at all, except to cut them down—except that second one which shows the balls falling. Like I say, it was at least 1200 feet long originally. It was then cut down to a hundred feet to make it match "Guacha Guero." What Jonas Mekas calls "The Magic Feature" (*#12*) was originally about six hours long, and then

it was edited down, first to a two-hour version, and then
down to a one-hour version. There was also an enormous
amount of material made for that picture. None of the
really good material that was constructed for that film was
ever photographed. There was a Noah's Ark scene with
really fantastic animals. I started out with the poorer stuff.
The really good things were supposed to be toward the
end of the film, but being as the end of the film was never
made. . . .

On that Oz film, that expensive one, of course I had quite
a few people working; so that all kinds of special cut-outs
were made that were never photographed. I mean really
wonderful ones were made! One cut-out might take someone two months to make. They were very elaborate stencils
and so forth. All of my later films were never quite completed. Most of the material was never shot because the
film dragged on too long.

Those two optically printed films were made for the
Guggenheim Foundation. The three-dimensional one was
made from the same batch of stencils as the color one. First
I got a camera from Frank Stauffacher, which is when those
two films were made: the first is called *Circular Tensions*
(#5), I forget what the other one is called. The black-and-
white one (#4) precedes that.

PAS: *The black-and-white film (#4) begins with a shot of—*

—a painting. It is a painting of a tune by Dizzy Gillespie
called "Manteca." Each stroke in that painting represents
a certain note on the recording. If I had the record, I could
project the painting as a slide and point to a certain thing.
This is the main theme in there, which is a-doot-doot-
dootdoot-doot-doottadootdoot; those curved lines up there. See,
ta-doot-doot-doot-doot-dootaloot-dootaloot, and so forth. Each
note is on there. The most complex one of these is this one,
one of Charlie Parker's records, I don't remember the name
of it. That's a really complex painting. That took five years.
Just like I gave up making films after that last hand-drawn
one took a number of years, I gave up painting after that
took a number of years to make; it was just too exhausting.
There's a dot for each note and the phrases that the notes
consist of are colored in a certain way or made in a certain

path. The last paintings that I made were realistic things connected with the Tower of Babel. There was an extraordinary one of the control room of the Tower of Babel which was built into a railway car leaving it. That painting was derived from a scene in Buster Keaton's film *The General*, where he chops out the end of the boxcar. A special film was projected onto the painting so that all the machinery operates.

In a number of cases I've made special screens to project films. All those so-called early abstract films had special painted screens for them. They were made of dots and lines. All those things disappeared.

When I went to Oklahoma last year I decided to devote my attention to the Indians. I really was honored to be able to record those things from the Indians. I decided to devote the rest of my life to that one thing. It was an unusual opportunity because the Kiowa Indians are extremely conservative. They hadn't really been studied very much. Through various reasons I got involved with them so that they told me all their myths and everything. It seemed better to devote the conclusion to that. That's why I'm living in this hotel room. Despite the fact that I can't afford the hotel room—it's fifty dollars a week—I am more or less able to spend my time doing that one thing. It is a very elaborate series of records, you know. We're devoting far too much time to accessory subjects. Naturally I sort of goof on everything I'm doing.

PAS: *I'm very puzzled about your fascination to visualize music.*

That is an interesting question, isn't it? I don't know. When I was a child, somebody came to school one day and said they'd been to an Indian dance and they saw somebody swinging a skull on the end of a string; so that I thought, hmmm, I have to see this. I went to that. Then I fell in with the Salish around Puget Sound for a long time. I sometimes spent three or four months with them during summer vacation or sometimes in the winter while I was going to high school or junior high school. It all started in grade school. In an effort to write down dances, I developed certain techniques of transcription. Then I got interested in the de-

signs in relation to the music. That's where it started from.
Of course! It was an attempt to write down the unknown
Indian life. I made a large number of recordings of that
which are also unfortunately lost. I took portable equipment
all over that place long before anyone else did and recorded
whole long ceremonies sometimes lasting several days. In
diagraming the pictures were so interesting that I then
started to be interested in music in relation to existence.
After that I met Griff B. and went to Berkeley and started
smoking marijuana, naturally little colored balls appeared
whenever we played Bessie Smith and so forth; whatever
it was I was listening to at that time. I had a really great
illumination the first time I heard Dizzy Gillespie play. I had
gone there very high, and I literally saw all kinds of colored
flashes. It was at that point that I realized music could be
put to my films. My films had been made before then, but
I had always shown them silently. I had been interested in
Jungian psychiatry when I was in junior high school. I found
some books by Jung in the Bellingham library. The business
about mandalas and so forth got me involved. I would like
to say I'm not very interested in Jung anymore: it seems
very crude now.

Incidentally this whole thing can probably be printed,
if you want to print it for me, like some kind of poem. In
that way this constant shifting back and forth can be
eliminated.

Later I borrowed a camera from Hy Hirsh. He had a
pretty good camera, a Bell and Howell model 70 something and had seen my films. The San Francisco Museum
showed that one of the grill works (#4) that precedes *Circular Tensions* and he came up and spoke. That's when I
asked for a camera. I've never owned a camera; I've usually
just borrowed one, then pawned it. That's always an embar-
rassing scene: trying to explain to the person where his or
her camera is. I can remember Frank Stauffacher saying to
me, "Now you haven't pawned the camera, have you?"
He said this jokingly, but it was pawned. Usually people
get their cameras back, eventually. My later films were
made with one that belonged to Sheba Ziprin. The "Mysteri-
oso" film (#11) and the long black-and-white film (#12)
were shot with her camera, which is now in a pawn shop in
Oklahoma City. The main parts of my film in Oklahoma

last year were shot on a camera that belonged to Stuart Reed.
That camera is in a barber shop in Anadarko, Oklahoma, where
Mr. A.'s Wollensack also is, unfortunately.

After I first stopped making films, I made those paintings
that you point at. Unless you've seen those, it's hard to
describe what they really are. They are at least as good as
the films. I'd been able to hear Charlie Parker and Thelonious
Monk, both of whom had come to San Francisco, but
wanted to make one final thing, another painting of Thelonious.
When I came to N.Y.C. I realized that it would be
impossible to make it in the form of a painting because
his music was so complex and it would be better to make a
film. I hadn't made films for at least five years by then.
#10 was a study for the "Mysterioso" film. Generally speaking
those films were made by trying to collect interesting
pictures, cutting them out, and then filing them. I had
enormous files possibly only two or three percent of which
was shot. I had worked on this one thing for twenty years,
having collected a lot of that stuff before; but then when I
left San Francisco I gave it to Broughton because I felt that
he might do something with it; but he obviously never did.

After I came here I started building again. Toward the
end I had everything filed in glassine envelopes: any kind
of vegetable, any kind of animal, any kind of this that and
the other thing, in all different sizes. Then file cards were
made up. For example, everything that was congruent to
that black-and-white film (#12) was picked out. All the
permutations possible were built up: say there's a hammer
in it, and there's a vase, and there's a woman, and there's
a dog. Various things could then be done—hammer hits
dog; woman hits dog; dog jumps into vase; and so forth.
It was possible to build up an enormous number of cross
references.

This was all written on little slips of paper, the file cards—
the possible combinations between this that and the other
thing. The file cards were then rearranged in an effort to
make a logical story out of it. Certain things would have to
happen before others: dog-runs-with-watermelon has to occur
after dog-steals-watermelon.

I tried as much as possible to make the whole thing
automatic, the production automatic rather than any kind
of logical process. Though at this point Allen Ginsberg

denies having said it, about the time I started making those films he told me that William Burroughs made a change in the Surrealistic process—because, you know, all that stuff comes from the Surrealists—that business of folding a piece of paper: one person draws the head and then folds it over and somebody else draws the body. What do they call it? The Exquisite Corpse. Somebody later, perhaps Burroughs, realized that something was directing it, that it wasn't arbitrary, and that there was some kind of what you might call God. It wasn't just chance. Some kind of universal process was directing these so-called arbitrary processes; and so I proceeded on that basis: try to remove things as much as possible from the consciousness or whatever you want to call it so that the manual processes could be employed entirely in moving things around. As much as I was able I made it automatic.

I must say that I'm amazed, after having seen the black-and-white film (#12) last night, at the labor that went into it. It is incredible that I had enough energy to do it. Most of my mind was pushed aside into some sort of theoretical sorting of the pieces, mainly on the basis that I have described: first I collected the pieces out of old catalogues and books and whatever; then made up file cards of all possible combinations of them; then I spent maybe a few months trying to sort the cards into logical order. A script was made for that. All the script and the pieces were made for a film at least four times as long. There were wonderful masks and things cut out. Like when the dog pushes the scene away at the end of the film, instead of the title "end" what is really there is a transparent screen that has a candle burning behind it on which a cat fight begins—shadow forms of cats begin fighting. Then all sorts of complicated effects; I had held these off. The radiations were to begin at this point. Then Noah's Ark appears. There were beautiful scratch-board drawings, probably the finest drawings I ever made—really pretty. Maybe two hundred were made for that one scene. Then there's a graveyard scene when the dead are all raised again. What actually happens at the end of the film is everybody's put in a teacup, because all kinds of horrible monsters came out of the graveyard, like animals that folded into one another. Then everyone gets thrown in a teacup which is made out of a head, and stirred up. This is the Trip to Heaven and the Return, then the Noah's Ark, then The Raising of the Dead, and finally the Stirring of Everyone in a Teacup. It was to be in four parts. The script was made up for the whole works on the basis of sorting pieces. It was exhaustingly long in its original form. When I say that it was cut, mainly what was cut out was, say, instead of the little man bowing and then standing up, he would stay bowed down much longer in the original. The cutting that was done was really a correction of timing. It's better in its original form.

#13 had all the characters out of Oz in it. That was assembled in the same way: I naturally divided Oz up into four lands because Oz consists of the Munchkins, the Quadlings, the Gillikins, and the Winkies; and then the Emerald City is in the middle; that is where the wizard's balloon had landed. I had built that thing many times as a child. I had fairly severe hallucinations and I had built something called my Fairy Garden for many years. I actually used to see little gnomes and fairies and stuff until I was seven or eight. It's a typical psychic phenomenon; I mean, I wasn't nutty or anything; all children see that stuff. Up until I was eighteen or so I worked hard on my Fairy Garden, and then started building Oz. It was a fairly large place because we had blocks and blocks of property in Anacortes. I built Oz a number of times; the final form though was for this film. It was to be a commercial film. Very elaborate equipment was built; the animation stand was about the size of a floor and exactly fourteen feet high. Oz was laid out on it, then seven levels built up. It was like the multiplane camera of Disney except that I was using a Mitchell camera that moved around. That's how I got into so many difficulties. Van Wolf had not paid rent on the camera, which was a thousand dollars a week. He was the producer, but he was taking far too many pills to do much but try to wiggle out of situations that developed. He got various people to pay for it: Huntington Hartford, Harry Phipps, Peggy Hitchcock, Elizabeth Taylor, and so forth invested in the film.

It was divided into different things. I ditched the Munchkins, Quadlings, Gillikins, and Winkies in their original form. What I was really trying to do was to convert Oz into a Buddhistic image like a mandala. I can't even remem-

ber what those lands were. One of them was Hieronymus
Bosch Land: all of Bosch's paintings were carefully dissected.
Another one was Microscopia taken from the books of
Haeckel, who was the Viennese biological artist and very
wonderful. The things he made are just marvelous; he
picked out every possible grotesque object that there was.
There was another land that was entirely made out of flesh.
Enormous vistas for miles were made out of naked people
from dirty mags. That would have been a nice film! most of
my material was prepared for it and over six hours of tests
were shot to get the apparatus to operate correctly. Only
the little piece in the drawer there was ever synchronized
to the music. In this particular section, the ballet music
from *Faust*, The Tin Woodman performs magic before leaving
for the Emerald City. The sound track was made up for
the whole film.

Dr. Leary had me interested in that black-and-white film
(#12), although, you realize, that "Heaven and Earth
Magic," whatever it's called, was a color film at that point.
It ran through a special machine that projected slides. This
is the first one that occurs: as the first head is on the
screen, the slide of the same image is projected around it.
There was a fader that obscured the screen out at the edges.
You don't realize that it's an oblong image; it's just that
there's another head the same as this—that's the telephone
operator who made the greatest number of phone calls in
the United States in some particular year. Where everything
dissolves into the bridge, you see it's taking place on the
moon; when the machinery is all operating, it's inside a
watermelon. The slides themselves run through another color
apparatus and the seats in the theatre were to be on some
kind of electrical contact or rubber pads so that as the audience looked at the film if a certain number of them would
lean in one direction that would activate little lights in the
projection booth which indicated that the audience, who
were in dentist chairs, watermelons, and so forth, were
thinking about a watermelon or about a dentist chair and
so forth. Then I would slip that slide in, since any one of
the slides could go with any portion of the film. They are
now in an order that was convenient. It was an attempt to
employ feedback phenomenon. It was executed to a degree
in Steinway Hall. Mr. Phipps set up a sort of presentation

there. The whole thing was set up and I arbitrarily guessed what the audience was thinking of from their responses. We didn't have any special chairs for them to sit in though.

I never did finish that sentence about the relation of Surrealism to my things: I assumed that something was controlling the course of action and that it was not simply arbitrary, so that by sortilege (as you know, there is a system of divination called "sortilege") everything would come out all right. #14 was made on this basis. Although I kept a record that such and such was shot in such and such an area of the screen, it was completely arbitrary.

PAS: *Was it your decision to leave the Kodak leader between rolls of film?*

I stole that idea from Andy Warhol. Everything that was shot was put in. A great number of images are missing. The staff to which the most effort was devoted doesn't even show at all. A very large amount of material for some reason just isn't on the film. Peter Fleischman, who made that last film with me, and I spent weeks shooting objects that must have been all underexposed. I assumed when Ansco said that the film had a rating of 300 that it did have a rating of 300. Most of what was shot at the beginning and the end of the film disappeared because of that. The central portion was not developed for a long time; it was left lying around in the hot weather for about six months so that it faded out and became white. I like the effect of the thing: it's all black at the beginning and the end, white in the middle; it looks good. Mr. Casper at Filmtronics made extremely good prints of the middle part. They are better than the original but nonetheless it didn't come out anything like I'd expected it to.

I started to get people for a film some months ago . . . how did that start? I think I asked Andy if he wanted to make a film, and he said "Yeah!" So I said, "Look, can I have three hundred dollars?" He said "Yeah." Who was it I asked next? I think Jack Smith. Then Robert Frank. At that point it seemed ridiculous to make an underground movie, but to make a really elaborate super-underground movie for showing in neighborhood theatres. That would be the only one I would make. The project keeps bogging down, basically because I haven't been able to find anybody that knows enough about films in regular theatres. Arthur and Huth Young have the money for it. I called them in a drunken condition and asked them for two million dollars, and Arthur said they perhaps would do it if they thought there were any possibility of producing an actual thing. In fact I called them last Tuesday or Wednesday again and they have been waiting all this time to look at films. They are interested in astrology. It is necessary to get some handsome producer to produce the film; not to produce money but to decide whether it's to be a short feature, or a short, like a Bugs Bunny length, so it can be distributed in first run theatres.

It would be like a trip around the world. Various people would come in. It would be marvelous; for instance, if Andy were able to supervise maybe a twenty minute color picture of Mount Fuji, but with a really good cameraman and technicians and everything so it would be really his beauty. Stan VanDerBeek was going to work on it. What he would do would be to go to northern Australia and animate aboriginal bark paintings. It will be produced eventually. Mr. Young once sent me a lavish check because he didn't like *Taras Bulba*. I'd called him the night before asking for money to go to Hollywood to try to salvage the Oz film. He said, "No, no, no, no, we're going to the movies, we're going to the movies, we don't have any time to talk with you now, Harry. And we're not interested in films. And anyhow you're drunk. You're calling me a fart." However the next morning a check did come in the mail and he wrote, "We didn't like *Taras Bulba* at all and we decided to see if you could do better." However I took the money and went to Miami Beach to see Peter's mother instead of going to Hollywood. I've been afraid to phone them for a long time.

I don't think I'll make any more animated films. They're too laborious and bad for the health. Sitting under those lights for hours is terrible. I've made enough of those; just like I've made enough hand-drawn films. I would like to make an "underground" movie that could be shown everywhere in little towns, because it was seeing art films, or whatever they used to call them, that first got me interested in these things. Now there must be lots of kids all over the world that would make films if they saw some of the things that are being made now.

There was another very good series of films I saw during the late 1920's. It always started with coming up to a door that had a little grillwork in it, a mysterious little thing; the going in there, through it. Isadora Duncan was in one of those. You'd go through this door and then there would be some Turkish or Chinese exotic operations. Those and the Fu Manchu movies were the ones that influenced me most. Naturally I would like to make some kind of artistic film that would be helpful to the progress of humanity. And that's the best one I can think of. There's no doubt in my mind that eventually someone is going to make a so-called "underground" movie that will revive Hollywood as Kenneth Anger writes of it.

"CULTURE: INTERCOM" AND EXPANDED CINEMA
A Proposal and Manifesto

by Stan VanDerBeek

Stan VanDerBeek is best known for his invention of the Movie-Drome, a domed theater in which the entire interior surface of the dome serves as a cinema screen. He completed construction of the first movie drome in 1965 at Stony Point, New York. In this article VanDerBeek discusses his radically new approach to the technology of mass communication.

Two of Stan VanDerBeek's films received prizes at the Brussels Experimental Film Competition in 1958, and in 1959 he was the recipient of a Rockefeller grant for work in non-verbal communication. Mr. VanDerBeek is the author of articles that have appeared in Film Quarterly, Film Culture, *and* Popular Photography. *He has lectured and screenings of his films have taken place at various universities and colleges, including Harvard, Cornell, and Pratt Institute.*

It is imperative that we quickly find some way for the entire level of
world human understanding to rise to a new human scale.
This scale is the world . . .

The risks are the life or death of this world.

The technological explosion of this last half-century, and the
    implied future

are overwhelming, man is running the machines of his own
    invention . . .

while the machine that is man . . .

runs the risk of running wild.

Technological research, development and involvement of the
    world community

has almost completely out-distanced the emotional–sociological
    (socio-"logical")

comprehension of this technology.

It is imperative that each and every member of the world
    community,

regardless of age and cultural background, join the 20th
    century as

quickly as possible.

The "technique-power" and "culture-over-reach" that is just
    beginning to

explode in many parts of the earth, is happening so quickly
    that it has put

the logical fulcrum of man's intelligence so far outside himself
    that he

cannot judge or estimate the results of his acts before he
    commits them.

The process of life as an experiment on earth has never been
    made clearer.

It is this danger . . . that man does not have time

to talk to himself . . .

that man does not have means to talk to other men . . .

the world hangs by a thread of verbs and nouns.

Language and cultural-semantics are as explosive

as nuclear energy.

It is imperative that we (the world's artists) invent a new
    world language . . .

that we invent a non-verbal international picture-language . . .

I propose the following:

That immediate research begin on the possibility of an
    international

picture-language using fundamentally motion pictures.

That we research immediately existing audio-visual devices, to
    combine these

devices into an educational tool, that I shall call an "experience machine"

or a "culture-intercom" . . .

The establishment of audio-visual research centers . . . preferably on an

international scale . . .

These centers to explore the existing audio-visual hardware . . .

The development of new image-making devices . . .

(the storage and transfer of image materials, motion pictures, television,

computers, video-tape, etc . . .)

In short, a complete examination of all audio-visual devices and procedures,

with the idea in mind to find the best combination of such machines for

non-verbal inter-change.

The training of artists on an international basis in the use of these image

tools.

The immediate development of prototype theatres, hereafter called

"Movie-Dromes" that incorporate the use of such projection hardware.

The immediate research and development of image-events and performances

in the "Movie-Drome" . . .

I shall call these prototype presentations: "Movie Murals,"
"Ethos-Cinema,"
"Newsreel of
Dreams,"
"Feedback,"
"Image
Libraries" . . .

The "movie-drome" would operate as follows . . .

In a spherical dome, simultaneous images of all sorts would be projected

on the entire dome-screen . . . the audience lies down at the outer edge of

the dome with their feet toward the center, thus almost the complete field

of view is the dome-screen. Thousands of images would be projected on this screen . . . this image-flow could be compared to the "collage" form of the

newspaper, or the three ring circus . . . (both of which suffice the audience

with an abundance of facts and data) . . . the audience takes what it can or

wants from the presentation . . . and makes its own conclusions . . . each member

of the audience will build his own references from the image-flow, in the

best sense of the word the visual material is to be presented and each

individual makes his own conclusions . . . or realizations.

A particular example . . .

to prepare an hour-long presentation in the "movie-drome" using all sorts

of multi-plex images, depicting the course of Western civilization since

the time of the Egyptians to the present . . . a rapid panoply of graphics

and light calling upon thousands of images, both still and in motion

(with appropriate "sound-images"). It would be possible to compress the

last three thousand years of Western life into such an aspect ratio that

we, the audience, can grasp the flow of man, time, and forms of life

that have led us *up to the very moment* . . . details are not important, it

is the total scale of life that is . . . in other words . . . using the past and

the immediate present to help us understand the likely future . . .

endless filmic variations of this idea are possible in each field of

man's endeavor . . . science, math, geography . . . art, poetry, dance,

biology, etc. . . . .

endless variations of this idea by *each* culture group and nationality

that take it on as a project . . . to be presented in turn to each other culture group . . .

The purpose and effect of such image-flow, and image density (also to

be called "visual-velocity"), is to both deal and logical understanding,

and to penetrate to unconscious levels, the use of such "emotion-pictures"

would be to reach for

the "emotional denominator" of all men . . .

the basis of human life thought and understanding that is non-verbal

to provide images that inspire basic intuitive instincts of self-realization to inspire all men to good will and "inter and intro-realization" . . .

When I talk of the movie-dromes as image libraries, it is understood

that such "life-theatres" would use some of the coming techniques

(video-tape and computer inter-play) and thus be real communication

and storage centers, that is, by satellite, each dome could receive

its images from a world wide library source, store them and program

a feedback presentation to the local community that lived near the

center, this newsreel feedback, could authentically review the total

world image "reality" in an hour-long show that gave each member of

the audience a sense of the entire world picture . . . the let us say

world's work of the month put into an hour.

"Intra-communitronics," or dialogues with other centers would be likely,

and instant reference material via transmission television and tele-

phone could be called for and received at 186,000 m.p.s. . . . from any-

where in the world . . .

Thus I call this presentation, a "newsreel of ideas, of dreams, a movie-mural . . ."

an image library, a culture de-compression chamber, a culture-inter-com . . .

my concept is in effect the maximum use of the maximum
    information

devices that we *now* have at our disposal. . . .

Certain things might happen . . . if an individual is exposed to
    an over-

whelming information experience . . .

It might be possible to re:order the levels of awareness of any
    person . . .

it certainly will re:order the structure of motion pictures as we
    know

them . . .

cinema will become a "performing" art . . . and image-library.

I forsee that such centers will have its artist in residence who
    will

orchestrate the image material he has at his disposal . . .

and will lead to a totally new international art form . . .

That in probing for the "emotional denominator," it would be
    possible

by the visual "power" of such a presentation to reach any age
    or

culture group irregardless of culture and background

the "experience machine" could bring anyone on earth *up
    to the 20th*

century.

As the current growth rate risk of explosives to human flesh
    continues,

the risk of survival increases according . . .

it now stands at 200 pounds of T.N.T. per human pound of
    flesh . . . per human

on earth.

There are an estimated 700 million people who are unlettered
    in the world . . .

we have no time to lose

or mis-calculate . . .

The world and self-education process must find a quick solu-
    tion to

re:order itself, a revision of itself, an awareness of itself . . .

that is each man, must somehow realize the enormous scale of
    human

life and accomplishments on earth right now . . .

Man must find a way to measure himself, to simultaneously

   grow and keep
in touch with himself . . .
Man must find a way to leap over his own prejudices, and
   apprehensions . . .
The means are on hand . . . here and now . . .
in technology and the extension of the senses . . .
To summarize:
My concern is for a way for the over-developing technology of
   part of the
world to help the under-developed emotional-sociology of *all*
   of the world
to catch up to the 20th century . . . to counter-balance technique and logic—
and to do it now, quickly . . .
My concern is for world peace and harmony . . .
the appreciation of individual minds . . .
the interlocking of good wills on an international exchange
   basis . . .
the interchange of images and ideas . . .
a realization of the process of "realization" of self-education
that now must occur before the "fact" of education . . .
in short: a way for all men to have fore-knowledge
by advantageous use of past and immediate knowledge . . .
Mankind faces the immediate future with doubt on one hand
and molecular energy on the other
He must move quickly and surely to preserve his future . . .
he must realize the present . . .
the here and the now . . . right now.
An international picture-language is a tool to build that
   future . . .

SHOOTING UP

by James Stoller

*James Stoller, born in Brooklyn in 1941, is one of the first
critics to write on the films of Warren Sonbert, and he has
also written with enthusiasm on the works of the Kuchar
Brothers. He is founder and editor of the magazine* Moviegoer.

It takes a lot to get a movie made—not bread alone, but an
expense of energy that in the case of even the simplest 16mm
short is as much a matter of hustling and muscling as it is
of sustaining the creative fire. Artists seldom being the most
practical or worldly people around, depending on which
way you look at it, it's either a small wonder so few good
films get made, or a miracle so many do. Hearteningly, under
these circumstances, recent developments in the New York
"underground" have encouraged a more permissive approach
to filmmaking, in which the distillation process leading to art
is not so much a purification of sensibility through hard work
and technique, but involves a prior labor liberating the sensibility itself.

Writers like Jonas Mekas have anticipated an era when
films will be created as cheaply as poems, but a related
trend is equally apparent: the trend toward "films" in which
the filmmaker, on the face of it, has in one sense or another
had comparatively little filmmaking to do, and in which,
bypassing many of the standard managerial fiats of the
medium, he has produced something less answerable to
cinema's traditional properties but correspondingly more
personal, and perhaps more moving. Such a film, in fact,
may be more moving as experience than as film: for a
central (and anti-McLuhanist) statement consider Peter
Emanuel Goldman's "Any medium will do; film just happens to be the best" (imagine that from Eisenstein or Welles,
Brakhage, or even Truffaut!). And for seminal work Andy

180

Warhol's, where the recording camera sits in its place with never a need for a cut (hence for a splice).

A heart-stopping film by Warren Sonbert called *Amphetamine*, which runs maybe ten minutes and is accompanied by records of the popular Detroit rock 'n' roll group, The Supremes, was screened at the Film-Makers' Cinematheque recently. Completely symptomatic of the filmmaking revolution I have suggested, it seems paradoxically to come to terms with its subject in a way which might be seen as "cinematic" in the essence despite its forthright rejection of much of the apparatus of traditional filmmaking, which we are left to suspect might bear finally the kind of relation to "cinema" that syntax bears to direct expression: auxiliary but, in certain states of heightened consciousness, peculiarly dispensable.

Amphetamine presents various takes of a boy at a party "shooting up," his face exceptionally mobile. Then there are (subjective?) shots of a kind of exquisite blur. Then a shock cut to two boys, presumably high, locked in a primal embrace. Although the progress of these uncomplicated shots has an exactly felt, almost dialectical logic, it is hard to see what makes the images themselves so electrifying, other than that we feel ourselves witness to faces and bodies in attitudes that have not appeared on a screen before. Some will complain that this is an "obvious" way to capture an audience—as it is obvious also, not ironic or even especially clever, to play "I Hear a Symphony," with its ecstatic *Tristan*-like progressions, over these images of boys who are drugged. But what's the difference, if the viewer is enthralled and moved and the filmmaker has not been ashamed to be . . . obviously obvious? As in a sexual experience there is similarly no need to fear the "obvious," between the receptive spectator and the filmmaker a tacit agreement may spontaneously arise, a kind of communion unimpeded by guise and guile. To this loosening of classical requirements of "art" the filmmaker Peter Goldman can again bear witness: "The first scene I shot in *Echoes of Silence* was the one of the three girls putting on makeup. . . . When I saw the footage I realized how much could be said by just shooting the right faces and nothing more."

Sonbert is not yet 20 and will do more ambitious things;

too much should not be allowed to hang on his first effort, auspicious as I think it is. Still it is exemplary of other work that has preceded it and more that will follow—though it breaks with, say, Warhol's "static" films in that its images are much less cool, more emotionally charged, evoking much less desire in the spectator to proceed beyond them to a literary interpretation. What they are is what they are, and that is enough. Where *Amphetamine* is especially symptomatic is in its intimation that the filmmaker has not performed enough *work* for this to be art. But I would suggest that the work has indeed been done, although principally in an unaccustomed direction: the direction of freeing the imagination first so that a statement could be made for which, in its transparency and unpretentiousness, there was no comfortable precedent. The result is beautiful and pure: behind the bald surface we feel, first, that many inessentials have been cleared away, and then, that the *need* for them has been cleared away.

Warren Sonbert has since made two more short films, by comparison with which *Amphetamine* looks chiefly like a shocker.

In *Where Did Our Love Go?* a hyperactive and uncommitted camera gives us fleeting views of a number of favored Manhattan scenes and the beautiful and vacant-looking children who inhabit them. The latter appear and reappear in various combinations and alignments that reportedly make reference to their real life at the time the film was shot. If its "in" aspect were not hopelessly lost on me, I might like this lovely small film less. As it is, I'm grateful for it: largely craftless and undemanding, it has the consistency and sureness of a sustained, endlessly surprising, intuitive perception.

A series of meetings and greetings in the city (a New York seen magically in color, reminiscent of the New York of Frank O'Hara's poems) is wedded to a series of unfulfilled chases, not only the people but the camera following repeatedly through doors, down corridors, across streets, after what must be gone, or lost, or never was. Sonbert's restless, rushing fragmentation of incident frees modish gestures and attitudes from their temporal context and freezes them in an immutable past tense, so that everything we see seems to have happened long ago. The pervasive camera-

Warren Sonbert: From *Where Did Our Love Go?*, 1966

consciousness contributes to this effect by giving whatever anyone does the look of having been done precisely to be recorded on film, and the wonderful dreamy old rock 'n' roll songs on the sound track—the Shirelles, the Ronettes—already sound like signals of a bygone time. Clips from movies and manifestations of local painting become continuous with the "real" life of the film, settings its tone and its color and creating a lively interplay.

Where Did Our Love Go? feels like both a valentine and a farewell to a generation, as well as being simply a portrait which is tender, distant, accurate, somewhat high, and sad. In one brief and emblematic image near the end, a group of kids huddles in a semi-circle on a sofa, neither really touching nor completely apart, and you can feel all the ambiguity and the uncertain liveliness of the teenyboppers in the street—the generation which no one, probably, understands but which Sonbert, in a series of tender and moving moments, has revealed to us. I could watch this film a hundred times; it made me feel older than I am, but it also opened my eyes and my heart.

Sonbert's third film is *Hall of Mirrors*, with René Ricard and Gerard Malanga, opening with a funny and disturbing re-cut of some of the most peculiar Hollywood footage imaginable, and progressing to a graceful and poetic re-evaluation by Sonbert of the same motif. The three parts of this mysterious film didn't coalesce for me, yet it is partly because of it that Sonbert has become the 16mm filmmaker now working in New York whose new work I find myself awaiting most eagerly, and with the greatest assurance that it will be not just surprising, but self-renewing.

The Kuchar Brothers have lit out on their own, with George Kuchar's *Hold Me While I'm Naked* already a mainstay on the Bridge-Gate-Cinematheque circuit. As the filmmaker who directs hot lovemaking but gets none himself, Kuchar looks marvelously adolescent and deprived; to heighten his wretchedness he has shot himself in heroic poses from the worst possible angles and pushed the result into incongruous romantic scenery; there are red splotches on his face which you might suspect he painted there himself. Nonetheless his film betrays an anomalously happy heart, stripping the subject of lewdness, grimness, self-pity; it is endearing in something like the way that certain Beatles songs, Paul McCartney shrieking "Got to get you into my life," are endearing. With much of the flair of his great Hollywood near-namesake (George Cukor), Kuchar creates bright, pure specific imagery that gives the theme of sexual frustration its definitive comic due. In the last minutes of the film he rotates 360 degrees in the shower, then bangs his head quietly against the bathtub wall, while television antennas vibrate on rooftops outside—omnipresent communication signals counterpoising his loneliness. On the screen Kuchar's ideas work and are likable at the same time. I think they are the real thing: poetry without poetics.

Kuchar's habit of having everyone, including his various plump bare-breasted sexpots, speak in dubbed-in Bronx rasps is somewhat revolting, but it encourages a comfortable anti-arty feeling and scarcely undermines the precise, colorful, sensuous images, which speak their own good language. It also serves another purpose. It is one thing, after all, to be merely horny; it is another thing entirely, as Kuchar now recalls to us, to be horny in a lower-middle-class Bronx (Flushing, Brooklyn) apartment redolent with the unaccountably anaphrodisiac aroma of Mother's potato pancakes, cabbage soup, or whatever she happened to brew on rainy afternoons. In the Kuchar kitchen it is a feast of steak and tomatoes that the sodden and enervated hero emerges from his shower to face, and never have so many vitamins seemed so much beside the point.

This film could cheer an arthritic gorilla, and audiences, apparently sensitized by its blithely accurate representation of feelings few among them can have escaped, rise from their general stupor to cheer it back. Here are the words of Kuchar's own program note: "Zesty color that makes you nice to be near, helps to elevate the flowing film to the level of liquid consciousness that is so poignant it floats!" *Leisure*, which accompanied *Hold Me* at some recent screenings, was a delicate and funny footnote.

Brother Mike Kuchar has been less successful to my taste, with his recent *Green Desire* and *The Secret of Wendel Samson*, similarly about sex problems. These films have good things but seem basically arty and even humorless; more precisely, you can't tell whether or not he's kidding. You sometimes can't with George either; the difference is that it doesn't matter.

NOTES FOR *THE DEVIL IS DEAD*
by Carl Linder

Carl Linder's notes for The Devil Is Dead, *from which an extract follows, reveal the way in which one particular filmmaker handles his material. Of special interest is Linder's unconventional, literary approach to characterization.*

Carl Linder is a filmmaker whose cinematic works include The Devil Is Dead, Skin, *and, most recently,* Womancock, *and* Closed Mondays. *Originally he was associated with the West Coast filmmaking group in San Francisco. He now lives in New York and teaches filmmaking at the School of Visual Arts.*

Notes on a Male Character for *The Devil Is Dead*

The boy is hard, full of nails.

He hears the excitement of tearing. Meaning that he should tear, cloth perhaps, perhaps panties, perhaps.

He needs protection, seeking shelter under a mattress.

All of his life is devoted to fools, he takes to dolls, and then knives.

What he has in his head is a gut string, wearing the end of a whip around his head, tightening, he loathes on his face, the tightening of fidelity, for isn't this against the grain, sawing.

Perhaps he finds himself sawing, grinding a thing of beauty in half, a thing of contempt like a child's potty, or perhaps beautiful in the way of a penis, grinding a penis against stone. And this represents his poverty to hold onto life respectably.

He looks out of openings, through holes, in paper, and he applies these holes to himself, around his foot.

The boy wears gloves, protection against being caught, and then being able to handle the situation. This is a real gloved boy, and he places his hands in stickiness.

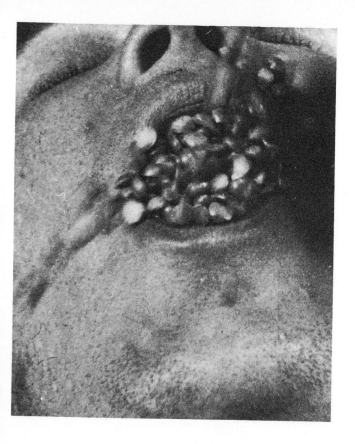

Carl Linder: From *The Devil Is Dead*, 1964

His life is gelatinous, his kind friends are too, but this is represented by a stick sticking in the floor, while he kicks it, then bends it, helping it to reach the floor, the way he does his friends, making them more ignoble to pass out the whole matter quickly.

Quickness is necessary, and a shot of scything wheat, or comparable is necessary.

The boy needs shaving. He needs a haircut, and a bout with the devil.

He wears a handiron on his wrist, and knuckles on his hind end. These are caught out of a pattern of fornication, outhouses, dirt, shit, finite, blond excretion, cum, little wads of spent sputum.

These are his mistresses, he loves on the buttocks of love. The fineness of granite, and glass, and grass.

This is his pedestal, his church, temptuousness.

His hair is rung with grass.

His chest is spun from glass.

His pectorals are brought out of the ovens for a feast.

His head is heady, large, begging, pleading for lard.

His stomach resembles a cannibal waiting for a shark, a man-eating stomach, full of pearls, laden with pearls, and socking gloves. This is a man's belly, of snaky flesh, rubbed tight.

His legs stand as if in a pasture, apart, hugging the ground.

His feet protrude in a glass way, forging a rigging of chains on the ground.

All this crowns his body

And his attitude is one of pleasure, all around.

His posture one of Caesars, or of some great Catherine, a feminine Pope perhaps.

His shoulder is stuck out, as if penetrating the paper eye of a follower.

His side is thrust too, outward in a revolving way.

All of him undulates like a giant sea left in a sphere of hurt and pus, and nastiness.

His halter turns up at the thought, Leave me! He says lugubriously.

Some actor, he can't even act if he tries.

But his presence evokes a commonness, a simple greed, a

snatching of yourself perhaps, a snatching gesture perhaps.
His face indicates a great land mouse, or something akin
to a prison.
His ears are lifted from smut.
His nose a gesture of defiance and submission.
He waits to be chained, grated down, degraded, fooled
with.

Impression of work that is real, and artificial, co-existent,
a triumph of elements, neither false, nor true, real, etc., and
so this as applied to film, a real person, exacting normal
things from surroundings, juxtaposed to weird happenings,
projectings, Tions, odd water creatures, entering, leaving the
environ of real self, all as if a mixture of self and not, which
truer than all one, a mix of foreign elements, of strange
occurence, self admixed with the oil, and emulsion taking
place, a forming, forcibly of the unreal with the real, without excuse, with the pretense of the existence of itself to
justify it. This is the art. A self-realization of nature as it
were. Here is a bottle, next to a block of lead, or a body
kneading the dough between legs, this is the enterprise, the
thing which adamants the occurrence be only of the tough
thread of being, occurrence, someone's intention, and so,
let it be.

Notes on a Female Character for *The Devil Is Dead*

The girl has a broken neck.
She reads the papers and vomits.
She is eligible for a fling against the wall.
Standing on her tiptoes, gesturing lewdly, awfully.
Something edible in her hand.
She has to have dinner.
She loves to play with hooks.
The girl is manly, tired, looking ugly.
She finds pennies in the sewer.
She looks for ants. She looks for a find in a pocket.
She has to find all there within her self.
She comes in a great haste.
She is wearing purple.
She comes in in a hand basket.

She worms in.

She brings with her a blanket.

She lays on it.

She is at home. Home is in her self where she has her hand.

This is a waste she says to herself. She screws up her nose.

She looks for wormy crinkled paper. We know that it is wormy by the color green, and by the way it stands when you let it go.

We are letting the basket of fruit go. It goes in the air as if thrown. In the mirror with it. Disgusted, it looks like a windstorm, we know it is a windstorm by the flagellation in the wood above the eye. The wood waves, greens with age, it saps and oozes.

Her legs are filled with a raw wood.

Her buttox is soft, white, wound in rubber, or paper, a paper towel will do.

She poses wrapped in toilet paper.

She looks for her lost sword, her knife to peel the onions. These we have, but where. We have them in a basket for fruit.

THREE FILMMAKERS *
Andy Meyer * Charles Boultenhouse *
Storm De Hirsch

by Gregory Markopoulos

Gregory Markopoulos is one of the major figures in the new school of filmmakers. His works include Twice a Man, Galaxie, *and* The Illiac Passion. *Markopoulos has pioneered an editing technique that makes use of single images and in-camera editing. He has written for several film journals, has published a volume of poetry, and has lectured about his films at Columbia University, and at Hunter and Queens colleges. His films have been shown at several film festivals and at the Museum of Modern Art. Markopoulos is Associate*

* Reprinted from *Film Culture*, No. 35, Winter, 1964–65.

*Professor and director of the program in cinematography at
the Chicago Art Institute School. He lives in New York City.*
*The widely divergent approaches and techniques of the
three filmmakers discussed in the following article are indica-
tive of the broad spectrum of talent covered by the artists
in the New York film school.*

The filmmakers of the New American Cinema are not only
unlike any other filmmakers of the past—unlike the avant-
gardists of the 1920's, the politically oriented filmmakers of
the 1930's, or the avant-gardists of the 1940's, or even the
midwest school of filmmakers of the middle and late 1950's—
they are also unlike each other in their mode of filmic conception as any birth from coenogenesis, ectogenesis, and
parthenogenesis. The foundation of the New American
Cinema is molded out of invisibility and decorated in in-
divisibility. Within such a foundation, films are begun like
quick-fire even as others are being completed. . . .
   The celestial body of New American Cinema has an extensive range. There is the amazing first work performed in
8mm by Andy Meyer. Reference is made to his film *Shades
and Drum-Beats.* In the same millimeter, there are the
humorously detailed comedies spoofing Hollywood by the
young Kuchar brothers. On another level, there is the 16mm
work of Charles Boultenhouse—his motion picture *Handwritten,* and his more recent work *Dionysius,* with its extraordinary ending conceived in the tradition of the satyr play.
And recently there has appeared the fine work of the
poet and filmmaker Storm De Hirsch, whose *Goodbye in the
Mirror* contains that visual wisdom from which too many
individuals working in the motion picture medium have become disengaged. Nor can one ignore the continuous work in
progress of Marie Menken. . . . .
   I would like to concentrate here on several newly completed films by three of the above-mentioned filmmakers.
The youngest of the three is Andy Meyer, who at this writing
has returned to Brandeis University to continue his studies.
Through exceedingly limited means, Mr. Meyer has glo-
riously, with the use of an 8mm motion-picture camera,
created one of those remarkable films incensed with the
values which everyman forgets, caught as he is in the sedge

flats he calls his streets. It is these disowned values that Mr. Meyer obstinately, and with the greatest of poise, works with and surprises his film spectator. Unimportant at this juncture of the young-filmmaker's career is the fact that his film does not pretend to technical achievement. The spirit of an artist transcends the idea of technical achievement. The anguish and delirium of *Shades and Drum-Beats* is enhanced by that form of editing which envelops the filmmaker; and out of the available materials before him, he creates his world for the first time, and thereafter, with each new work or experiment.

The world of *Shades and Drum-Beats* has no need for sound; the film frames become the filmic grammar. They speak and contain the words, the sentences that reveal to the engrossed film spectator the spirit of Meyer's work. Those who are fortunate in viewing *Shades and Drum-Beats* will come away having inhaled the most precious of aromatic barks.

Charles Boultenhouse's 16mm work *Dionysius,* so vastly different from the work of Meyer, contains an abundance of riches which one may gladly say is never for one moment thrust toward the spectator, as occurs in the recently and much publicized commercial motion picture *Topkapi,* by Jules Dassin. *Dionysius* is divided into more than several parts, during which time the soundtrack is first spoken in English, then in French, and finally in Greek. Both the poetry, which enhances the images, and the spoken word are handsomely invented. One is reminded of the complex musical levels of the composer Charles Ives. Though the title *Dionysius* suggests the legend of the Greek god of wine, the film remains supremely American. Inspired by that happy hour of its creation, Mr. Boultenhouse has used as a chorus a group of filmmakers which becomes the visual sonata form of his film. Because the film spectator cannot help but become possessed during the viewing of *Dionysius,* as one becomes possessed in the face of the sensuous temple homes of Frank Lloyd Wright in the films of Kenneth Anger, the consequences of his share as a film spectator become an extraordinary catharsis. The only point upon which Mr. Boultenhouse might be taken to task is the fact that he did not photograph the figures of Pentheus and Dionysius naked.

The third filmmaker in this triumvirate is Storm De Hirsch.

Of the several films to her credit, the most impressive are *Divinations*, with its exciting soundtrack, its hand-colored images, and her first feature work, *Goodbye in the Mirror*, which is completely unpretentious both in the selection of theme (concerning a young woman who goes to Rome to find herself a husband) and its presentation on the screen. From the very inception of the credit titles, the film spectator feels the power of one of the most fascinating cities in the world—Rome. From the beginning to the end of the film, the spectator's pleasure and understanding are enhanced on the same social filmic scale of that grand experimentalist Rossellini. Though the images in most films are easily forgotten, such is not the case with those of *Goodbye in the Mirror*. Best retained and rooted are the images and episodes of the turning streetcar; the central characters Maria and Marco; the sweeper; the scurrying nuns; the steps to the water supply tank (homage, perhaps, to Maya Deren's *Meshes of the Afternoon*); the well-documented bathroom scene; the very amusing song "I Wish I was a Fascinating Bitch"; the visual melodies as conceived in the walk episodes which alternate between one character and another; Marco's performance; the grapes being washed and the paper bag crumpled by the same two lovers. One is reminded that here is a sense of existence as in the famous *Sous les toits de Paris* by René Clair.

Miss DeHirsch has paid the closest attention to her soundtrack. For instance, the scene where the English girl is picked up and goes riding in a horse-drawn carriage: the buildings, the Colosseum looming towards the spectator, past, beyond, and returning to him, the trot of the horse, the sound of the jingling bells, the street lamps in the late afternoon, the chuckles of the couple in the carriage, and then *direct cut*—it is evening, a descending Mediterranean evening. Still another area to which Miss De Hirsch has paid vivid attention is the performance of the actors and, in particular, the way in which they use their hands.[1] There is the expert scene of the guitar lessons with Maria instructing herself, a scene which is beautifully intercut with the contrasting despair and hope that take place in Maria's apartment between Maria and her two

[1] "Every part of the human frame should contribute to express the passions and emotions of the soul. Action must be graceful and appropriate to the words. . . ."—*Thespian Preceptor, or A Full Essay of the Scenic Art*, published in 1810.

boarders, an English girl and a Swedish girl. Character delineation is seldom so eloquently conceived as at this point in
Goodbye in the Mirror. There is the sublime visit of the lovers
(Maria and Marco) to the sculpture studio of Marco's friend,
Brooks. The whole sequence is encompassed by Rosa Pradell's
performance as she views the sculptures of Brooks for the first
time. Not a word of dialogue, and yet the whole feeling in this
initial presentation of Marco's fiancée to his friend is achieved.
Only Anna Magnani has revealed the same depth under the
inspired direction of Rossellini in *The Miracle.* Lastly, one
should not forget the busy noonday episode of the English girl
reciting her "Friends, Romans, Countrymen" speech to the
unsuspecting passersby below her balcony.[2] There is no doubt
that Storm De Hirsch is one of those rare artists to whose new
works the film spectator eagerly looks forward.

BRUCE CONNER AND HIS FILMS[*]
by Brian O'Doherty

*Brian O'Doherty emphasizes the revolutionary nature of Bruce
Conner's films—particularly in their special use of material
originally made for other purposes and "found" (Duchamp
prefers to say, in this case, "chosen") for new use by the filmmaker. Conner, in this author's opinion, is characteristic of the
new artists in that his work falls both within and without the
traditional concept of fine art.*

Mr. O'Doherty was an art critic for The New York Times
*from 1961 until 1964. His collected criticism is being pub-
lished by Simon and Schuster.*

Since art has turned itself inside out—from the self to the environment, from total abstraction to the object—there have
naturally been changes in the way artists function. Instead of

---

[2] Ron Rice did equally well in the Hamlet parody in his unfinished film, *The Queen of Sheba Meets the Atom Man.*

[*] Printed in a slightly different version in *The New York Times,*
April 26, 1964.

the artist as pure artist, his horizon physically limited by the four sides of a canvas, and his eye turned inward on the clash of self-renewing forces, we are apparently getting a different kind of animal—the all-rounder who can perform within the category of what we think of as "art," and outside it, in other areas, when he so feels.

In recent years we have had the artist as a sort of pre-theatrical impresario (Happenings), as performer (notably Robert Morris and Robert Rauschenberg), and more recently as moviemaker—including Andy Warhol and today's example, Bruce Conner. The artist as moviemaker is an old story—Man Ray, Cocteau, and Dali produced the classics—but there's a difference now, in much the same way that neo-Dada turned out not to be Dada at all, but Pop, although some persist in not seeing the difference.

Thus one can look at Bruce Conner's exhibition at the Alan Gallery, and his two films *A Movie* (1958) and *Cosmic Ray* (1962)—12 and 4 minutes long respectively—as expressions of the same attitude and fundamentally the same technique applied to a different medium. At the moment assemblage as a technique is permeating all the arts with extraordinary vigor.

Conner's assemblages have curtained off a special horror-corner in art in recent years. Deeply melodramatic, they provoke hostility by their careful offensiveness. There is a love of ugliness presented with a *fin-de-siècle* sense of connoisseur-ship—vulgarity and bad taste (or what we associate with them) consciously invited in and preserved in an environment where they retain enough to shock but not to disrupt. Take one piece: a scorched, melted head with a few teeth biting out from it; nearby a bride from a wedding cake whose groom is laid out under glass nearby. It's called "November 22nd, 1963."

It is Grand Guignol with a difference. Most of his pieces find the same sore spot and rub; flowers take on the paralysis of graveyard bouquets; girlie photos make the viewer feel like a corpse remembering former pleasures; lace associates directly with arsenic; flickering votive lamps desecrate instead of sanctify. The detritus and debris of old nylons, comic strips, wrappers, beads, cigarette butts, are accumulated in a sort of inspired excess that becomes a curious digestive process in which fire seems catalytic—everything burned and singed so it looks as if one puff of air would disperse the whole flimsy structure. The afterlife of these discarded things is as precarious as an assemblage of shadows.

In *A Movie* the technique is exactly the same—a montage of found materials from fact (newsreels) and fiction (old movies). Clichés and horrors make a rapid collage in which destruction and sex follow each other in images of pursuit (cowboys and Indians, all kinds of cars, engines, an elephant) and falling (parachutes, bombs, planes) until finally a diver disappears through a hole in the bottom of the sea—the ultimate exit. The entire thing is prefaced by a girl from a shady movie lazily undressing. By the time *A Movie* is over she has retroactively become an Eve or Circe or Prime Mover.

Some of the collage images are so well known (the *Hindenberg* in flames, Mussolini and Petacci hanging upside down, the Tacoma suspension bridge undulating like a piece of malignant rubber) that they send the mind pinwheeling out of the movie on a tangent while the next sequence is also demanding attention—a very new kind of split-level effect the way Conner does it.

For the film clips of reality are used as object—not as objects prompting surrealist associations, but as objects from real life loudly claiming attention while being forced into a relationship to contribute to the movie. The movie is split open again and again by real life hurting through it. This is remarkably like the effect Robert Rauschenberg gets in his latest paintings.

The shorter film ties up closely with a piece called *Spiral Flesh* from the exhibition at the Alan Gallery—an elbow-shaped jig-saw of what looks like fingers rotating to prompt serialized associations of the human form. *Cosmic Ray* turns the female nude into a piece of animated protoplasm that pulses, expands, bursts like a bubble, overlaid by a measles of blips and flashes and numbers (and eventually more sinister images)—like an X ray of a teen-ager's mind when Ray Charles sings "What Did I Do?" which he does on the accompanying soundtrack. It is a Pop art masterpiece, with a sophistication of means, a control of ambigious effects and expressive intent far removed from Surrealism. Conner clarifies the artistic usage of "reality" —objects and photographs and film clips—in a new way of coping with the environment. His films are revolutionary.

OBJECTIONS TO THE NEW
AMERICAN CINEMA

by Dwight Macdonald

In these notes, Dwight Macdonald criticizes the New Ameri-can Cinema, and directs his remarks toward films by the Mekas brothers. As Mr. Macdonald points out, Jonas Mekas is, indeed, the "patron saint of the New American Cinema." It can be said that this movement owes its entire existence to the efforts of Jonas Mekas. A Mekas film that Mr. Macdonald does not concern himself with here is The Brig, *one of the outstand-ing products of the new film movement.*

Mr. Macdonald approaches these films with what may be considered conventional critical apparatus, yet at the same time he is always aware of the critical procedure he employs. He articulates the critical dilemma so many movie-goers en-counter when confronted with a new cinematic system.

The author has written criticism for numerous publications, including Esquire *and* The New York Review of Books.

Culture has now become so fashionable that the danger is no longer what it has traditionally been, neglect of original talent, but rather the opposite: an indiscriminate encouragement of everything, which is producing a cultural inflation reminiscent of what happened to the *Reichsmark* after the First World War. This victory of the avant-garde is ironic because it comes long after the creative force has been spent: Joyce, Picasso, Matisse, Yeats, Eliot, Cézanne, Stravinsky, and the other in-novators have had epigones rather than heirs. The one impor-tant exception is cinema, in which directors like Truffaut, Resnais, Antonioni, Fellini, Kurosawa, and Bergman have in the last decade been working out a new aesthetic that, after an interregnum of thirty-five years, has resumed the develop-ment of the art at the point at which it was left by the great American, Russian, and German silent directors.

There is another irony: the victory has been too complete.

The philistines are now so intimidated by the monotonous success of the avant-garde, from Flaubert and Manet on, together with the equally monotonous defeat of one generation after another of well-entrenched, self-confident philistines, that they now accept almost anything with pretensions to being "serious" and "advanced." This process may be seen clearly in the cinema, where the gale of new avant-garde has pulled along in its wake all kinds of debris.

Jonas Mekas is editor of *Film Culture,* movie columnist of *The Village Voice,* and patron saint of the New American Cinema, from which I'm still hoping for something Cinematic, whether New or American. I write "saint" without irony: he is dedicated, selfless, and courageous. He has recently invited martyrdom by exhibiting two sexually explicit, and perverse, movies, Smith's *Flaming Creatures* and Genet's *Un Chant d'Amour;* the New York cops have accepted the invitation and have arrested him. The films seemed to me artistic rather than pornographic in intention, but intention is not execution and I don't see how one could honestly testify in court that either was of much artistic value. Like the Beat littérateurs, the moviemakers of the New American Cinema are moralists rather than artists. After the showing of *Flaming Creatures,* one of them denounced me as a stuffed shirt—another one thought my trouble was that nobody over forty could possibly understand it—because I insisted it was monotonous and unimaginative. "You'll see," he predicted. "In ten years there'll be intercourse on the screen!" As I said, they're primarily interested in morals.

Guns of the Trees

Mr. Mekas's first movie, *Guns of the Trees,* was billed by Cinema 16 as "controversial . . . the best-loved or most-hated film on this year's program." I detect a note of desperation here: when an entrepreneur so advertises a cultural product, one suspects the first reactions have been hostile, as in the case of *Les Liaisons Dangereuses* (see below) which got adverse notices—Brendan Gill's rave in *The New Yorker* is currently displayed in lonely splendor in front of the theatre—and whose promoters were reduced to running one of those pro-and-con ads with an exhortation to the public to decide for themselves. Flattering, but why don't they ever ask us to decide about hits?

Guns of the Trees got off to a good start with an impassioned leaflet by its creator which I read with nervous appreciation (will I dig it? am I a square?) before the house lights went down. It was headed, with a jaunty echo of dry-cleaning establishments, "WHILE-U-WAIT," and its text raised considerable expectations. In the interests of cultural history, I reproduce the salient passages:

"There is no story. Telling stories is for peaceful and content people. And at this juncture of my life I am neither content nor peaceful. I am deeply and totally discontent. Do I have to list the reasons why? Haven't you read your *Times* and your *Pravda* today? Why do you wonder, then, that poets are beginning to get uneasy?

"Yes, the artists are abandoning the beautiful, happy, entertaining, self-glorifying stories. They are beginning to express their anxiety in a more open and direct manner. They are searching for a freer form, one which permits them a larger scale of emotional statements, explosions of truths, outcries of warnings, accumulations of images—not to carry out an amusing story but to fully express the tremblings of the consciousness of man, to confront us eye-to-eye with the soul of modern man. . . .

"It's not through the mind and order that I create. I create through my ignorance and chaos. Order doesn't interest me. I know that through my chaos I have a chance of arriving somewhere, of catching some secret movements of the subconscious, of Life, of Man. . . .

"It is from this anxiety that my discontent grows. And I am throwing it against all those who are for death. It is not that I believe in changing them. They are perhaps not even worth saving, not worth the breath of a single flower trampled under their Power. It's only that my patience has run out. It's only that I had to make this gesture of solidarity for those who think and feel the same way I do, are angry about the same things I am—for all the others my film will have no meaning. My film is only a letter of solidarity to the friends of an existential discontent, no matter in what continent, what country —a letter from the mad heart of the insane world, WHILE-U-WAIT."

Then the film began. George Jean Nathan once wrote a

piece about the opening of the Paramount Theatre in New
York circa 1926. He described in detail the platoons of
epauletted, cloaked, shakoed ushers, the spotlights and the
red carpets, the hand-painted oil paintings that lined the walls
(they still do), the Baroque profusion of the gold-leafed interior, the stupendous obligato on the mighty Wurlitzer organ,
and then—I quote from memory—"the great golden curtains
parted and we saw a movie in which a floozy seduced a bond
salesman." Such, *toute proportion gardée*, was my reaction to
Guns of the Trees after reading Mr. Mekas's eloquent leaflet.

I expected something profound and difficult. What I got
was two contrasting love stories which were all too easily
followed (once one got used to avant-garde cutting) since
they represented Good and Bad, Creative and Destructive,
Life and Death, or, existentially speaking, Authentic and In-
authentic. The Creative, Authentic, etc., couple was colored,
the Destructive, etc., couple was white. "The small people
don't learn," says the Negro girl, who was embarrassingly
smug, to the tense white girl, who later kills herself, "but
people like you and me should learn from everything." (This
is the Salinger complex, the We Happy Few syndrome.) This
labored fable takes place in a welter of "avant-garde" effects
that don't come off, as in the stylized mimes that open and
close the film. The settings were grimly "realistic," in the
mode that I remember from similar art-film efforts in the
Thirties: railroad yards, city dumps, crumbling walls and
alleyways, frowzy parks, kitchens that could do with a little
dishwashing. Shot 210 is described in the script as: "Somewhere in the Bronx. A field of broken glass, junk, sun—Gregory walks across the junkyard, slowly, looking down, black."
Meanwhile, back at the dump. . . .

All that is spontaneous in *Pull My Daisy* is self-conscious
here; Ginsberg is inferior to Kerouac as a narrator because he
is really rhetorical while Kerouac is mock-rhetorical; here Ginsberg alternates with folk songs, the last refuge of the American
left; he is too pompous and they are too simple. All those
MacLeishian questions: "What is man?" "Perhaps just to be."
"Will it ever change?" No reply from Ben Carruthers's co-
star, Adolfas Mekas, Jonas's brother, who is perhaps the most
stolid movie actor since Francis X. Bushman.

The symbol of police brutality is some cops timidly pushing
around folk-singers in Washington Square—maybe Eleanor

Roosevelt or the New York *Post* will object; in the Thirties the cops were, with not too much hyperbole, called "Cossacks" and they really roughed up Communist demonstrators in Union Square; a clear gain in civil liberties, but not much of a symbol of Power trampling underfoot those Flowers of Life. Sorry, forgot the climactic expression of rebellion: Carruthers pissing on my bank—Manufacturers Hanover Trust Company branch at Fifth Avenue and 43rd Street—or, to be accurate, *almost* pissing on it; he gets his fly open, but he is drunk and his pals lead him away before the awful deed is done.

Gregory (Francis X. Mekas) has a big scene with a "social worker"—the quotes are in the script, perhaps to imply that the "social worker" is not a social worker really though why it's not bad enough to be actually a social worker I don't see— which runs as follows: (Gregory speaking) "There is nothing wrong with Fidel Castro." "You compare yourself with Fidel Castro?" "No, I identify with him." "You realize Fidel Castro is a revolutionary. Are you revolting against something?" "Yes I am." "What are you revolting against?" (TV scripts run on this way but at least it's from hunger.) "Against dishonesty, corruption." "What do you want? To change the world? Is that your idea?" "I think everybody wants to change the world, no?" There then comes a blank white screen, which is Mr. Mekas's ingenious transition device, after which we hear the portentous tones of Mr. Ginsberg:

"What do you think of America? You who run America, vote hypocrite, edit school books, make foreign wars, appoint aldermen and football coaches?

"You who therefore are America, the land that opens its mouth to speak with four hundred billion dollars of armaments and two cents' worth of measly foreign aid [anybody checked these figures?] all for bombs and horror, fraud, dope fiends, Syngman Rhee, Batista, Chiang Kai-shek, madmen, Franco— who else God knows. I refuse to read the paper."

This is cut into (shot 187): "Frances, somewhere in the fields, standing by a pile of burning autumn leaves." So even that most charming and nostalgic ceremony of American life is twisted into an emblem of our allegedly death-oriented society.

Instead of transitional music, Mr. Mekas uses an electronic squeak of varying pitch. Very avant-garde but after a while it gets on one's nerves just like Hollywood's mood music. But he does score one coup: he has dug up from somewhere a line that still haunts me: "Where are the snows of yesteryear?" Now where could he have found *that*?

Hallelujah the Hills

Adolfas Mekas, with brother Jonas as assistant director, has made a feature-length comedy that might be called Variations on Themes from Mack Sennett. Despite its avant-garde provenance, and despite a record number of "in" spoofs of and allusions to other movies, I didn't like it.

(1) The performers mugged it up amateurishly, their efforts at improvisation being especially painful since they had no technique, unlike Sennett's comedians who were either trained by him in a style as formalized as classical ballet or else, like Keaton and Chaplin, had learned their trade in such rigorously disciplined schools as the American vaudeville and English music hall. The male leads, Peter Beard and Marty Greenbaum, substituted vigor for skill, like musclebound wrestlers trying out for Balanchine. This must have been the director's fault, since Jerome Raphael, who was so good as Solly in *The Connection*, comes out here unintentionally oafish —and as nervously uncertain as the others.

(2) This kind of zany comedy, as Sennett knew very well, needs a strongly accented rhythm and a clear form precisely because it is so freewheeling. For the same reason, it needs a counterpoint of reality—what could be more prosaic than a policeman, the raw material of a Keystone cop? But here the opposite: formless, unrelieved fantasy. I left after the first hour, when I finally realized that literally anything could happen next, since there were no limitations, either realistic or artificial. Infinity in art is boring.

(3) I don't think it is necessarily funny for a comedian to trip himself and fall down, not even when he does it five times in rapid succession, not even when he is bare-assed. Nor do I think it a sure laugh if he squeezes his face out of shape against a windowpane, nor if he crams food overflowingly into his mouth at a Thanksgiving dinner (two comedians doing it are twice as unamusing). The food cramming, I suppose, was suggested by Chaplin's force-feeding by the machine in *Modern Times*, but that was part of a satiric idea and

was also executed with style, timing, and other technical graces.

Except for Ed Emshwiller's superb photography, *Hallelujah the Hills* is worth noticing only because of its *succès d'estime.* (I doubt audiences liked it—embarrassingly few laughs at the show I attended.) Ever on the alert for the latest thing in the *faux bon,* the Lucepapers puffed it in *Time* and huffed it in that double issue of *Life* devoted to the movies which was as appetizing as a double portion of cotton candy, though not as nutritious. It was invited to more international film festivals last year than any other American movie, and by now has opened in Paris, Milan, London, Amsterdam, etc. As an American cultural export it has been received with the same mixture of romantic illusion and condescension as greeted Pocahontas and Buffalo Bill. "One of the most completely American films ever made, in its combination of anarchistic wackiness with a nostalgic sense of the lost frontier and the magic of youth" (*Sight and Sound,* London). "Imagine a combination of *Huckleberry Finn, Pull My Daisy,* the Marx Brothers, and the complete works of Douglas Fairbanks, Mary Pickford, and D. W. Griffith, and you've got it . . . deliriously funny and ravishingly lyrical" (*The Guardian,* London). The Parisian press was, predictably, even sillier; the French love their fantasy image of us, compounded of Al Capone and the Cisco Kid, almost as much as they hate our reality. "Love and knowledge of the cinema enabled Mekas to go beyond everything that the art of the film has achieved until now" (*Le Figaro Littéraire*). "The young American cinema has never before shown us such spontaneity, such clarity, such health. . . . It is a film where the god Pan still lives. He wanders through the hills and, once again, everything sings" (*Arts;* don't know about Pan but "the young American cinema" is an interesting formulation; thought we all started equal there, at least, and indeed that its oldest old master was our own D. W. Griffith). ". . . a true joy for the spectator who can relax and curl up voluptuously in his theatre seat as if it were the couch of a hashish smoker" (*France-Observateur;* and maybe some pot would help, popcorn is definitely not enough). "*Hallelujah the Hills* has the charm of conserving its tonic effect when the immediate pleasure has passed; it attains in each of us some secret prolongation, beyond fantasy and simple amusement" (*Le Monde*). I offer this last, from a normally sober journal,

as an all-purpose sentence for aspiring movie critics, though it
probably wouldn't work in English.

The note seems forced. These rhapsodies are in fact conditioned reflexes triggered by some chic stimuli the Mekas
brothers have been lucky or shrewd enough to hit on: Experiment, Improvisation, Wild & Woolly America, the Cult of
Cinema, and that Nostalgia for Slapstick which includes them
all. At the preview, it was preceded by "a recently discovered
Mack Sennett short" that I thought might have been left in
oblivion. (Dare one say that a Sennett comedy can be un-
funny? Homer nodded, it was said, but that was before *auteur*
criticism. Now it must be revised: Homer nods, but Hitchcock
doesn't.) Still, hastily botched together as it was, I thought it
more satisfying than the self-conscious pastiche that followed;
it had at least the interest of a period piece. In February 1962,
I reviewed a similar pastiche, Louis Malle's *Zazie*. That was a
far more skillful effort and it even had a few laughs, but it
split on the same rock: History. "A man cannot become a
child again, he can merely become childish," I wrote then.
"The Sennett-Keaton-Chaplin world is gone; it is part of the
childhood of the cinema. *Zazie* faithfully reproduces it in all
its externals, but it misses the innocence and spontaneity and
lack of self-consciousness that make these externals charming.
And funny." I think it was Heraclitus who observed that you
can't step in the same river twice.

JACK SMITH'S *FLAMING CREATURES*

by Susan Sontag

*This early appreciation of the work of Jack Smith was written
in 1964. It first appeared in* The Nation *and was reprinted in
Miss Sontag's collection of critical essays* Against Interpretation *(New York: Farrar, Straus & Giroux, 1966). She is also
the author of two novels,* The Benefactor *and* Death Kit.

Today, Flaming Creatures *is generally considered one of
the outstanding documents of the independent cinema move-*

ment in America. Susan Sontag's article is a highly perceptive critique of this film.

The only thing to be regretted about the close-ups of limp penises and bouncing breasts, the shots of masturbation and oral sexuality, in Jack Smith's *Flaming Creatures* is that they make it hard simply to talk about this remarkable film; one has to *defend* it. But in defending as well as talking about the film, I don't want to make it seem less outrageous, less shocking than it is. For the record: in *Flaming Creatures,* a couple of women and a much larger number of men, most of them clad in flamboyant thrift-shop women's clothes, frolic about, pose and posture, dance with one another, enact various scenes of voluptuousness, sexual frenzy, romance, and vampirism—to the accompaniment of a sound track which includes some Latin pop favorite (*Siboney, Amapola*), rock 'n' roll, scratchy violin playing, bullfight music, a Chinese song, the text of a wacky ad for a new brand of "heart-shaped lipstick" being demonstrated on the screen by a host of men, some in drag and some not, and the chorale of flutey shrieks and screams which accompany the group rape of a bosomy young woman, rape happily converting itself into an orgy. Of course, *Flaming Creatures* is outrageous, and intends to be. The very title tells us that.

As it happens, *Flaming Creatures* is not pornographic, if pornography be defined as the manifest intention and capacity to excite sexually. The depiction of nakedness and various sexual embraces (with the notable omission of straight screwing) is both too full of pathos and too ingenuous to be prurient. Rather than being sentimental or lustful, Smith's images of sex are alternately childlike and witty.

The police hostility to *Flaming Creatures* is not hard to understand. It is, alas, inevitable that Smith's film will have to fight for its life in the courts. What is disappointing is the indifference, the squeamishness, the downright hostility to the film evinced by almost everyone in the mature intellectual and artistic community. Almost its only supporters are a loyal coterie of filmmakers, poets, and young "Villagers." *Flaming Creatures* has not yet graduated from being a cult object, the prize exhibit of the New American Cinema group whose house organ is the magazine *Film Culture*. Everyone should be

Jack Smith: From *Flaming Creatures*, 1963

grateful to Jonas Mekas, who almost singlehandedly, with tenacity and even heroism, has made it possible to see Smith's film and many other new works. Yet it must be admitted that the pronouncements of Mekas and his entourage are shrill and often positively alienating. It is absurd of Mekas to argue that this new group of films, which includes *Flaming Creatures*, is a totally unprecedented departure in the history of cinema. Such truculence does Smith a disservice, making it unnecessarily hard to grasp what is of merit in *Flaming Creatures*. For *Flaming Creatures* is a small but valuable work in a particular tradition, the poetic cinema of shock. In this tradition are to be found Buñuel's *Un Chien Andalou* and *L'Age d'Or*, parts of Eisenstein's first film, *Strike*, Tod Browning's *Freaks*, Jean Rouch's *Les Maîtres-Fous*, Franju's *Le Sang des Bêtes*, Lenica's *Labyrinth*, the films of Kenneth Anger (*Fireworks*, *Scorpio Rising*), and Noël Burch's *Noviciat*.

The older avant-garde filmmakers in America (Maya Deren, James Broughton, Kenneth Anger) turned out short films which were technically quite studied. Given their very low budgets, the color, camera work, acting, and synchronization of image and sound were as professional as possible. The hallmark of one of the two new avant-garde styles in American cinema (Jack Smith, Ron Rice, *et al.*, but not Gregory Markopoulos or Stan Brakhage) is its willful technical crudity. The newer films—both the good ones and the poor, uninspired work—show a maddening indifference to every element of technique, a studied primitiveness. This is a very contemporary style, and very American. Nowhere in the world has the old cliché of European romanticism—the assassin mind versus the spontaneous heart—had such a long career as in America. Here, more than anywhere else, the belief lives on that neatness and carefulness of technique interfere with spontaneity, with truth, with immediacy. Most of the prevailing techniques (for even to be against technique demands a technique) of avant-garde art express this conviction. In music, there is aleatory performance now as well as composition, and new sources of sound and new ways of mutilating the old instruments; in painting and sculpture, there is the favoring of impermanent or found materials, and the transformation of objects into perishable (use-once-and-throw-away) environments or "Happenings." In its own way *Flaming Creatures* illustrates this snobbery about the coherence and technical finish of the work of art. There is, of course, no story in *Flaming Creatures,* no development, no necessary order of the seven (as I count them) clearly separable sequences of the film. One can easily doubt that a certain piece of footage was indeed intended to be overexposed. Of no sequence is one convinced that it had to last this long, and not longer or shorter. Shots aren't framed in the traditional way; heads are cut off; extraneous figures sometimes appear on the margin of the scene. The camera is hand-held most of the time, and the image often quivers (where this is wholly effective, and no doubt deliberate, is in the orgy sequence).

But in *Flaming Creatures,* amateurishness of technique is not frustrating, as it is in so many other recent "underground" films. For Smith is visually very generous; at practically every moment there is simply a tremendous amount to see on the screen. And then, there is an extraordinary charge and beauty to his images, even when the effect of the strong ones is weakened by the ineffective ones, the ones that might have been better through planning. Today indifference to technique is often accompanied by bareness; the modern revolt against calculation in art often takes the form of aesthetic asceticism. (Much of Abstract Expressionist painting has this ascetic quality.) *Flaming Creatures,* though, issues from a different aesthetic: it is crowded with visual material. There are no ideas, no symbols, no commentary on or critique of anything in *Flaming Creatures.* Smith's film is strictly a treat for the senses. In this it is the very opposite of a "literary" film (which is what so many French avant-garde films were). It is not in the knowing about, or being able to interpret, what one sees, that the pleasure of *Flaming Creatures* lies; but in the directness, the power, and the lavish quantity of the images themselves. Unlike most serious modern art, this work is not about the frustrations of consciousness, the dead ends of the self. Thus Smith's crude technique serves, beautifully, the sensibility embodied in *Flaming Creatures*—a sensibility which disclaims ideas, which situates itself beyond negation.

Flaming Creatures is that rare modern work of art: it is about joy and innocence. To be sure, this joyousness, this innocence is composed out of themes which are—by ordinary standards—perverse, decadent, at the least highly theatrical and artificial. But this, I think, is precisely how the film comes by its beauty and modernity. *Flaming Creatures* is a lovely specimen of what currently, in one genre, goes by the flippant name of "Pop art." Smith's film has the sloppiness, the arbitrariness, the looseness of Pop art. It also has Pop art's gaiety, its ingenuousness, it exhilarating freedom from moralism. One great virtue of the Pop-art movement is the way it blasts through the old imperative about taking a *position* toward one's subject matter. (Needless to say, I'm not denying that there are certain events about which it is necessary to take a position. An extreme instance of a work of art dealing with such events is *The Deputy*. All I'm saying is that there are some elements of life—above all, sexual pleasure—about which it isn't necessary to have a position.) The best works among those that are called Pop art intend, precisely, that we abandon the old task of always either approving or disapproving of what is depicted in art—or, by extension, experienced in life. (This is why those who dismiss Pop art as a symptom of a new conformism, a cult of acceptance of the artifacts of mass civilization, are being obtuse.) Pop art lets in wonderful and new mixtures of attitude, which would before have seemed contradictions. Thus *Flaming Creatures* is a brilliant spoof of sex and at the same time full of the lyricism of erotic impulse. Simply in a visual sense, too, it is full of contradictions. Very studied visual effects (lacy textures, falling flowers, tableaux) are introduced into disorganized, clearly improvised scenes in which bodies, some shapely and convincingly feminine and others scrawny and hairy, tumble, dance, make love.

One can regard Smith's film as having, for its subject, the poetry of transvestitism. *Film Culture,* in awarding *Flaming Creatures* its Fifth Independent Film Award, said of Smith: "He has struck us with not the mere pity or curiosity of the perverse, but the glory, the pageantry of Transylvestia and the magic of Fairyland. He has lit up a part of life, although it is a part which most men scorn." The truth is that *Flaming Creatures* is much more about intersexuality than about homosexuality. Smith's vision is akin to the vision in Bosch's paintings of a paradise and a hell of writhing, shameless, ingenious bodies. Unlike those serious and stirring films about the beauties and terrors of homoerotic love, Kenneth Anger's *Fireworks* and Genet's *Un Chant d'Amour*, the important fact about the figures in Smith's film is that one cannot easily tell which are men and which are women. These are "creatures," flaming out in intersexual, polymorphous joy. The film is built out of a complex web of ambiguities and ambivalences, whose primary image is the confusion of male and female flesh. The shaken breast and the shaken penis become interchangeable with each other.

Bosch constructed a strange, aborted, ideal nature against which he situated his nude figures, his androgynous visions of pain and pleasure. Smith has no literal background (it's hard to tell in the film whether one is indoors or outdoors), but instead the thoroughly artificial and invented landscape of costume, gesture, and music. The myth of intersexuality is played out against a background of banal songs, ads, clothes, dances, and above all, the repertory of fantasy drawn from corny movies. The texture of *Flaming Creatures* is made up of a rich collage of "camp" lore: a woman in white (a transvestite) with drooping head holding a stalk of lilies; a gaunt woman seen emerging from a coffin, who turns out to be a vampire and, eventually, male; a marvelous Spanish dancer (also a transvestite) with huge dark eyes, black lace mantilla and fan; a tableau from the *Shiek of Araby*, with reclining men in burnooses and an Arab temptress stolidly exposing one breast; a scene between two women, reclining on flowers and rags, which recalls the dense, crowded texture of the movies in which Sternberg directed Dietrich in the early thirties. The vocabulary of images and textures on which Smith draws includes pre-Raphaelite languidness; Art Nouveau; the great exotica styles of the twenties, the Spanish and the Arab; and the modern "camp" way of relishing mass culture.

Flaming Creatures is a triumphant example of an aesthetic vision of the world—and such a vision is perhaps always, at its core, epicene. But this type of art has yet to be understood in this country. The space in which *Flaming Creatures* moves is not the space of moral ideas, which is where American critics have traditionally located art. What I am urging is that there is not only moral space, by whose laws *Flaming Creatures* would indeed come off badly; there is also aesthetic space, the space of pleasure. Here Smith's film moves and has its being.

THE CAMERA EYE—MY EYE *

by Stan Brakhage

Stan Brakhage has been making experimental films since the early 1950's. His first works were, in the words of P. Adams Sitney, "in the part-neo-realist-and-part-dream-vision-psycho-dramatical genre." Since his marriage in 1958, Brakhage's films have developed as a mythopoeic exploration of his relationship with his wife and children.

The following essay is excerpted from Metaphors on Vision, *a long aesthetic statement by Brakhage to which* Film Culture *devoted its entire issue for Fall, 1963.*

Imagine an eye unruled by man-made laws of perspective, an eye unprejudiced by compositional logic, an eye which does not respond to the name of everything but which must know each object encountered in life through an adventure of perception. How many colors are there in a field of grass to the crawling baby unaware of "Green?" How many rainbows can light create for the untutored eye? How aware of variations in heat waves can that eye be? Imagine a world alive with incomprehensible objects and shimmering with an endless variety of movement and innumerable gradations of color. Imagine a world before the "beginning was the word."

To see is to retain—to behold. Elimination of all fear is in sight—which must be aimed for. Once vision may have been given—that which seems inherent in the infant's eye, an eye which reflects the loss of innocence more eloquently than any other human feature, an eye which soon learns to classify sights, an eye which mirrors the movement of the individual toward death by its increasing inability to see.

But one can never go back, not even in imagination. After the loss of innocence, only the ultimate of knowledge can

* This material has been excerpted from *Metaphors on Vision* by Stan Brakhage, New York: A Film Culture Book, 1963.

balance the wobbling pivot. Yet I suggest that there is a pursuit of knowledge foreign to language and founded upon visual communication, demanding a development of the optical mind, and dependent upon perception in the original and deepest sense of the word.

Suppose the Vision of the saint and the artist to be an increased ability to see—vision. Allow so-called hallucination to enter the realm of perception, allowing that mankind always finds derogatory terminology for that which doesn't appear to be readily usable, accept dream visions, day-dreams or nightdreams, as you would so-called real scenes, even allowing that abstractions which move so dynamically when closed eyelids are pressed are actually perceived. Become aware of the fact that you are not only influenced by the visual phenomenon which you are focused upon and attempt to sound the depths of all visual influence. There is no need for the mind's eye to be deadened after infancy, yet in these times the development of visual understanding is almost universally forsaken.

This is an age which has no symbol for death other than the skull and bones of one stage of decomposition . . . and it is an age which lives in fear of total annihilation. It is a time haunted by sexual sterility yet almost universally incapable of perceiving the phallic nature of every destructive manifestation of itself. It is an age which artificially seeks to project itself materialistically into abstract space and to fulfill itself mechanically because it has blinded itself to almost all external reality within eyesight and to the organic awareness of even the physical movement properties of its own perceptibility. The earliest cave paintings discovered demonstrate that primitive man had a greater understanding than we do that the object of fear must be objectified. The entire history of erotic magic is one of possession of fear thru holding it. The ultimate searching visualization has been directed toward God out of the deepest possible human understanding that there can be no ultimate love where there is fear. Yet in this contemporary time how many of us even struggle to deeply perceive our own children?

The artist has carried the tradition of vision and visualization down through the ages. In the present time a very few have continued the process of visual perception in its deepest sense and transformed their inspirations into cinematic experiences. They create a new language made possible by the moving picture image. They create where fear before them has created the greatest necessity. They are essentially preoccupied by and deal imagistically with—birth, sex, death, and the search for God.

The Camera Eye

O transparent hallucination, superimposition of image, mirage of movement, heroine of a thousand and one nights (Scheherazade must surely be the muse of this art), you obstruct the light, muddy the pure white-beaded screen (it perspires) with your shuffling patterns. Only the spectators (the unbelievers who attend the carpeted temples where coffee and paintings are served) think your spirit is in the illuminated occasion (mistaking your sweaty, flaring, rectangular body for more than it is). The devout, who break popcorn together in your humblest double-feature services, know that you are still being born, search for your spirit in their dreams, and dare only dream when in contact with your electrical reflection. Unknowingly, as innocent, they await the priests of this new religion, those who can stir cinematic entrails divinely. They await the prophets who can cast (with the precision of Confucian sticks) the characters of this new order across filmic mud. Being innocent, they do not consciously know that this church too is corrupt; but they react with counter-hallucinations, believing in the stars, and themselves among these Los Angelic orders. Of themselves, they will never recognize what they are awaiting. Their footsteps, the dumb drum which destroys cinema. They are having the dream piped into their homes, the destruction of the romance thru marriage, etc.

So the money vendors have been at it again. To the catacombs then, or rather plant this seed deeper in the undergrounds beyond false nourishing of sewage waters. Let it draw nourishment from hidden uprising springs channeled by gods. Let there be no cavernous congregation but only the network of individual channels, that narrowed vision which splits beams beyond rainbow and into the unknown dimensions. (To those who think this is waxing poetic, squint, give the visual objects at hand their freedom, and allow the distant to come to you; and when mountains are moving, you will find no fat in this prose.) Forget ideology, for film unborn as it is has no language and speaks like an aborigine—monotonous rhetoric. Abandon aesthetics—the moving picture image without religious foundations, let alone the cathedral, the art form, starts its search for God with only the danger of accepting an architectural inheritance from the categorized "seven," other arts its sins, and closing its circle, stylistic circle, therefore zero. Negate technique, for film, like America, has not been discovered yet, and mechanization, in the deepest possible sense of the word, traps both beyond measuring even chances—chances are these twined searches may someday orbit about the same central negation. Let film be. It is something . . . becoming. (The above being for creator and spectator alike in searching, an ideal of anarchic religion where all are priests both giving and receiving, or rather witch doctors, or better witches, or . . . O, for the unnamable.)

And here, somewhere, we have an eye (I'll speak for myself) capable of any imagining (the only reality). And there (right there) we have the camera eye (the limitation, the original liar); yet lyre sings to the mind so immediately (the exalted selectivity one wants to forget) that its strings can so easily make puppetry of human motivation (for form as finality) dependent upon attunation, what it's turned to (ultimately death) or turned from (birth) or the way to get out of it (transformation). I'm not just speaking of that bird on fire (not thinking of circles) or of Spengler (spirals neither) or of any known progression (nor straight lines) logical formation (charted levels) or ideological formation (mapped for scenic points of interest); but I am speaking for possibilities (myself), infinite possibilities (preferring chaos).

And here, somewhere, we have an eye capable of any imagining. And then we have the camera eye, its lenses ground to achieve 19th-century Western compositional perspective (as best exemplified by the 19th-century architectural conglomeration of details of the "classic" ruin) in bending the light and limiting the frame of the image just so, its standard camera and projector speed for recording movement geared to the feeling of the ideal slow Viennese waltz, and even its tripod head, being the neck it swings on, balled with bearings to permit it that Les Sylphides motion (ideal to the contemplative romantic and virtually restricted to horizontal and vertical movements (pillars and horizon lines) a diagonal requiring a major adjustment, its lenses coated or provided with filters, its light meters balanced, and its color film manufactured, to produce that picture post card effect (salon painting) exemplified by those oh so blue skies and peachy skins.

By deliberately spitting on the lens or wrecking its focal intention, one can achieve the early stages of impressionism. One can make this prima donna heavy in performance of image movement by speeding up the motor, or one can break up movement, in a way that approaches a more direct inspiration of contemporary human eye perceptibility of movement, by slowing the motion while recording the image. One may hand hold the camera and inherit worlds of space. One may over- or under-expose the film. One may use the filters of the world, fog, downpours, unbalanced lights, neons with neurotic color temperatures, glass which was never designed for a camera, or even glass which was but which can be used against specifications, or one may photograph an hour after sunrise or an hour before sunset, those marvelous taboo hours when the film labs will guarantee nothing, or one may go into the night with a specified daylight film or vice versa. One may become the supreme trickster, with hatfuls of all the rabbits listed above breeding madly. One may, out of incredible courage, become Méliès, that marvelous man who gave even the "art of the film" its beginning in magic. Yet Méliès was not witch, witch doctor, priest, or even sorcerer. He was a nineteenth-century stage magician. His films *are* rabbits.

What about the hat? the camera? or if you will, the stage, the page, the ink, the hieroglyphic itself, the pigment shaping that original drawing, the musical and/or all other instruments for copula-and-then-procreation? Kurt Sachs talks sex (which fits the hat neatly) in originating musical instruments, and Freud's revitalization of symbol charges all contemporary content in art. Yet possession through visualization speaks for fear-of-death as motivating force—the tomb art of the Egyptian, etc. And then there's "in the beginning," "Once upon a time," or the very concept of a work of art being a "Creation." Religious motivation only reaches us through the anthropologist these days—viz., Frazer on a golden bough. And so it goes—ring around the rosary, beating about the bush, describing. One thread runs clean through the entire fabric of expression—the trick-and-effect. And between those two words, somewhere, magic . . . the brush of angel wings, even rabbits

leaping heavenwards and, given some direction, language
corresponding. Dante looks upon the face of God and Rilke is
head among the angelic orders. Still the Night Watch was
tricked by Rembrandt and Pollock was out to produce an
effect. The original world was a trick, and so were all the
rules of the game that followed in its wake. Whether the
instrument be musical or otherwise, it's still a hat with
more rabbits yet inside the head wearing it—i.e., thought's
trick, etc. Even The Brains for whom thought's the world, and
the word and visi-or-audibility of it, eventually end with a
ferris wheel of a solar system in the middle of the amusement
park of the universe. They know it without experiencing it,
screw it lovelessly, find "trick" or "effect" derogatory terminology, too close for comfort, are utterly unable to comprehend
"magic." We are either experiencing (copulating) or conceiving (procreating) or very rarely both are balancing in
that moment of living, loving, and creating, giving and receiving, which is so close to the imagined divine as to be more
unmentionable than "magic."

In the event you didn't know "magic" is realmed in "the
imaginable," the moment of it being when that which is
imagined dies, is penetrated by mind and known rather than
believed in. Thus "reality" extends its picketing fence and
each is encouraged to sharpen his wits. The artist is one who
leaps that fence at night, scatters his seeds among the cab-
bages, hybrid seeds inspired by both the garden and wits-
end forest where only fools and madmen wander, seeds needing several generations to be . . . finally proven edible. Until
then they remain invisible, to those with both feet on the
ground, yet prominent enough to be tripped over. Yes, those
unsightly bulges between those oh so even rows will find their
flowering moment . . . and then be farmed. Are you really
thrilled at the sight of a critic tentatively munching arti-
chokes? Wouldn't you rather throw overalls in the eventual
collegic chowder? Realize the garden as you will—the growing
is mostly underground. Whatever daily care you may give it
—all is planted only by moonlight. However you remember
it—everything in it originates elsewhere. As for the unquotable
magic—it's as indescribable as the unbound woods it comes
from.

(A foot-on-the-ground-note: The sketches of T. E. Lawrence's "realist" artist companion were scratches to Lawrence's

Arab friends. Flaherty's motion picture projection of *Nanock
of the North* was only a play of lights and silhouettes to the
Aleutian Islander Nanook himself. The schizophrenic does see
symmetrically, does believe in the reality of Rorschach, yet he
will not yield to the suggestion that a pin-point light in a
darkened room will move, being the only one capable of
perceiving its status correctly. Question any child as to his
drawing and he will defend the "reality" of what you claim
"scribbles." Answer any child's question and he will shun
whatever quest he'd been beginning.)

Light, lens concentrated, either burns negative film to a
chemical crisp which, when lab washed, exhibits the blackened
pattern of its ruin or, reversal film, scratches the emulsion to
eventually bleed it white. Light, again lens concentrated,
pierces white and casts its shadow-patterned self to reflect
upon the spectator. When light strikes a color emulsion, multiple chemical layers restrict its various wave lengths, restrain
its bruises to eventually produce a phenomenon unknown to
dogs. Don't think of creatures of uncolored vision as restricted,
but wonder, rather, and marvel at the known internal mirrors
of the cat which catch each spark of light in the darkness and
reflect it to an intensification. Speculate as to insect vision,
such as the bee's sense of scent thru ultraviolet perceptibility.
To search for human visual realities, man must, as in all other
homo motivation, transcend the original physical restrictions
and inherit worlds of eyes. The very narrow contemporary
moving visual reality is exhausted. The belief in the sacredness
of any man-achievement sets concrete about it, statutes becoming statues, needing both explosives and earthquakes for
disruption. As to the permanency of the present or any established reality, consider in this light and through most individual eyes that without either illumination or photographic
lens, any ideal animal might claw the black off a strip of film
or walk ink-footed across transparent celluloid and produce
an effect for projection identical to a photographed image. As
to color, the earliest color films were entirely hand painted
a frame at a time. The "absolute realism" of the motion picture image is a human invention.

What reflects from the screen is shadow play. Look, there's
no real rabbit. Those ears are index fingers and the nose a
knuckle interfering with the light. If the eye were more perceptive it would see the sleight [of hand] of 24 individual pic-

tures and an equal number of utter blacknesses every second of
the show. What incredible films might ultimately be made for
such an eye. But the machine has already been fashioned to
outwit even that perceptibility, a projector which flashes adver-
tisement at subliminal speed to up the sale of popcorn. Oh,
slow-eyed spectator, this machine is grinding you out of
existence, its electrical storms are manufactured by pure white
frames interrupting the flow of the photographed images, its
real tensions are a dynamic interplay of two-dimensional
shapes and lines, the horizon line and background shapes
battering the form of the horseback rider as the camera moves
with it, the curves of the tunnel exploding away from the
pursued, camera following, and tunnel perspective converging
on the pursuer, camera preceding, the dream of the close-up
kiss being due to the linear purity of facial features after
cluttersome background, the entire film's soothing syrup being
the depressant of imagistic repetition a feeling akin to counting
sheep to sleep. Believe in it blindly, and it will fool you—
mind wise, instead of sequins on cheesecloth or max-manu-
factured make-up, you'll see stars. Believe in it eye-wise, and
the very comet of its overhead throw from projector to screen
will intrigue you so deeply that its fingering play will move
integrally with what's reflected, a comet-tail integrity which
would lead back finally to the film's creator. I am meaning,
simply, that the rhythms of change in the beam of illumination
which now goes entirely over the heads of the audience would,
in the work of art, contain in itself some quality of a spiritual
experience. As is, and at best, that hand spreading its touch
toward the screen taps a neurotic chaos comparable to the
doodles it produces for reflection. The "absolute realism" of
the motion picture image is a twentieth-century, essentially
Western, illusion.

Nowhere in its mechanical process does the camera hold
either mirror or candle to nature. Consider its history. Being machine, it has always been manufacturer of the medium, mass-
producer of stilled abstract images, its virtue—related variance,
the result—movement. Essentially, it remains fabricator of a
visual language, no less a linguist than the typewriter. Yet
in the beginning, each of an audience thought himself the
camera, attending a play or, toward the end of the purely
camera career, being run over by the unedited filmic image
of a locomotive which had once rushed straight at the lens,

screaming when a revolver seemed fired straight out of the
screen, motion of picture being the original magic of the
medium. Méliès is credited with the first splice. Since then,
the strip of celluoid has increasingly revealed itself suited
to transformations beyond those conditioned by the camera.
Originally Méliès's trickery was dependent upon starting and
stopping the photographic mechanism and between times
creating, adding objects to its field of vision, transformations,
substituting one object for another, and disappearances, re-
moving the objectionable. Once the celluloid could be cut, the
editing of filmic images began its development toward Eisen-
steinian montage, the principal of 1 plus 2 making 3 in moving
imagery as anywhere else. Meantime labs came into the picture, playing with the illumination of original film, balancing
color temperature, juggling double imagery in superimposition,
adding all the acrobatic grammar of the film inspired by D. W.
Griffith's dance, fades to mark the montage-sentenced motion
picture paragraph, dissolves to indicate lapse of time between
interrelated subject matter, variations in the framing for the
epic horizontal composition, origin of Cinemascope, and vertical picture delineating character, or the circle exclamating a
pictorial detail, etc.
     The camera itself taken off the pedestal, began to move,
threading its way in and around its source of material for the
eventual intricately patterned fabric of the edited film. Yet
editing is still in its 1, 2, 3 infancy, and the labs are essentially
still just developing film, no less trapped by the standards
they're bearing than the camera by its original mechanical
determination. No very great effort has ever been made to
interrelate these two or three processes, and already another is
appearing possible, the projector as creative instrument with
the film show a kind of performance, celluloid or tape merely
source of material to the projectioning interpreter, this expression finding its origins in the color, or the scent, or even
the musical organ, its most recent manifestations—the increased programming potential of the IBM and other electronic
machines now capable of inventing imagery from scratch.
Considering then the camera eye as almost obsolete, it can at
last be viewed objectively and, perhaps, view-pointed with
subjective depth as never before. Its life is truly all before it.
The future fabricating machine in performance will invent
images as patterned after cliché vision as those of the camera,

and its results will suffer a similar claim to "realism," IBM being no more God nor even a "Thinking machine" than the camera eye all-seeing or capable of creative selectivity, both essentially restricted to "yes-no," "stop-go," "on-off," and instrumentally dedicated to communication of the simplest sort. Yet increased human intervention and control render any process more capable of balance between sub-and-objective expression, and between those two concepts, somewhere, soul. . . . The second stage of transformation of image editing revealed the magic of movement. Even though each in the audience then proceeded to believe himself part of the screen reflection, taking two-dimension visual characters as his being within the drama, he could not become every celluloid sight running through the projector, therefore allowance of another viewpoint, and no attempt to make him believe his eye to be where the camera eye once was has ever since proved successful—excepting the novelty of three-dimension, audiences jumping when rocks seemed to avalanche out of the screen and into the theatre. Most still imagine, however, the camera a recording mechanism, a lunatic mirroring, now full of sound and fury presenting its half of a symmetrical pattern, a kaleidoscope with the original pieces of glass missing and their movement removed in time. And the instrument is still capable of winning Stanford's bet about horse-hooves never all leaving the ground in galloping, though Stanford significantly enough used a number of still cameras with strings across the track and thus inaugurated the flip-pic of the penny arcade, Hollywood still racing after the horse. Only when the fans move on to another track can the course be cleared for this eye to interpret the very ground, perhaps to discover its non-solidity, to creat a contemporary Pegasus, without wings, to fly with its hooves, beyond any imagining, to become gallop, a creation. It can then inherit the freedom to agree or disagree with 2,000 years of Western equine painting and attain some comparable aesthetic stature. As is, the "absolute realism" of the motion picture image is a contemporary mechanical myth.

Consider this prodigy for its virtually untapped talents, viewpoints it possesses more readily recognizable as visually non-human yet within the realm of the humanly imaginable. I am speaking of its speed for receptivity which can slow the fastest motion for detailed study, or its ability to create a continuity for time compression, increasing the slowest motion to a comprehensibility. I am praising its cyclopean penetration of haze, its infra-red visual ability in darkness, its just developed 360-degree view, its prismatic revelation of rainbows, its zooming potential for exploding space and its telephotic compression of same to flatten perspective, its micro- and macroscopic revelations. I am marveling at its Schlaeran self capable of representing heat waves and the most invisible air pressures, and appraising its other still-camera developments which may grow into motion, its rendering visible the illumination of bodily heat, its transformation of ultra-violets to human cognizance, its penetrating X ray. I am dreaming of the mystery camera capable of graphically representing the form of an object after it's been removed from the photographic scene, etc. The "absolute realism" of the motion picture is unrealized, therefore potential, magic.

My Eye

My eye, tuning toward the imaginary, will go to any wavelengths for its sights. I'm writing of cognizance, mind's eye awareness of all addressing vibrations. What rays pass through this retina still unretained by mind? How long has sight's center continued pupil to other men's imaginings? This sensitive instrument must respond to all the gods who will deign to play upon it. Now as with the other four receptacles it too much fears The Devil, postulates "sights" as the end of its vibratory travels, remains bottled against any sinking, sticks to the surface to avoid ballooning into unfamiliar waves of unknown spaces, humanly preferring the certain breakers which will eventually shore it, scattering fragments, reflective surfaces, and magnifiers of a word here, and a moving picture there, of what was once an internal continuing composition. For the one sea, once seen, becomes a wavering weary-summation, dulls, palls receptivity to the distant surf hush, known Siren only when beyond all but a smashed salvation. Even the inside-out decomposes belief in the message heavenly destined for the sole comprehension of God-the-Beachcomber. Still, within these limitations, my eye begins a movement toward realms less imagined than the sands of heaven, risks more than ordinary flight, plots land escaping to a sub-terrain.

It all begins with the art, the necessity to create—for what? —that explanation changing time to Time, the young man dreaming of deification, not seeing himself as mere star— immortality rather casting his whole name in astral lights, spelled correctly for all time—beginning this pursuit patterned after others, in an essentially non-religious era "The Lives of the Artists" becoming initiates' Bible, all ending as youth loses sense of growth for ever, scents his decay, and comes to know, for all the remembering of him, he will die. In that instant he either falls spiritually on the spot or begins to bend at the knees. In anger at his uneternalness, that he'll never see his biography unless he autos it himself, the aesthete begins cocooning toward his innards by demanding immediate internal return, release in creation, self-knowledge, etc. When each expression refuses echo and he discovers art unmirrors, this budding Narcissus either builds a boat, sits banked waiting his reflection, or plunges in. From here on out all endeavor depends on depth, and all reasoning only confuses each issue. He exhausts excuses until each art work seems more sneeze than statement. His entire being becoming instrument for the expression of incomprehensible forces, he finds *these,* not *his,* expressions mold him after the fashion they will any attenuated audience. Being the medium, however, he's more familiar with the material than most, inherits worlds of words if poet, sounds if composer, etc., these gifts, given only when unasked after, exclude from the early epileptic "fall-out," the floater, and the reflective one. Yet all fall, the artist "in" and only surviving through a formal resistance granting the illusion of bottomless descent.

My eye, then, inspiraling, frictioning style-wise, being instrument for striking sparks, is bequeathed visions at every illumination it's struck to create. . . . Similar vistas being available to any viewer willing to release his eye for comparable movement. My eye so lost in space that fall feels ascensional, so style-beguiled as to know no "reality," sea running down-up hill willy-nilly, waves not known by their phosphorescence but through aesthetic reflection only . . . similar illuminations possible for any viewer capable of understanding his very vision as a metaphoric creation either directly inspired by nature or watered down by the cliché sights of others. My eye, again, then, beginning its non-color, life-giving, continually created coursing, follows rainbows, no thoughts of a pot of gold allowed the mind, pursuing light, seeking to stare straight into the sun, yet humbly shunning no reflections, searching even electrical filaments, all fires. A bent black tube, toy spectroscope, broke up a light beam to shelve the colors in very neat rows for formal introduction, as lacking-daisical and hypocritical as histories on tombstones; still I began to differentiate in the shuffling of shelves, spectrum change, from light source to light source, came to know at least each mask, sun's mask, neon's mask, etc. Then began the identification of light source through the guise of reflection, sun's rays grass costumed, house bulb by way of rug, etc. Finally came the discovery of what costume added to the light source character, the subtlety of the shelving in the merging of "color" spanch to "other-color" spanch within the bent tubing, and cognizance of the vibrations between and within those, once thought of as dominant "color" solids, in discovering the moon's transformation of sun's rays, the "brown" varnished furniture's enchantment of fire source light, etc. The spectroscope itself then shelved, except for occasional reference in the contemporary game of also-being-somewhat-scientific which I am fortunately only childishly prey to, and the eye's flight discovery of its internal ability to produce prismatic sensations directly, without extraneous instruments. The original influence of this added venture was the prism, quickly discarded in the game and replaced by squint, allowance for the eyelashes to diffract the illumination prismatically. Finally, eyes wide open, the raylike structure of the path of light, obviously still too influenced by Western sense of perspective, finding one vanishing point among bulb's filaments or at sun's center and radiating horizontally to the four corners of twin-trained eyes, and vertically to shatter among the lashes, contains within its web indescribable rainbows, still too influenced by the spectroscope and the prism, being imitative of each in arrangement of colors—"red-yellow-green-blue-purple"—yet exhibiting color oddities when the eye has been uninfluenced by scopism for a period of time. Under extreme non-concentration, fixed by effortless fascination, akin to self-hypnosis, my eye is able to retain for cognizance even those utterly unbanded rainbows reflecting off the darkest of objects, so transitory as to be completely unstructionable, yet retaining some semblance in arrangement to the source of illumination, bearing incredible resemblances to eyelid vision, patterning their tonal dance to the harmonics of all closed vision, yet differing in just that spectroscopic arrangement. I am stating my given ability, prize of all above pursuing, to transform the light-sculptured shapes of an almost dark-blackened room to the rainbow-hued patterns of light without any scientific paraphernalia. I am even enabled to impose arbitrary selection upon this newly discovered sense ability, to choose one color toning, eye only filtering out all others, and perceive all light, either source or reflection, according to inclination . . . this cast of eye-dye finding its parallel in everyday ordinary vision due to lack of perception rather than selectivity—i.e., the seeing of a snow scene at twilight as essentially black and white or black and blue-white to the exclusion of all other coloration. I am finding now that all my seemingly speculative color pursuits have had precedence in my filmic statements, subconscious invitations which unfortunately needed the conscious approval, my low level taking more cognizance of the gadget, the science toy, than of my own aesthetic visionary encouragement. As eyes become freed of their introductory influences, they become increasingly subject to the inspiration of the art. Many will see this only as intro-spectrum. I say all is.

There is, too, an akin-to-soft-focus-vision dependent on special indefiniteness. Self-hypnosis here is approximated through a fixity, rather than laxity, of gaze. Willful attention, forced beyond the natural capacity for mental absorption, produces a willy-nilliness less memory-dominated than when one is ungoed. Here one seems more practitioner than patient, and patience is not as necessary. One feels less hypnotic and more as if hypnotizer of the object, "objectivity" a descriptive of this process. All optic nerves must remain strained, beyond any ordinary attentive sighting, until they are as truly, though oppositely, involved with "the linear" as one is when focally negating alignment. The nerve ends must be as if drawn out to see all objects as if penciled. They must become identified with "the line" beyond any delineation. "Space" is what must cease to exist. The rationality which will be activated by these procedures must be turned to the destruction of all two- or three-dimensional logic. One may, for instance, feed the mind with the fact that in contemporary mathematics many problems are "solved" by allowing the problematical existence of many more dimensions than the realist, essentially Western Renaissance, three. Or one may simply allow the brain to wander among the multiple vanishing points and horizon lines of many Renaissance masterpieces and exhaust mental restrictions within those labyrinthine expressions. One cannot here diminish-vert-or-stract the intellect but must maintain a sense-originating argument with all its restrictive manifestations. Thus concentrated once upon my wife's arm, elbow to hand, my eyes drew every possible line out of it until all seemed strands separated as if in a dissection of its light and shadow surface. Then a semi-reformation produced multiple arms, moving independently in this re-defined space, superimposing over each other all differently drawn. The shaded area of the knuckles, the inbetween finger cast shadows, the very hair of the arm and the crackling blackened wrinkles produced a number of finely-drawn caricatures afloat without apparent interdependence. Eventually it became impossible for me to discern the originating image. At this point my mind, seeking to redefine "reality," wondered if my own hand to split-up would have a complementary image of itself for reaching out to touch or otherwise sense, to grasp or otherwise move in interrelationship, with each of my wife's imagistic offspring; and it then postulated an attempt to connect parent hands to this intent. The instant the singular image of my blundering fingers began to pry into this multiple exposure— the vision vanished, all lines snaking to their source. As in all previous examples of supernatural vision, my wife and I have both experienced a number of more successful eye adventures in this respect, which are completely beyond any linguistic expression whatsoever.

If one were to turn an adventuring eye to literary correspondence, facsimilating visual adventure with similarly adventuring literature, transforming optic abstract impressions into non-representational language, enchanting non-sights into non-words, one could write only sound poems, the audio manifestations of letters not being restricted to a predetermined logic and rather communicating on an emotional level only distantly related to all the known word origins of any written sound. Within that distant relationship is the embryonic form of a purely onomatopoetic art. The visual parallel of this art is being created by men termed "Abstract Expressionist," who are fashioning the symbol—cuneiform—hieroglyphic letters for future communication. The moving picture image enables the development of continuity and therefore an evolution upon

language as we contemporarily know it. All contained within
this book has died in the womb. I abort it to save the living
organism, its origins . . . itself a specimen . . . at best a
museum piece . . . of value only to the anatomical eye.

THE WORK OF BRUCE BAILLIE
by John Bragin

*Bruce Baillie makes his films in the West, where he lives. He
has been associated with the New American Cinema longer
than most. In this article John Bragin discusses several of
Baillie's films. Bragin is preparing a book on Michelangelo Antonioni and writes criticism for* Film Culture *and* Film Quarterly.

Bruce Baillie is one of the true poets of the New American
Cinema. He is sensitive to the form, texture, color, line,
pattern, and movement of both the world of nature and of the
material, industrial world created by man. His work is marked
by two salient characteristics: the first is the use of the conflict between the world of nature, which Baillie sees as poetic
and lyric, and the world man has made, which is often bar-
baric, ugly, coarse, and mechanical; the second is tension
inherent in each work, a tension that comes from a conflict
between the lyric and poetic style of the film, and the horrors
of modern Western civilization. Most strongly felt when he
presents these horrors in the same poetic style as that in which
he presents the world of nature, this tension is Baillie's trademark. His early films tend to dwell on the haziness of the
borderline between external horrors and those created from
within the mind. In his later films this ambivalent terror
expands from the aberration of a single character to one that
pervades our whole society. In Baillie's most recent films he
has left social comment behind and concentrates on the creation of visual and aural effects for their own sake.

On Sundays (1960), *The Gymnasts* (1960–61), *Have You
Ever Thought of Talking to the Director?* (1961), and *A
Hurrah for Soldiers* (1962) comprise most of the output of his
first period, with *A Hurrah for Soldiers* beginning the transi-

tion to his second period. The first three films are built around the experiences of a single character, and the film remains tied to these experiences in a conventional story-line. In the films the characters are relatively passive; they move through their worlds without showing much feeling concerning their involvement in situations that would conventionally elicit heavily charged emotional responses. Baillie moves his characters like chess pieces through the world he wishes to explore. Their existence is merely a dramatic excuse to give a simple structure to his films. The filmmaker is not so much interested in exploring character and motivation as he is in exploring the physical world of objects and things which vibrate with a life apart from man. As presented by Baillie, in almost pantheistic terms, this world absorbs much of the emotion generated from man.

On Sundays opens with pleasant shots of San Francisco cable cars, of old men in the park, and a girl playing on a grassy mountain slope above the city. All the objects comprising the city, and the grass and rocks of the mountain, have a tactile quality, through which Baillie draws the viewer into the film. The first intimation of danger is an Iron Cross hanging around the neck of a German shepherd.

In the next sequence the girl explores an old, deserted house. Patterns of charred wood, streams of diffused light, reflecting broken glass, sharp blacks and whites, and long slow movements of the girl and the camera create a visually exciting sequence. There are some brief glances out of the window at the city, and some long shots of the house. Everything seems at peace. But, suddenly, a man appears. At first we are not sure if he is something she is imagining or not. She runs from the house, and we retrace her path through the house which before had seemed so pleasing, and which now seems to hide terror behind every corner. The man appears and disappears several times, but makes no attempt to approach the girl. This first appearance of the man, a tramp, is the girl's first realization of a squalor which exists as much inside her as in the outside world. As she returns to the city, and the park, the man reappears. Slowly, with overt actions on his part, his solidity and reality increase, until she has no alternative but to submit herself to his direction. He leads her through the squalid world which he inhabits, but makes no attempt to force himself on her.

Finally, at night, she ends up in a bar frequented by this man and his friends. She does a frantic little dance on top of the bar, with no expression in her face or body. After this she simply walks out of the bar with another tramp we have hardly seen, and the film ends.

Through her Baillie explores the details of the physical reality which make up the world which the tramps inhabit. He does this in much the same way, and with much the same attention to texture, feeling, and sensuality, as Genet did in *Our Lady of the Flowers*. And, like Genet, he does not attempt to enforce some metaphysical system on top of the world he explores, but draws one from that world by involving himself in it as deeply as he can. There is no dramatic conflict, but a conflict which arises from a tension between the subject matter and Baillie's poetic presentation of that subject matter.

In *The Gymnasts* Baillie shows the form and feeling of men in movement. The film begins with shots of large hallways, diffusely lit, pillars and stairways in sharp patterns of black and white, and a non-descript man getting towels and gym shorts from a check-out window. He goes through another large, deserted and crumbling arena, which is a passageway between the normal world we have just seen and the gym room he finally arrives in. There is echoing laughter on the soundtrack, which further detaches us from reality. The gym is empty, but, suddenly, we hear circus music and the room is alive with acivity. Men are swinging on bars, parallels, rings, and side-horses. Sometimes we see only parts of bodies such as arms, legs, hands, and chests. Baillie uses close-ups of these to emphasize and explore rhythm and movement as well as the texture of muscles and skin. We are drawn closer into the feeling, tone, and texture of these gymnasts to the point where physical reality begins to become oppressive. The camera swings around, taking every conceivable angle of the activity. The music ends as suddenly as it began. The man returns through the crumbling arena, back to the crowded hall, where he returns his towel and shorts at the check-out window.

Throughout the sequence in the gym the man stands in his street clothes, passively observing the scene. After awhile we are no longer aware of his presence, until the music stops. It could be said that this whole spectacle took place somewhere beyond normal life, in a region of the man's mind, just like the girl who seemed spontaneously to generate and reinforce a vision within her own mind, until she succumbed to it.

The soundtrack of *Have You Every Thought of Talking to the Director?* alternates between the music of a banjo and piano and the voice of the main character talking to the director of the asylum to which he has been committed. The meaning of the images is more complex than the character's simple, factual statements. There is the same basic tension as in his first films between the lyricism of Baillie's presentation of the subject matter and the subject itself. We are shown the protagonist's recollections—compounded of memory and hallucination—of his life before commitment; in them the figure of the asylum director appears several times in various guises. This bearded figure becomes an obsession and pulls the protagonist closer and closer to the real director who runs the asylum. The film begins and ends with slow tracking movements through the corridors of the asylum where the man who has been committed sits, alone and lost in thought. Throughout the film Baillie breaks down the banality of objects, people, and nature. He invests them with a tenuous, unreal quality which draws us closer to experiencing them as themselves, apart from limited, learned, habitual patterns of perception.

A Hurrah for Soldiers marks a new departure, for in it Baillie discards the tie to a sequence of events experienced by a single character. The film is in color, which Baillie uses to heighten his presentation of the tactile quality of the physical world. For the most part, the film takes place on or near a single stretch of beach, but the feeling is not one of a limited location. Then sensation of greater scope comes from the fragmentation and rearrangement of details, destroying obvious continuity in favor of a heightened awareness of reality. The tension between the beauties of the scenes at the beach and the brutal events and images interspersed throughout the film is increased in this way. In Baillie's second period the protagonist is eliminated, but the terror remains. It is no longer created by the aberration of one man's mind, but by the aberration of an entire society. *A Hurrah for Soldiers* grew out of the Congo situation, which represented for Baillie a contemporary form of the ignorance and brutality that has come to dominate the earth.

The three films of Baillie's second period are his finest

works: *To Parsifal* (1963), *Mass for the Dakota Sioux* (1963–64), and *Quixote* (1964–65). It is here that we find the fullest realization of the tension and conflict that are Baillie's main themes. In his later films Baillie indulges more in visual and aural sensation for its own sake, and does not maintain the individuality and incisiveness which characterized his second period. *To Parsifal* is in color, has a soundtrack from Wagner's opera, and is divided into two parts. The first part concerns the sea. The film begins with scenes of grass and flowers blown by the wind, followed by shots of waves crashing against a rocky shore, and then scenes taken further out at sea. Into this lyric pattern Baillie weaves shots of the rigging of a fishing boat swinging against the sea and sky. For an instant we see an undefined bright red form, then back to shots of the sea, sky, and rigging. When we return to a longer, clearer shot of that red form we see that it is the guts of a fish spilling out under the knife of a fisherman. This is the climax of the first part. Man has impinged on the calmness and beauty. Gulls swarm above the bloody deck.

The first part of the film ends with a slow tracking shot of the Golden Gate Bridge, shrouded in midst. This denouement draws us away from the blood and back to a more serene setting.

The second part of the film deals with man's invasion of the high mountains. The serenity and peace of the rocks and pines are disturbed by the building of a railway. The nude body of a young girl represents a mean between the vast expanses of nature and its detail of brooks, streams, and flowers. She is also the link to the world of man which is invading both these realms of nature.

The second part of the film ends with the peak of a soprano's aria punctuated by a screaming train whistle. At the same time we see the rough arm of a man grasping the girl around the waist and pulling her back. Next the camera draws back again for longer shots of the mountains, pines, and railway. The wheels of the railroad cars create a stroboscopic pattern against the sky, and harmony has returned.

Of *Mass for the Dakota Sioux* Willard van Dyke has said: "There have been many documentary films representing the horrors of city life, but Baillie's *Mass* goes far beyond documentation, providing us with a deeply felt and deeply moving film that is truly cinematic in concept and in execution."

In *Mass* Baillie uses black and white, negative, slow and fast motion, multiple imagery, changes in exposure, stock footage, and most of the other devices usually associated with experimental films. Using for soundtrack a Gregorian Chant recorded at a Trappist Monastery in Vina, California, Baillie shows the destructive, contradictory elements of the civilization which developed the Mass, and went on to destroy the race of the Sioux Indian.

The film begins with a man writhing in death pangs on a street corner. From this the Introit follows: It is a slightly overexposed sequence of multiple images of factories, chimneys, housing tracts, etc., the buildings of Western man. Despite the fact that these effects were done in the camera, not carefully executed by a laboratory, the images dissolve and recombine in patterns that are not only visually satisfying, but carry great force in exposing the mechanical sameness of the objects, houses, and factories. The Kyrie is a lingering, melancholy section in which long, gliding tracking shots follow a motorcyclist across the San Francisco Bridge. In the central part, entitled the Epistle, the absurdity of the images and objects of the modern world is presented. Material photographed directly from the TV screen is made more outrageous because of the scanning lines, and some film footage from Hollywood is cut into Baillie's own scenes. The Mass is heard, now louder, now softer, throughout the sequence. The Gloria follows: The plaintive, terror-filled face of Ray Milland from *The Man with the X-Ray Eyes*, and a 1933 Cadillac going along the Bay Bridge and disappearing into a tunnel. The Offertory is a procession of lights accompanied by another chant. The Consecration and Communion follow: We see again the dying man on the pavement; the Cadillac arrives and the body is covered, consecrated, and removed; the car drives off and the Mass ends. Baillie has not made such a tight, incisive, and beautiful film since *Mass*.

Quixote falls far below the level of *Mass* even though it has some advances in technique. The film is 45 minutes long, and lacks the feeling of a unified whole that pervades *Mass*. The material comes from scenes shot all over the United States, from television and movie footage, from Vietnam newsreels and from dramatic scenes created by Baillie himself. The soundtrack includes natural sounds, synchronous dialogue, music and sound effects altered by tape speed and

direction, and all manner of sounds ranging from the lyric
and very beautiful to the screeching and disconcerting. Except for the last section, the film falls apart from bigness and
overextension. The last section is introduced by a man riding
a black horse in silhouette and slow motion. There is jazz on
the soundtrack. We see shots of New York City, including
a beautiful one of an American flag at the UN waving in the
wind and covering and revealing a bright sun. The hand of
a girl is superimposed, at intervals, over a procession of Negroes. The hand is writhing and clutching in pain. Fighting
in Vietnam is intercut with scenes from daily life in this
country. The sequence builds to a climax and ends on the
red face of a girl, lying on her back, shaking her head back
and forth. This one, specific image communicates the total
catastrophe pointed to by the film; Baillie says "The presentiment at the end of the film is of the end we have created
for ourselves."

Yellow Horse (1965–66) was shot at a motorcycle rally,
but, unlike Anger's *Scorpio Rising*, there is no attempt at
social statement. The machines, helmuts, chromium, and
bright colors in fast movement are patterned solely on the
basis of sensation. Baillie uses distorting devices to mutate
form and movement and remove objects and people from
their context.

Tung is a five-minute silent film in vivid color with much
superimposition, use of negative, and an entirely disjointed
continuity. Across the whole pattern moves the negative
image of a girl with flowing, ghostly white hair.

Castro Street is a very complicated look at the industries
and railroad along a stretch of street in Richmond, California. Its images of the modern world do not possess the
terror of Baillie's earlier films, and while just about every
effect of sound and sight found in experimental films is used,
there is a definite lack of cohesiveness, continuity, and point
of view. Baillie described this as his "coming of consciousness," and as "something for anyone to follow into on his
own." Baillie would like to have as much control of his
medium as the painter has available to him.

His last two films are *Still Life* (two minutes) and *All My
Life* (three minutes), both shot in the summer of 1966. Each
is one continuous take. The first shows a still life arranged
on a table; people move around behind the table and in front

of a window, changing the light falling on the back of the still life. Practically inaudible dialogue is heard. *All My Life* consists of a pan across a fence and brightly colored flowers on a sunny day. An old 78rpm recording of Ella Fitzgerald singing the title song is heard. These two short films are no more than diverting exercises.

Baillie seems to have totally lost the feeling for drama that was inherent in his earlier work, and is now simply involved in the pursuit of small pleasures. His last two periods are but shadows of his earlier accomplishments.

FOUR FILMS BY ANDY WARHOL *

by Gregory Battcock

Potentially the most influential of the New York filmmakers is Andy Warhol, a comparative newcomer to cinema, to which he turned only after having acquired a considerable reputation in the plastic arts. The early films of this artist were deceptively simple: they had a minimum of content and were made with a minimal technique. Warhol first became well known as a filmmaker for his use of the still image— the device whereby the action on the screen is reduced to small variations in the posture of a single image. Action is even further reduced, in most of Warhol's films made prior to 1965, by the filmmaker's refusal to move the camera. And it may not be farfetched to draw an analogy between this film approach, on the one hand, and the approach toward painting followed by the minimal painter, on the other, in which attitudes toward the surface, the shape of the canvas, and scale and proportion are criticized.

Early Warhol movies emphasized the cinema as a medium for experiencing time, rather than movement or event. They included *Empire*, made by focusing a camera on the Empire State Building for several hours, and *Sleep*, which applied the same technique to the subject of a sleeping man. In this period, Warhol made scarcely more effort to direct the action (or inaction) when making films with waking human actors than when working with a building or an "actor" who

* Portions of this article were published in *Film Culture* and the *College Art Journal.*

was fast asleep. Thus *Henry Geldzahler*, *The Thirteen Most Beautiful Boys*, *Eat*, and *Haircut*, the titles of which precisely delineate their contents, are essentially similar to *Empire* and *Sleep*. The following observations on *Empire* can be applied, with only slight modifications, to all the other films in this group.

Since it may be assumed that the first purpose of *Empire* is to present the essential character of film as a medium, it may then be asked why wasn't a blank or exposed film simply run through the projector? Simply because, while doing so might suffice as a provocative statement, the use of plain film, which is uniform in color, would make impossible the exhibition of contrast and gradations between black and white; and the black-and-white dialectic is probably the second most important restriction and distinction of the film medium. The decision to film *an object* thus made possible the presentation of the full range of tones from black to white. It might be argued here that filming a block of wood could certainly present the full range (black, white, grey) of tones. Why, then, was the Empire State Building used?

If a block of wood were filmed, the audience would be forced to consider that block of wood as *art*, as sculpture—junk or "found," Abstract Expressionist or Dada; a concern that would be irrelevant to the purposes, or subject, of the movie. The choice of the Empire State Building seems logical. It's not some faceless building in Queens that demands identification or clarification, nor is it a building from which any aesthetic pleasure or stimulation can be gained (at least not at this time). It is, simply, a big nothing—perhaps the biggest nothing, except for the Pan Am Building, around. It's better known, more familiar, seemingly more permanent than the newer colossus uptown. It's New York, America—yet not a moment like the Statue of Liberty with which one can identify emotionally, either in glorification or vilification.

As if to emphasize that the selection of the Empire State Building is primarily a device by which to present the full range of tones from black to white, the first reel of this long (eight-hour) movie shows the dramatic change of all the original darks or blacks to lights, and the original lights gradually moving through the entire spectrum to blacks.

Andy Warhol: Two frames from *Empire*, 1964

During the first fifteen minutes the image of the building is obscured almost entirely by fog. This provides a dramatic beginning, and one that acknowledges traditional methods of film art. It recalls the first appearance of Garbo in *Anna Karenina*, when the face of the actress is almost totally obscured by steam from a train. Dramatic evolution is confined to the first reel, leaving the rest of the film free to concentrate on a more important limitation of the medium.

In this work Warhol has clearly dismissed the idea that "movement" is an essential characteristic of movies. Movement can, after all, be presented and experienced in other media—the dance, theatre, now even sculpture—so Warhol has chosen not to deal with it in this film essay on the re-identification of the essential message of cinema. Sound is dispensed with also, and its absence is consistent with the object photographed, since the Empire State Building does not, *qua* building, make noise.

Silence has been dramatically employed in films almost since sound became available. Generally, sound has been erased from portions of films to heighten the dramatic impact of certain scenes, such as the mirror scene in the Marx Brothers film *Duck Soup* (1933). The documentary, or nonfiction character of *Empire* is not altered by the absence of sound, and its message is appropriate to the electronic age. Black and white and everything in between is one subject of this film. Another, even more important, is time.

Warhol's decision to film the slow passing of dusk and night emphasizes the importance that he as artist gives to the element of time. In commercial films events are rarely presented in their full time span. Time is distorted in such films—usually by compression. The time in *Empire* is distorted in a different way. It is distorted, perhaps, simply by its *not* being distorted when one would reasonably expect it to be. In addition, the action in the first reel is clearly speeded up, possibly so that the change from day to night, the major "event" in the film, could be summarily disposed of in order to clear the way for the timeless "real" time of the unchanging image of the building. Time is perhaps the most important single element that distinguishes film from the other visual art forms. In looking at still objects, the viewer chooses his own time. In dance and the theatre, time is, to some extent, controlled by the director and performers. Warhol then, may not force the viewer to look at his films—in which case there is only one thing left to do, and that is, to sit through them.

The intellectual content of *Empire* clearly overshadows the visual, and the exaggerated time element is in opposition to the "telescoping" of incidents typical of the commercial cinema. In *Empire* and his other early films, Warhol re-examines communicative procedures in art. In so doing, he has focused upon the very *presence* of the art object itself in a way that recalls modern handling of some commercial products. Indeed, the presence of an object, and its intrusion upon the audience, or consumer, is receiving renewed attention in several areas. Recent advertisements for a new television set read: "New Westinghouse Jet Set. Doesn't stare back at you. It's considerate television." In film, of course, the time is decided by the film—that is, by the film-maker. The projector runs at a predetermined speed; the projectionist is not yet an artist.

The subject of *Empire* is, then, an investigation of the presence and character of film—a legitimate if not a requisite concern for the artist. And the terms established for this investigation are the black and white of film technology and the obvious, yet frequently denied, limitation of time.

Empire is now a classic of the avant-garde. In a short period it has received extraordinary acceptance, which suggests it appeared at the right moment. Whatever influence it may have had, film will not be quite the same again. Neither, perhaps, will the Empire State Building.

From the deadpan "new realism" just described, with its mind-destroying concentration on insignificant incidents and situations, Warhol has recently moved on to more explicit ironies.

In *Horse* Warhol produced an apparently straightforward parody of the traditional Western—complete with oppressed Mexican (played by Tosh Carrillo), sheriff, boy outlaw, and cowboy—that yet succeeds in revealing the disguised eroticism of the genre. Ron Tavel, who wrote and directed *Horse* and *Vinyl*,[1] also wrote *Screen Test* (with Mario Montez)—a transitional work in both form and content. It is one of the first of Warhol's sound films, yet the still camera is retained.

In *Screen Test*, as in other still-image pictures, slight

[1] Starring Sedgwick and Carrillo.

variations of image become all the more important because of their scarcity. Presence of the Abstract Expressionist sensitivity heightens their impact and therefore makes the films much more interesting. The strong black-and-white contrasts in *Screen Test* demand a consideration of the flat negative-positive values of the surface, and as in a painting by Franz Kline, it is uncertain whether it is a line or a plane, a white picture on a black ground or a black on white—and it doesn't really matter. The usual half-tone pictorial characteristics seem somehow absent from the picture and bring the picture more toward painting; at the same time the film limitations, which give the work its identity, are not denied.

A single actor, "in drag," is shown on the screen for the entire duration of *Screen Test*. Mario Montez is certainly at his best here, for he seems to expose himself utterly in this new revelation of the duality of acting and experience. In effect, the experience cannot be separated from the acting, and the question of determining whether or not Montez is actually acting is thrust upon the audience. His totally convincing performance is heightened by the rather sloppily applied make-up and wig, which speak of Genet and Greenwich Avenue in a startlingly real and cruel manner. And if the wig, make-up, and sex are distortions, so also is the length of the screen test—seventy minutes.

The sound of *Screen Test* consists of two voices: the off-stage voice of Ron Tavel commands the actor to repeat over and over certain words and phrases self-consciously chosen and frequently vulgar and juvenile; Montez does so with embarrassed distaste.

The burden of appreciating the film rests squarely on the audience. The audience, never catered to, is abused, exposed, and ridiculed. It is, at the same time, very much considered. The use of film as a device to torment its audience may be understood as an intellectual challenge; certainly it forces an alert viewer to come to new terms with art. The popular value structure is shattered and not in the terms of the value structure. When engaged in the protest and destruction that is art, Warhol does not subscribe to the notion that calls for the toppling of the old order within the terms of the older order. By demonstrating consistent respect for his medium, he will challenge the existing order

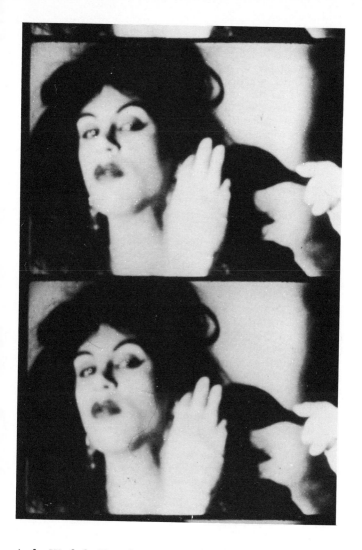

Andy Warhol: Two frames from *Screen Test* (1965) with Mario Montez

on all levels, using his own terms, even though they will be unacceptable to most people and delay acceptance of his art. Quick acceptance of a statement which attempts to subvert within the conditions and restrictions of the status quo and according to its lexicon is to be expected, even though that statement must ultimately be false. If *Sleep* or *Empire* were films to turn on to, *Screen* Test is actively interesting because the viewer is forced into an immediate and not altogether unfamiliar involvement.

As has already been intimated, the actual subject of all Warhol's early movies is film itself and its attendant hypocrisies. *Screen Test* is no exception, though its apparent subject may be transvestism. Here too the intellectual content dominates the visual; the film apes Hollywood and movies in general. In presenting these disturbing challenges to the nature of the medium, Warhol hinders understanding and sympathy by his choice of vehicle. However, sexual dualism as represented on the screen can be taken as further proof of Warhol's intent to unmask the sexual fraud of the contemporary cinema. The usual presentation of sex is a product of the art of packaging technology and it is illusion, facade, and gesture that we buy and that Montez's posturing lays bare.

Representative of the next stage in Warhol's development as a cinematic artist is *Kitchen*, a film noteworthy for the changes it introduces in the concept of the "superstar," a concept that Warhol is credited with contributing to the iconography of the underground cinema. In the introduction of this latest device, Warhol consciously refers, yet again, to the basic structure of the professional Hollywood cinema. This time the star system itself becomes the subject of scrutiny. In the early still-image movies, the so-called superstar was the sole figurative element recognizable on the screen. More recently, as critical attention has been directed to attempts to identify and license the superstar, Warhol has been engaged in changing the use and presentation of the whole idea. The changes can be seen moving in several directions. Peculiarities of the set, props, script, and audio elements are exploited in a leveling-off process that, in *Kitchen*, acts as a bridge between the earlier films and such new works as *The Chelsea Girls*. Paradoxically, the real superstar in *Kitchen* is the least obtrusive, and the one who behaves mostly like a prop. His participation in the film is less than marginal, and many of the props are assigned a more aggressive role. Though he is always on the set, only at the end of the film is the non-super superstar (played by René Ricard) allowed genuine human identity as he socializes on an equal level with the other people in the film. Here Warhol is obviously trying to equalize in prominence all figurative elements—both figures and objects. Thus the resultant redistribution of emphasis is of a type associated with painting. If the characteristic feature of the superstar in *Kitchen* is seen as a confusion of identity on one hand, coupled with a questioning of traditional patterns of communication on the other, then the real superstar is the most silent and inanimate one.

I should like to discuss the film with several considerations in mind—namely, the role of the set and props, the sound direction, and the superstar.

The title, the director, and the scenarist (Warhol and Tavel, respectively) are audibly introduced along with the actors and their parts, the set and its furnishings, and the procedure followed in making the film. The audience is reminded that the script is planned and that the actors deliver prepared lines, copies of which are distributed around the set in case they forget. Thus, the artist draws the audience into his confidence. No sentimentality is involved in the device, as it does not alleviate the responsibility demanded of the audience, which, as always in any meaningful art offering the promise of intellectual reward, is considerable. In the introduction, as in criticism of a painting, the various items, including format and figures, are given equal billing. Thus, early in the film, a special approach to the various figurative items is indicated. A sort of equalization is begun. The superstars, the ice box, and the kitchen table all have an equal start. All their identities are reshaped.

The spacial organization of the set in *Kitchen* is fixed and defined in a way that recalls the early Renaissance manner of Bouts, Campin, or Van Eyck. Walls, floor, and ceiling act as extension and reinforcement of the frame. Warhol does not move the camera in this film, and, once again, there is little reason for him to do so. The side and rear walls of the kitchen where the movie takes place determine the edges of the picture and the movements of people and things are confined within them. Warhol has telescoped, in a sense, the development of Renaissance space (of this type) from early to later stages, for his subsequent films do away with the rigid spatial delineation and the space is limitless— the entire studio in *Camp*, the great outdoors (filmed on location) for *My Hustler*, and the indefinite "unseen" limitation in *The Chelsea Girls*. These films are without fixed spatial limits, and both actors and, in a new departure for Warhol, camera wander. In them, the limitations of the surface are decided by the frame of the camera, rather than physical restriction by the set.

The clean white kitchen and its introduction as a "clean white kitchen" have special significance. It may not be a coincidence that the ubiquitous white walls of modern interiors are contemporary with the practical realization of the existential predicament. In any room with white walls the occupants are forced into a deeper awareness of and attitude toward the objects that the walls enclose. The antiseptic, unnatural, unfinished whiteness (bare like canvas waiting to be painted—then often not painted) rejects both objects and occupants equally and places them in an intimate relationship with each other. Moreover, white walls give a sense of limitless space, without actually providing the challenge of such a space in reality; decorated walls, on the other hand, decidedly confine space. As the urban environment has been extended beyond the walls of the city to include the entire globe (the "wild" spaces enclosed, protecting them from us), so the existential presence of white walls reflects a change of our position as regards the immediate landscape.

Quite naturally, the objects within the white non-limitation, in this case the kitchen, gain new importance; at the same time they are no longer "permanent" in the way that art could once be said to be. Permanence implies a type of decision alien and impractical to the modern philosophic process. Thankfully, the new unlimited environment contains only disposable items (appliances, mates, art objects, emotions); the environment itself becomes temporal and disposable—clipped, treated, planned, and renewed. The intellect, obviously, transcends the object; even the film doesn't have to be seen, and understanding may be experience. Description of the film can suffice; the experience the film offers

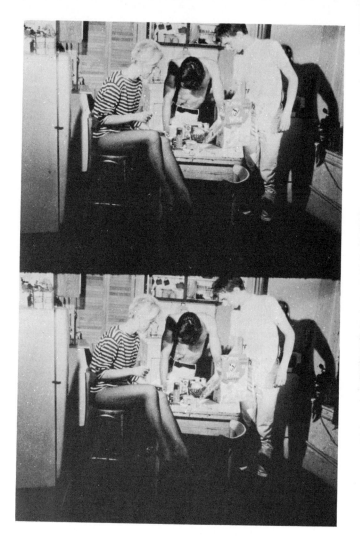

Andy Warhol: Two frames from *Kitchen* (1965) with Edie
Sedgwick (left) and Roger Trudeau (center)

is understanding, not seeing, it. Bookcases have movable shelves and paper books along with 33r.p.m. records are seen by the garbage. New books, better recordings, and new art (ideas) will and must replace them and accommodation for the replacements is built in ahead of time. Preparation is made for accommodation of the future rather than preservation of the past.

If Warhol forces a new appreciation of objects in *Kitchen*, he simultaneously urges a reconsideration of their relationship with people. The objects introduced at the beginning of the movie, and which play important roles include mixer, ice box, stove, kitchen sink, kitchen table, etc. Throughout, the kitchen table assumes considerable responsibility. It is placed in the center of the frame, and is used, abused, cluttered, sat on, exercised on, and when it is finally cleared, a murder takes place on it. In the end it is as it was in the beginning, ready to go through it all again. It alone among the objects and people in the movie seems to have followed a formal narrative and to have gone through a conventional pattern of communication with information and events radiating from centers to margins (if that is the conventional pattern), from beginning to end, as they perhaps no longer do. With its own clearly defined space, the table exists as something of a mirror-image; a play within a play. The disordered, compulsive cluttering on the table surface may represent the old order, and is accordingly ridiculed and abused.

The audio introduction of the parts and mechanics of the film is interrupted by the actors' sneezing. Throughout the entire film the male and female stars sneeze at one another, at intervals. The sneezes seem to acknowledge each other as they communicate some sort of information which, in this film, words or sexual behavior do not. Information and experience are not necessarily transmitted through the printed or spoken word, or by sexual contact or suggestion, or anything else. But sex and words are used to transmit information to the audience even though the actors do not communicate with each other by these means.[2]

[2] The dialogue between the actors is interesting and occasionally very amusing, though it is important only because it is there, and not for what it is about. It is based on obvious caricatures of Freudian psychology (e.g. "I've failed you. Both as a mother and

The new position of the dialogue is made clear late in the first reel of the movie. An electric malted-milk machine is turned on and the incessant noise from it all but obscures the remaining speech. Sometime in the second reel the machine is turned off, much to the relief of everyone, both actors and audience ("I can't stand that damn noise"). The direct and functional relationship between the dialogue and other sounds, and the fact that the film is on two reels, is demonstrated by the way the malted machine is used. As the second reel of the film begins, the actors are seen sitting around waiting, and the machine is turned off. After a spoken introduction to reel two, the actors arrange themselves and the machine is turned on again, symbolically representing the connection between the two reels. Warhol seizes on the physical fact of the separation between the two reels for particular attention, just as he has pointed up so many other hitherto ignored or obscured realities of film-making. Orderly, literary connection between the two reels of the movie exists solely in terms of the machine, not through dialogue or human behavior, both of which are deliberately interrupted in order to heighten further the separation.

At intervals, a photographer enters the set from the foreground and takes snapshots. Frequently the actors pause momentarily for the picture. The effect is to heighten certain moments in the film, and the device may be intended as yet another reminder of the unimportance of the plot, lest we get sufficiently carried away, even for a moment to become involved with the events portrayed.[3]

---

lover I've failed you." and "Isn't a mother a boy's best friend?"). So, too, sexual roles are at once confused and paradoxical. The two main characters are both sexy—Edie Sedgwick displaying lovely legs all over the place and Roger Trudeau in levis without a shirt. The male lead reveals he has just come from the shower where he had sex with Joe ("Which Joe, dear?"). And later in the picture, someone else finds he has sexually "attacked" the wrong person, because of a confusion in names. (Question: "Why does everyone in this movie have the same name?" Answer: "You don't have sex with a name, do you?")

[3] The use of the "photographer" reminds me of a peculiarity attendant to Warhol movies. Note that the "photographer" oc-

Whatever the reason, one cannot help but feel the gesture is a little obvious. In addition, it tends to distract from other more appropriate aspects of the film. But *Kitchen* is, on the whole, a dignified and honest attempt at realization of the sociological and aesthetic problems attendant on the new art.

Among Warhol's more recent films, *The Chelsea Girls* [4] is in some ways different from any of its predecessors, for it has the full complement of sound, movement, multiple images, and story line that the artist had laboriously discarded in his earlier cinematic work. The introduction of enriched content can be taken as yet another attempt by the artist to criticize formal cinematic procedure. For in this film, it is most particularly the way a movie is looked at and the way the information is assimilated by the audience that comes under scrutiny. As in *Screen Test*, the apparent and

---

casionally walks directly in front of the *camera* and obscures, momentarily, the picture. On several occasions during a recent screening of *Kitchen*, people in the front rows of the auditorium turned around to see who had walked in front of the projector. During the screening of Warhol's films (often on portable apparatus) people interject themselves between the projector and the screen with surprising frequency. Interestingly, the "less" there is on the screen, the more likely this is to happen. The action may be a demonstration of hostility toward the film which has apparently "nothing happening" on it. Similarly, "black" paintings by Ad Reinhardt are said to attract tactile attention at a high rate; they are protected by ropes at the Museum of Modern Art and by little platforms at the Betty Parsons Gallery. Equally, many people will not think twice about interrupting others' views of paintings by Barnett Newman or Kelly or Noland, although the same people will excuse themselves if they happen to obstruct the view of a Van Gogh (or a De Kooning, probably). Is Warhol perhaps protecting his work from this sort of thing by creating his own obstruction to preclude the necessity of further interruption?

[4] In this film, the familiar Warhol superstars appear without using fictional names. Of course, this is not an entirely new idea. The characters in the W.C. Fields movie *International House* (1933) also retained their own names.

the real subject are two different things.[5] In *The Chelsea Girls*
two different films are shown simultaneously side by side on a
wide screen. Occasionally they may overlap. The pictures are
said to suggest a series of rooms at the Chelsea Hotel (on
West 23rd Street in Manhattan) and to depict what goes on in
them. Each program is more or less the same, with the films
(some black and white and some in color) shown in the same
order. The films last about half an hour apiece and follow each
other without interruption. The series plays for about four
hours.

At each showing of *The Chelsea Girls* that has so far taken
place, the two movies have always been two different pictures; not two prints of the same picture.[6] It might indeed

[5] Critics writing in the popular journals have pointed out the
"dirty" subject matter of this film. Other writers have made an
analogy between the subject matter of *The Chelsea Girls*, on one
hand, and the napalm and torture of the Vietnam war, on the
other. In this sense, the popular critics may therefore be accurate
—however, it is the absence of sentimentality coupled with a total
and unfeeling dedication to *vérité* within this movie that makes
the comparison with the ghastly war in Vietnam an appropriate
one. A somewhat different view has been taken by Nicolas Calas,
writing in *Arts*, who feels that Warhol's selections are frequently
sentimental and that the film suffers because of this sentimentality.
Calas says: "Warhol is full of self-pity. One after another his
hermaphrodites dissolve into a Mimi and Mignon sentimentality
with canned soup in the tradition of Praxiteles and Cocteau."
(*Arts*, Vol. 41, #4, February, 1967.) A different observation is
noted by David Ehrenstein (*Film Culture*, No. 42, Fall, 1966), who
writes: "Warhol has no ax to grind, he's just an innocent bystander
at the scene of the accident. No moralizing, no message you can
wrap up and take home with you, just the facts." The movie must
have had some kind of moralizing effect on Ehrenstein, however,
for he ends his article: "Can our lives be filled with such intense
pain, our minds diseased, our souls ravaged?"

[6] Only one of the films, *Pope Ondine*, does not fit into the scheme.
It is about a Papal pretender and his response to an accusation
from an inept young coed who is making a confession. The film
is placed in an important spot in the sequence—at the end. Sound
for the accompanying film is always turned off, rather conspicu-
ously, when *Pope Ondine* begins. It's obviously a major event in a
situation which does not want a major event. *Pope Ondine* speaks
entirely for itself. Distraction is irrelevant. It's an extraordinary film

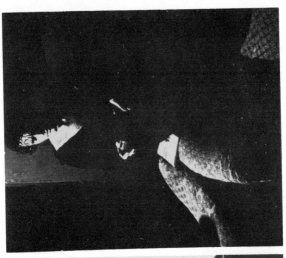

Andy Warhol: From *The Chelsea Girls* (1966) with Nico (left) and Pope Ondine (right)

be interesting to see two *identical* prints shown in this manner. In that event, however, critical attention would be directed elsewhere since the artist's concern would be with questions of comparison and time in the cinema image; questions that are not of the moment and not now of much interest. Moreover, the purpose of the experiment would immediately be clear, and, as Nicholas Calas writes in *Artforum*: "Not clarity but ambiguity rules art. . . ."

On some occasions one of the films on the screen has been black and white, the other in color. In some of the new color films, Warhol has used exceptionally vivid and travelogue-y color combinations. They have all been seen before and parts of them are abstract, in a way similar to figurative Abstract Expressionist painting of the fifties. These films appear equally dated and their emphasis seems to be misplaced. (That is, unless they were specifically made to be shown on a two-picture screen in the present manner.) Most of these movies are somehow a little bland. Did Warhol decide to show all these films two-at-a-time because he realized that they were unable to stand on their own? Or did he make them for this type of presentation? Whatever the answer, it is clear that *The Chelsea Girls* represents a new direction (predicted some time ago in *The Village Voice* by Mekas) in the films of Warhol.

Numerous problems that do not exist in the showing of ordinary films crop up in this special event. The whole point is that *The Chelsea Girls* is not an ordinary cinematic experience. Two films being shown at the same time can be considered a type of media-mixing, and simultaneously raise problems of display and presentation. The reader may ask

---

with exceptional presence. It's entirely engrossing with sharp wit and brilliant camera usage, and the message is something other than only the medium. In addition, the formal narrative is important, and it must be followed completely. Naturally, when one's attention is directed equally to two different events, it is impossible to follow the narrative of both at the same time. Warhol is only one of several artists who have contributed, in the past, to the ultimate destruction of formal narrative in film. The removal of this type of narrative or literary content from film form was an essential development and a prerequisite to the radical departure represented in *The Chelsea Girls*.

just how *The Chelsea Girls* differs from other Warhol experiments in media-mixing—such as *The Velvet Underground,* a
combination of noises, dancing, props, tactile effects, and films.
Although *The Chelsea Girls* employs only film, the most
important feature differentiating it from other inter-media
operations (including those of Whitman, Rainer, Cage,
Paxton, and Rauschenberg) is probably that *The Chelsea
Girls* takes place in a movie theater and the screen is where
it belongs—up on the stage in front. Thus everything about
the movie-going experience remains traditional except the
movies themselves. Attention is focused upon a re-evaluation
of the movie as movie and not as movie combined with the
various other effects—which in the long run may be less
outrageous and less offensive.[7] After all, the mixed-media
events of the artists noted above can be taken as positive
efforts to create a new art form; whereas Warhol's efforts,
true-to-form (and true to art), appear to subvert cinema
as an art medium. And, of course, they do.

If this conclusion is accepted, it is possible to see that
Warhol is then consistent with his earlier cinema projects.
He still questions the very nature of the medium and its
relationship with the cultural matrix and the contemporary
value structure—for which he clearly holds no brief. He is
determined to prove that only vital institutions can provide
vital art statements; his challenges to the medium serve
ultimately to assure its legitimacy. If in his earlier movies
he attempted to redefine the nature of film and to clarify
its limitations, the new works may be said to check out the
remaining restrictions of the art form. These include such
physical aspects as the two distinct types of images (the
retinal-visual and cerebro-visual), as well as the nature
of the auditorium, projection, and screen. Future Warhol
films will probably explore farther in the same direction.

One of the principal characteristics of many contemporary

[7] Other critics have pointed out an innovation of a different sort
—that in this film the camera is very close to the subject (figures).
The surrounding "background" material is cut away by the frame,
and the figures generally occupy the entire surface. It has been
suggested that this manner of Warhol recalls Caravaggio. It also
recalls a popular device employed by many makers of filmed television commercials.

Happenings, theater pieces, movies, and inter-media events is the role played by chance and accident; a role that is, as it were, built into the event. The concern with chance is a result of the direct and continuing influence of the Abstract Expressionist school of art. Typically and humanistically, the artist in this case is attempting to acknowledge the role of the audience, the unpredictability of existence, and the integrity of individual identities, by planning a spot in his work for the unplanned. He is, in effect, stepping back and at least pretending to give up control, to proscribe his Romantic position as god and seer; by so doing he may prove the role of the artist unnatural, obsolete, and unnecessary. The inevitable abrogation of Romantic responsibility in art has led toward the tendency to abstraction, the various "outrageous" forms, and the variety of "dehumanized" results. Thus, when the term "dehumanization" is appended to the new art, it is, to the modern artist an encomium. Such is his very goal.

One result of the intentional use of "accident" or "chance" in art events is that no two presentations of any given event will be exactly the same. Sometimes the differences may be slight, sometimes considerable. In any case, they will be noticeable even to the obtuse. Differences in performance of an elaborate theater-event can be observed in so many ways. There is no point in delineating the numerous possibilities for variation—the opportunities for error. Actual image differences in the various evenings in *The Chelsea Girls* are not very great. The major difference or changes apparent in the presentation from performance to performance are in timing by the projectionist and some of these changes are in reality beyond his control. Although he attempts to follow the same order in showing the various parts of the schedule it is impossible always to have the same two images complementing each other on the screen on every occasion. (Such precision could only be obtained by some sort of automated programming of projection.) Thus exact and dependable repetition, an expected feature within the film medium, is very simply and immediately challenged. At the same time, it's not at all obvious and my interpretation of the event could very well be entirely wrong.

The Chelsea Girls is, up to the present, the only one of Warhol's movies to have achieved a successful commercial presentation, and it has received fairly wide coverage by the popular press. It is dismaying to see how critics attuned to the productions of Hollywood, to conventional narrative in cinema, and to the European commercial cinema, have thoroughly managed to miss the point. An exception was Richard Goldstein in the *World Journal Tribune*, who handled the sociological aspects of the film with considerable perception, though giving relatively little attention to its artistic merits. Nearly all the other critics writing in the popular press dwelt with lugubrious insistence on the squalidness, sordidness, perversion, etc., of the lives depicted in the film.

In stripping the cinematic medium of its pretensions and decorations, Warhol has produced an art statement that is likely to be acceptable only to the very few. If they are to be seriously considered as art, Warhol's films demand a new aesthetic; their admirers would say the artist has already gone some way toward constructing one. Whatever one's opinion of the merits of the films, it must surely be admitted that Warhol has finally forced a realignment of the purpose, place, and function of the artist, who is no longer solely a technician or a decorator, but is now strictly an idea man and director. Much of his subject matter is, in one way or another, the subject matter of the commercial artist; in this manner big business and the immediate past, probably the two most difficult things for the contemporary artist to come to terms with, become for Warhol both the content and the product of his art.

In this procession of films, there is no pause for reflection and little self-indulgent repetition. If, by now, the earlier works are classics of the avant-garde, the newer ones continue to present the challenge, uncertainty, and polemic that is art.

INDEX

253